88 Hints for CAT LOVERS

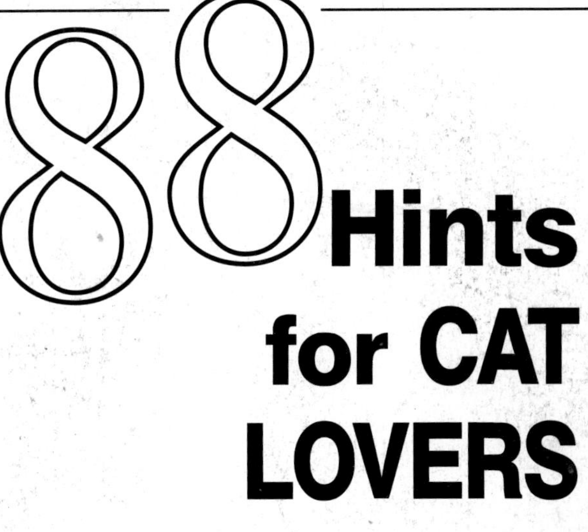

88 Hints for CAT LOVERS

By Marie Říhová

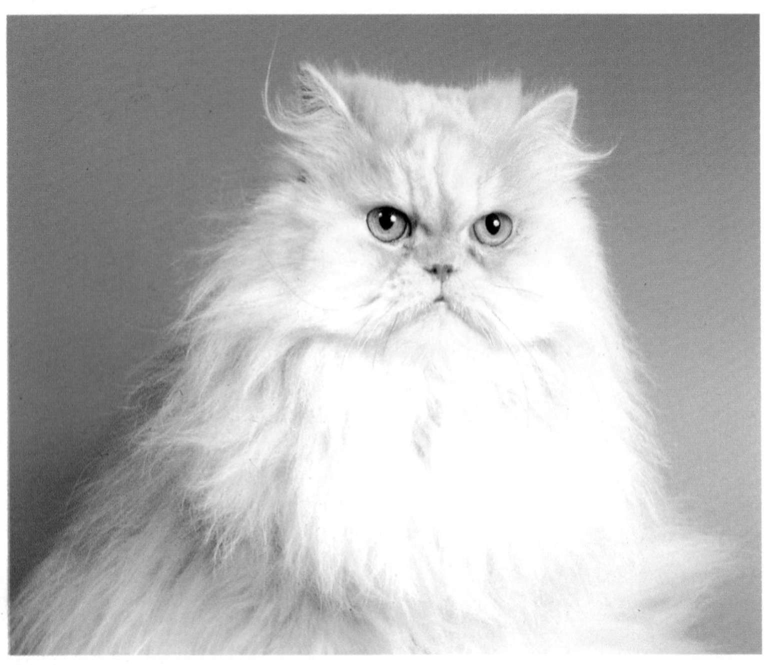

Designed and produced by Aventinum Publishing House
Prague, Czech Republic
English language edition first published 1995
by Sunburst Books, 65 Old Church Street, London SW3 5BS

Text by Marie Říhová
Translated by Ruth Tosková and Joy Moss Kohoutová
Illustrations by Jiří Polák
Photographs by Antonín Les and Petr Zhoř

ISBN 1 85778 060 4
Printed in the Czech Republic
3/22/01/51-01

Introduction

Dear Reader,

Have you chosen a cat as a companion? I want to help you learn to understand your cat better so that both of you enjoy living together. I am sure that in today's busy and over-mechanized times you will find in this small animal a representative of a natural world that is missing from the lives of many people. The cat is becoming an increasingly popular domestic animal because it is relatively undemanding and able to adapt to the dimensions of a city flat.

The cat is a handsome creature with a wide variety of coloration; few domestic animals can boast such a wide palette of colours as the cat. Even though the cat is turning into an ever more social animal, to this day it has certain economic importance. There are still plenty of 'working cats' that are kept to destroy rodents.

This book provides the cat-owner with basic advice that he or she needs, whether the pet is an ordinary household moggy or a rare-breed animal being raised for shows and breeding purposes.

Breeding cats, as anyone who has raised a litter of kittens knows, is a great hobby. Caring for a cat is a creative way of spending leisure time. Nor should one overlook the educational influence of an animal on children. But I also want to speak for the cat you intend to raise. Love your cat and act responsibly towards it. If you have decided against a rare breed with a pedigree and want only a plain, ordinary kitten, don't forget that in the nearest animal shelter there will certainly be a number of abandoned but delightful cats who would be only too appreciative of a warm and caring home.

The Autho

Contents

1 Cats and Man

Cats began associating with man about ten thousand years ago, when the first human communities abandoned the nomadic life. But the first definite evidence of the domestication of cats is little more than four thousand years old. At first there was a very loose arrangement; cats moved about human settlements and it took a long time before people gradually began to tame them. Egypt is generally regarded as the cradle of breeding and keeping cats. A huge amount of evidence has been found there about cats and people living together. Dozens of pictures of cats and many cat mummies have been found in Egypt, where the cat was revered and enjoyed great privileges. In fact some gods, such as Bast (or Pasht), the goddess of fertility, and the sun god Ra, were depicted as cats.

•

Egyptians had good reason to value cats because they protected granaries against rats and mice. Since there were no other ways of wiping out

◁ Strong emotional bonds are often established between children and cats.

these rodents, and since a single cat catch over 1,000 mice a year, the value of such an animal was obvious.

●

Today we call cats raised to kill rodents 'working cats', and until about a hundred years ago it was the sole reason why cats were kept. To this day, although mankind now has at its disposal highly effective chemicals to wipe out rodents, there are instances when the cat is without competition. The good old cat seems to be just about the best rodent remover, getting into almost inaccessible places or where poison would contaminate food.

●

But in the past century the cat has been bred for decidedly different reasons. It has become a social animal and hundreds of thousands of people throughout the world keep cats. The advantage of a cat is that it can be kept without difficulty in a city flat, and unlike a dog it does not have to be taken out for walks. More and more people who would find it irksome or difficult to keep another animal as a pet are deciding to get a cat.

●

This has brought about certain changes for the cat in human society. At one time the idea of breeding cats would have been ridiculed. Today, however, national and international organizations are devoted to establishing and defining cat breeds and for setting standards for regional, national and international shows and exhibitions.

The Sumerian goddess Basteet is depicted here as having a human body with a cat's head, and is accompanied by a feline group of 'ladies in waiting'.

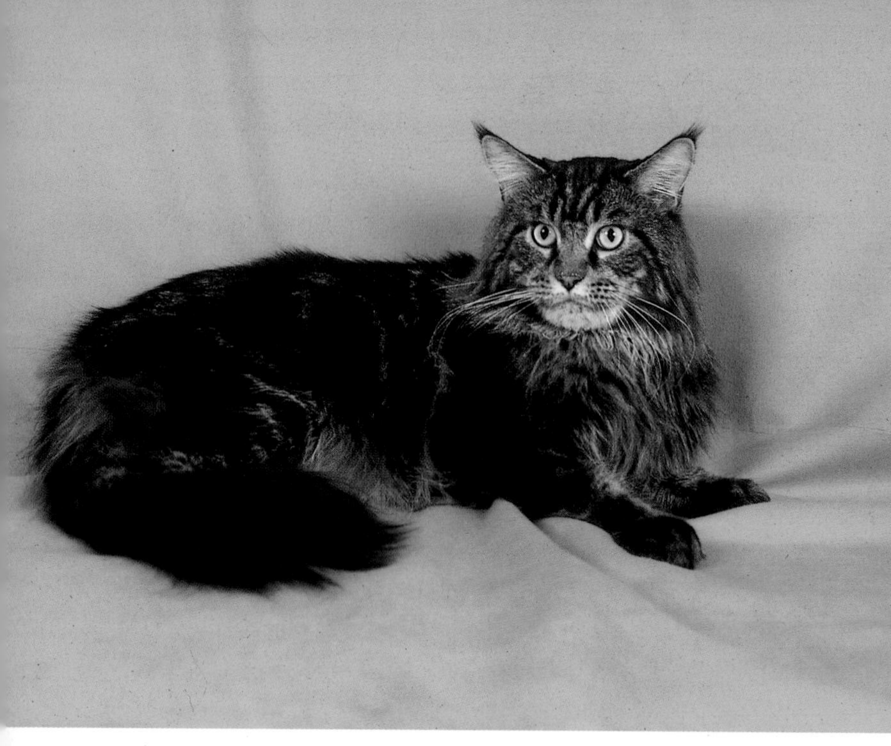

2 Cats: Plus Points and Minus Points

There is no doubting the usefulness of cats, although sometimes it is a subject for debate. Given the high number of rodents that a free-living cat may hunt down, there is no question that the latter's activities are useful. A cat, however, can be useful in other ways. Many people keep cats as a hobby, something that helps them to spend their leisure time creatively. A cat may be the sole companion of old people who live alone. The obligation to look after a live creature is a strong psychological stimulus that favourably influences what may seem to be an otherwise monotonous and lonely life. It has been proved scientifically that the presence of a household pet has a benecial effect on a sick person or invalid. Children in families that have cats have the chance of learning how to get along with live creatures, to look after them and to be responsible for them.

•

In considering the possible harmfulness of cats one must begin from the fact that most problems are due to the irresponsibility of human beings. Vagrant cats and their uncontrolled numbers of offspring are the biggest prob-

◁ The Maine Coon, a large and resilient breed, was originally bred in America as a working cat. Today, it is very popular at cat shows.

lem. Because of their often bad physical condition, these animals are prey to any number of infections. A cat that has been given sufficient attention — good quality food, vaccinations, regular health checkups — is more resistant to infection, and if basic rules of hygiene are observed it is extremely unlikely that the animal will transmit any infection to people. There is a reliable vaccine even against rabies, the most serious of the animal diseases communicable to man, and a cat can be substantially free of parasites through modern medicaments.

●

Most cats like to hunt birds. However, a cat usually cannot catch a healthy adult bird; its victim is more likely to be a sick or very young bird. If a cat is too fond of this activity, one can put a small bell on its collar to warn birds of its approach. But a cat can cause real damage to birds at nesting time. This can be prevented by a fairly simple device, such as putting a cat-proof 'collar' around the trunk of a tree that has a nest.

During the bird-nesting season it is advisable to attach a bundle of straw or a collar device made of tin, wood or some other material around a tree trunk to prevent cats from climbing to the top of trees.

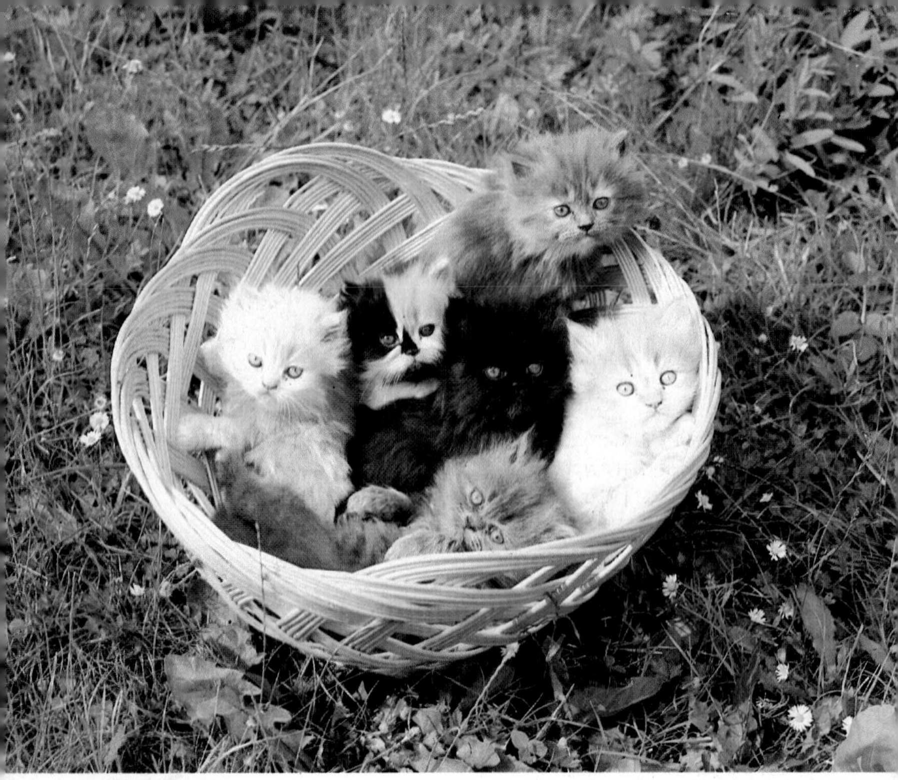

3 Choosing a Cat

There are so many breeds of cats today that everyone can choose according to taste. The individual breeds differ not only in appearance but also in temperament, character and their requirements for breeding and care. The large, longhair Persian cats are known for their placid and phlegmatic nature, but their coats require regular and consistent care. Semi-longhair breeds are not so demanding when it comes to their coats, but they are more temperamental and are very fashionable at the present time. In this group one finds a number of big differences as regards appearance and character. Shorthair cats, in general, are relatively lively and temperamental, and their coats need less looking after. These are animals suitable for persons in full-time employment who do not have the time off to regularly comb and brush a cat's coat. Rex cats belong to the shorthair breed; they are cats with a curly coat that demand a warm environment and are best suited to keeping indoors. The Siamese and Oriental breeds are the liveliest and most demanding in their desire for human company. They communicate wonderfully with people, are intelligent, and somewhat noisy: they positively insist on close contact with their owners.

A frequent dilemma is to decide whether to take a female cat or a male cat. The advantage of male cats is that they usually have a sweet nature and are fond of

◁ At this stage a varied litter of Persian kittens all have blue eyes.

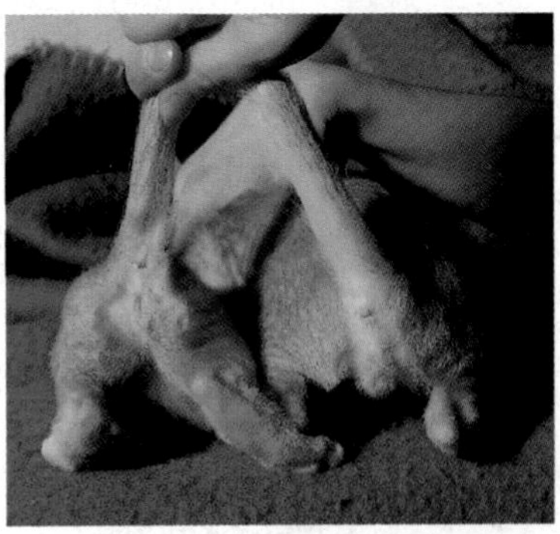

people. A male cat who, unlike a female, is not busy with maternal duties, really demands human company. The disadvantage of male cats, however, is their marking of territory by urination and their penchant for getting lost, which can cause problems. Not all male cats mark out their territory; it seems to depend not on the breed but on the individual cat. If a male is not intended for breeding there is a simple solution: neutering. After being neutered a cat becomes calmer and even more cuddly. Female cats do not mark their territory, but if allowed to roam freely they always have kittens. It is clear from this that fertile female cats cannot be allowed out on their own. Some females are decidedly noisy when in heat. If the owner is not interested in looking after kittens, the best solution is spaying — that is, having the female's ovaries removed. After being spayed, a female cat also becomes more serene and responsive to her owner's affection.

The kitten's sex may be best distinguished immediately after birth or after five weeks. Female kittens (left) have their anal and vaginal openings fairly close together; male (right) have their anal opening and penis farther apart. Between the two openings in the male is the scrotum, difficult to see immediately after birth.

Most identifying marks of individual breeds are apparent in the cat's head. A substantial difference is evident when comparing the heads of the Persian (left) and the Oriental cat (right).

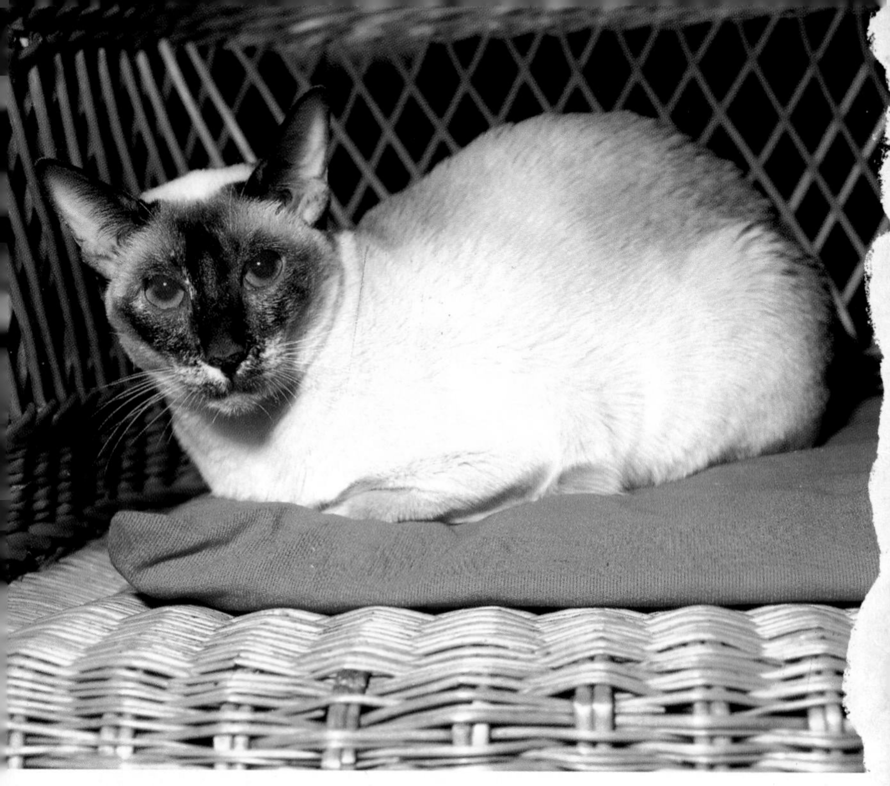

4 Will You Make a Good Cat Owner?

Before acquiring a cat you should consider very carefully whether you are able and willing to take on the responsibility of looking after it for many years. A cat commonly lives for 15 years and more, so effectively you will be acquiring another family member.

A cat needs enough living space. It is estimated that one cat requires about nine square metres, so keep only as many cats as will not suffer from overcrowding or get in each other's way. In a group of cats living in confined quarters a hierarchy is formed in which the weaker members are at a disadvantage and live under constant stress.

•

If you decide on a kitten of a certain breed, buy it from a registered breeder. You thereby have a guarantee that you are buying a healthy kitten and you will get sound advice on its daily regime, what it eats, what its hygienic habits are. If you are interested in breeding cats, it is better to buy older kittens. You can better see the signs of their breed, and there is less chance

◁ Siamese cats soon become family members. They demand a great deal of attention and are highly intelligent.

that later on some defects will appear that reduce the cat's breeding value.

Examine the kitten you intend to buy very carefully. A healthy kitten is lively and playful. Never buy a kitten that has been weaned too early. Breeding regulations stipulate that the youngest age at which kittens can be sold is 10 to 12 weeks, which means a time when they are already independent and eat solid food. If you buy a kitten that is too young you lay yourself and the animal open to a number of potentially serious problems. When visiting the breeder note how the kitten reacts to being petted. A well-balanced animal is not particularly shy. Also, look closely at kitten's living quarters; examine its mother, its siblings, and if possible its father. Its appearance and temperament often tell you a lot about your future adult cat. Obviously, a kitten must not show any signs of illness (coughing, a running nose, eyes or ears, diarrhoea, parasites and the like). It is best to take someone along who owns a cat or at least knows something about them.

●

You can also acquire a kitten or cat from an animal shelter. If you decide to acquire such a cat, your first trip should be to the vet for a check-up, where the animal can be examined thoroughly and the dates of vaccination scheduled. Until you are absolutely certain that the animal is healthy, keep it isolated from any other animals in your home.

Playfulness and mobility are an indication of these Oriental kittens' good condition. The owner should take sufficient time to select the kittens and observe their behaviour in a domestic environment.

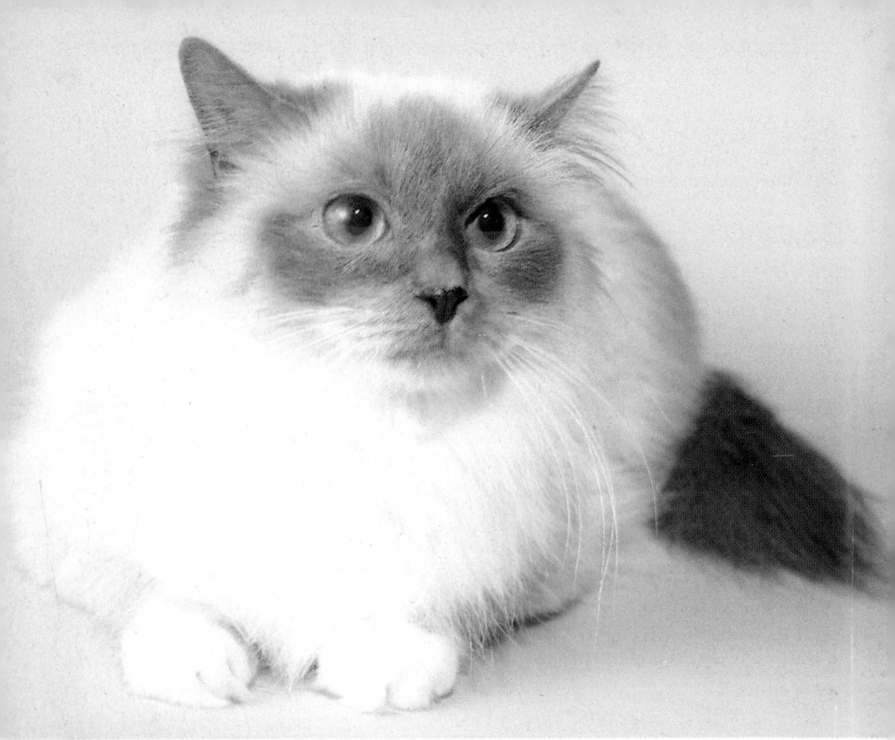

5 Making the New Arrival Feel at Home

For the first few days you must pay special attention to the cat. If possible, bring it home before a long weekend or holiday. If you have bought a kitten that was used to the company of its mother and siblings, the change will be a big event in its life. It will mew, perhaps even at night. Let the kitten sleep near you if it wishes to. Do your best to provide the same conditions that it had at its previous home. Choose the same type of litter tray with the same things on it and put it in a similar place. Give the animal the food it likes on the same schedule as the breeder did; prepare similar bedding for it. Speak to it, take it in your arms and on your lap. If your new acquisition is the only animal in the house, it will probably want to stay close to the person who in the early days gave it the most attention. You can expect that at first a kitten will forget, temporarily, its otherwise good hygienic habits. Do not punish it, but calmly and consistently show it where to relieve itself.

When you bring a new kitten or cat into the house for the first time, close all the windows and doors. For the moment, the cat does not know its environs and if it ran away it would have a hard time finding its way back. It is best to keep the animal for several days in one room, and only then allow it into other parts of the house or flat. If you have young children, warn them to be quiet; the cat is nervous in an alien envi-

◁ The Burmese is a highly sought after and appreciated breed.

A favourite bed for a cat may be a wicker basket, best placed above floor level.

ronment and is easily frightened by unfamiliar or excessive noise. It is best, at first, not to allow little children who do not know how to handle animals to get too close.

If you have brought a new cat into a house where there is another cat, the animals must be allowed to get to know one another gradually. This acquaintance occurs very easily as a rule, especially with a new kitten among adult cats, and generally there are no problems with neutered or spayed cats. But it is more difficult if the new arrival is also an adult cat. What usually happens is that for several days, and sometimes for several weeks, there is much hissing and threatening, and on rare occasions a fight will break out. The new arrival is forced to accept a subordinate position, but later on relations become more settled. The length of this acquaintance process depends on the willingness of the new arrival to accept its position, on its temperament, and also on the owner's patience. It is essential for the owner to be present at the beginning, to prevent any unnecessary injury: never isolate cats that are newly acquainted but have not yet become friends. Always feed the cats separately: feeding offers many occasions for conflict. You must also devote sufficient attention to your first animal. If you just tend to the new kitten, the older cat will feel its rights and priviledges have been overlooked and it will begin to grow jealous of the newcomer.

Every cat needs a private space where it will not be disturbed. Providing your cat with a safe haven helps it to adjust more readily to its new environment.

The process of animals becoming acquainted with one another is a very individual matter. In an ideal situation the cats make their acquaintance immediately and become friends at once. This can even happen if there is a dog in the house. In acquainting a cat with a dog, one uses the same approach. It is quite amazing how often and how quickly a dog becomes the subordinate one in a relationship when there is a new kitten or cat. But one cannot rely on this. Caution is essential at the very beginning.

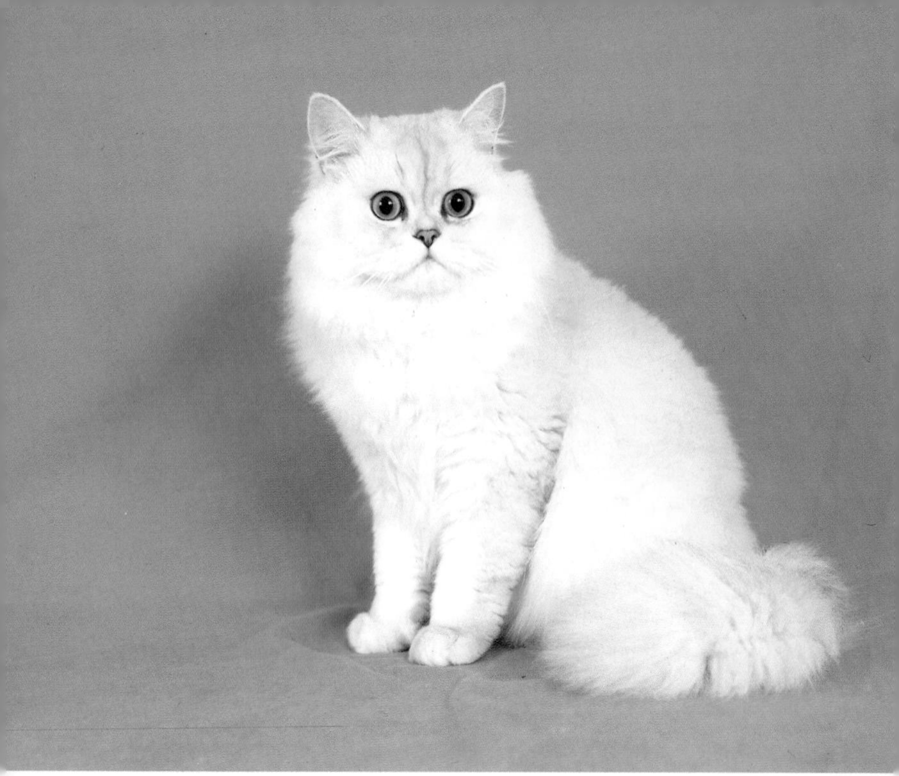

6 The Cat's Toilet

A litter tray is the most important item to be obtained before the cat comes into the house. There are many types of trays. They are made of plastic, which is easily washed and easy to disinfect. Choose the right place for the tray. It should be in a quiet part of the house to which the cat has access at all times of day and night — in a scullery, for instance, or the WC, the bathroom, under the stairs, and so on. It should stand on something with a washable surface — vinyl flooring or tiles. Cats are very fastidious and will not use the litter-tray filling a second time. If you are out of the house during the day, therefore, it is a good idea to have two trays.

•

If possible equip the litter tray with a lining with very good absorption qualities, so that even a non-neutered male cat leaves no odour. Put three to five centimetres of this lining in the tray, which must be cleaned daily. Solid faeces are picked up with a special trowel, as are the damp lumps that form after the faeces have been expelled. When the lining is changed completely, wash the tray thoroughly, disinfect it and, after it dries, fill it up again.

◁ To ensure the good appearance of white Persians the owner must attend regularly to their coat.

The best filling for the tray is one of many brands of cat litter available. Sometimes sawdust is used; it absorbs moisture well, but the cat carries it around the house on its paws. Sand is an unsuitable filling: it does not absorb the odour and quickly becomes wet. Some owners use a toilet with a double bottom; the top section is perforated but catches the faeces, while the urine goes through the openings to the lower tray. But such a toilet has to be cleaned immediately after use, otherwise the urine smells and the cat will not use it again. This system is more useful in an emergency or for a short-term solution.

•

If the cat soils the area around the tray, the floor should be washed thoroughly and disinfected. Otherwise the cat smells its faeces and there is a danger it will relieve itself in the same place all the time. The cat may, however, dislike the lingering smell of disinfectant, so you may need to move the tray to a new position.

A small trowel should be used to remove faeces and dispose of damp litter.

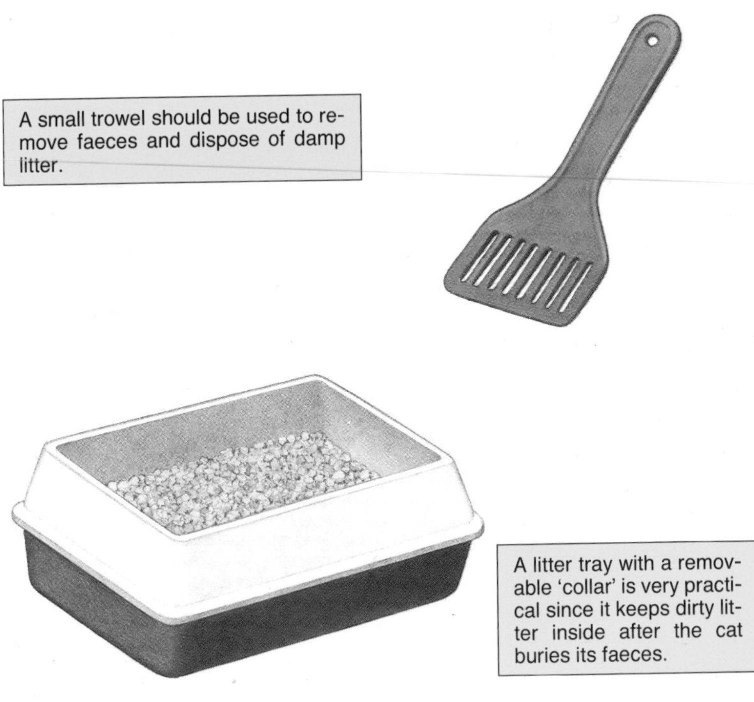

A litter tray with a removable 'collar' is very practical since it keeps dirty litter inside after the cat buries its faeces.

7 Making a Scratching Post

Cats love to sink their claws into upholstery. They must have something to sharpen their claws when they are growing and at the same time do away with the old outer sheath of each claw. You can never teach a cat not to claw: it is a basic instinct. Therefore a cat must have a scratching post. Some breeders have solved the problem by sacrificing an old armchair or another piece of upholstered furniture, leaving it to the cat to do with it as it pleases. If you choose a good scratching post that suits the cat you will soon find that it looses interest in the furniture or the carpets. It is better to bring home a scratching post before you bring home a kitten. Then it will learn not to claw or scratch furniture and you will not have to teach it to shake off a bad habit.

•

Scratching posts can be of any shape and made of all sorts of materials. A simple one consists of a piece of rug attached to the wall, or better still, to the corner of a wall, perhaps in the hall. You can also use a little softwood post, with or without a covering, or padded with a piece of carpet, or simply

◁ Use your imagination if you want to make a home-made climbing post.

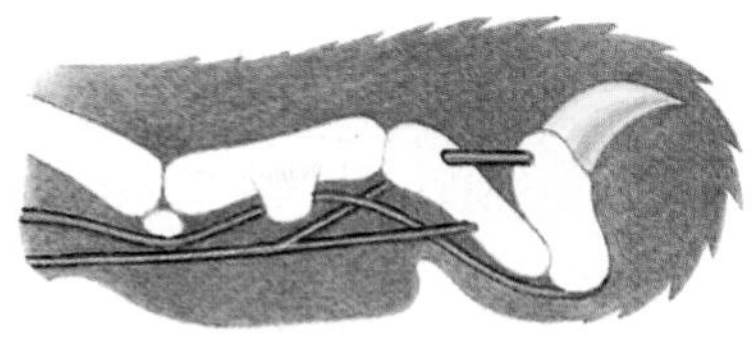

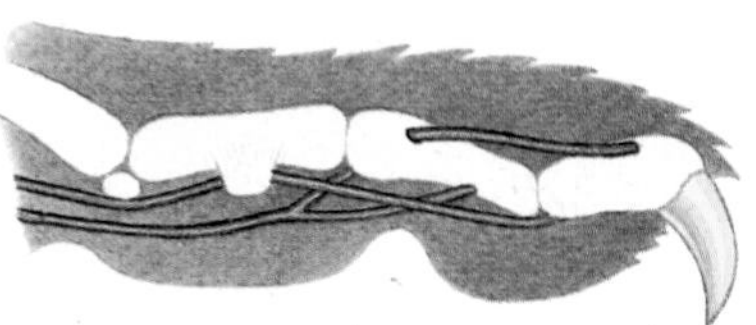

Retractable claws are not only important defensive and offensive weapons but make for better movement. After they have been clipped, some cats become unsure of themselves for a while and are afraid to jump, so claws should be clipped only in exceptional circumstances.

wrapped around with rope. It can be put vertically, sideways or horizontally. Use your imagination and place stumps or branches around the house which might also fulfil a decorative function. Shops sell many kinds of scratching posts. Put one in close to the cat's usual sleeping area; it likes to use it on awakening. One can also buy or make a whole set of furniture for a cat. This includes a combination of scratching posts, climbing poles, resting places and shelters. The material is usually wood covered with a carpet, and the climbing poles are covered with hemp rope. The cat will soon get to love such furniture. It is like physical training apparatus which brings the animal a little closer to natural conditions and improves its physical and mental well-being.

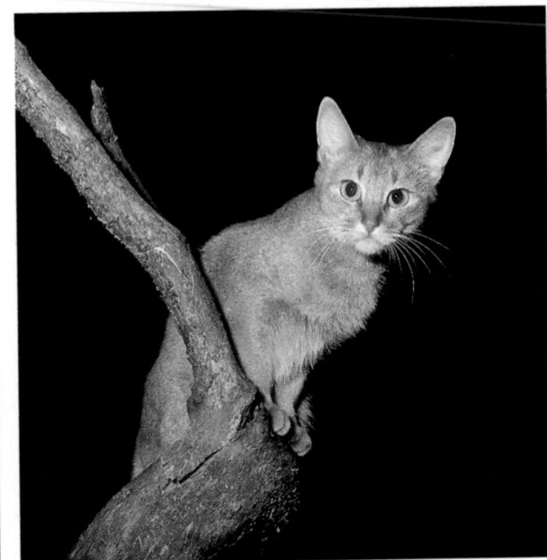

Climbing posts made of natural material are appreciated by housebound cats such as this Abyssinian Red. Moreover, such devices also enliven your home decor.

8 Creature Comforts

A satisfied cat is happy, playful and it is up to us to help make life more pleasant for it at home using certain little things. Like all living creatures the cat also needs its moments of privacy, a place to rest, where no one disturbs it. As a rule it chooses its favourite place itself. We can offer it a pleasant little nook — most suitable for such a purpose is a wicker basket, an ordinary basket or just an ordinary cardboard box lined with soft textiles. We must clean such a nook regularly, launder the blanket or put a slip cover on it that is changed often. We put the basket or box in a quiet, warm, sheltered place and never disturb the cat there. From time to time the cat changes its favourite place; many like to sleep well above floor level — on a chest of drawers or even on top of a wardrobe. Respect its choice if at all possible, but make sure that the chosen place is always clean.

A typical cat flap.

◁ Both kittens and adults are extremely fond of mazes, boxes or other hide-outs.

Cats, and more particularly kittens, need play to acquire greater nimbleness and just to be happy. Some cats maintain this playfulness into old age; neutered cats are often very playful. A cat is able to play for a long time with, say, a cotton-reel, a ping-pong ball, or a ball of string. You can make toys for the cat yourself or buy them in a pet shop. In making them, do not use brittle material that might injure the cat if they broke into pieces. Also the toys must be too large for the cat to swallow them.

•

Your cat must have its own feeding bowls: one for solid food and another for water. Cats do not like bowls that are too deep, so use shallow saucer-shaped ones. They must be sufficiently heavy and stable so that they do not easily overturn or slide along the floor. The bowls can be made of glazed ceramics, porcelain or Pyrex. The purpose-made plastic dishes that are widely available should be changed before their surface becomes roughened, making them hard to clean and thus a possible source of infection. Use a clean bowl every time you offer food; strict hygiene helps to prevent digestive disorders.

The two-way cat flap is a practical device built into a door panel that allows the cat to go in or out of the house without having to leave the door open all the time. The flap must be installed at a height that lets the cat pass through easily. Such flaps are made of wood or plastic and have springs or magnets that close it automatically after the cat has gone through. Teaching the cat to use this device requires a little patience. You can practise opening it with the cat, offering it enticements, such as its favourite food. Most cats learn to use their flap within a day or two.

If you keep a cat indoors exclusively, you should give it a chance to get some fresh air, at least through an open window or on a balcony. A cat's coat that has been aired is its best protection against fungal diseases, and being active outdoors helps to keep it fit. The sun's rays are important to produce vitamin D in the skin and this is especially necessary for growing cats. If you allow a cat to sit in an open window or on a balcony it must be safeguarded by wire mesh or netting so that it does not fall out. Non-poisonous creeping plants can be planted in flower boxes on a balcony. This serves not only to improve the appearance of the balcony; it also offers the cat refreshing shade.

Every housebound cat should be allowed to move around in sunshine and fresh air. A good idea is to install wire mesh or a net in the window frame.

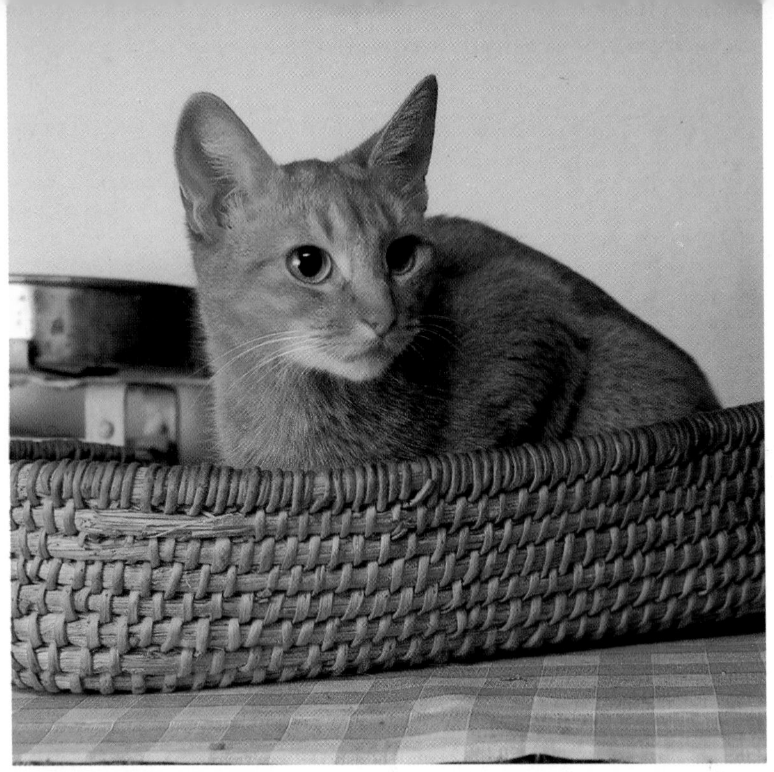

9 Dangers to Cats Inside and Outside the House

Only a properly vaccinated cat should be allowed to run outside. If you live on a busy street there is a danger that the cat will be run over by a car; traffic injuries are the commonest cause of cats' accidental death. The safest outdoor place for a cat is in a pen (see Hint 11) or, better, within a fenced-in garden to prevent the cat from getting outside. While running about freely cats can come into contact with pesticides, insecticides, and other chemicals used in garden or house. They can also catch and eat mice or rats that have eaten poisoned bait; such poison is often fatal to cats. Finally, there are some people who enjoy being cruel to animals.

•

You must also take certain measures to prevent accidents indoors. Make sure that heavy, unstable objects, such as a step-ladder, cannot fall on a cat. Kittens like to bite into electric cords. If they bite through the insulation they may receive an electric shock, so be sure to take all cords out of their sockets after using electrical appliances, and put them in a place where the cat cannot reach them.

◁ Abyssinian Red.

Other potential dangers include rope, thread, needles, pieces of tin foil, beads and other small objects that have been left lying about. A playful kitten may swallow such unsuitable play-things.

●

Make sure that any fireplace or stove is enclosed, so that the cat cannot get burned. (Most cats when young can be taught to avoid such dangerous objects in the home.) Household chemicals, such as detergents, washing powders and plant fertilizers, should be stored out of reach of cats as well as of children. Plastic bags are very dangerous. While playing, a kitten might crawl into one and suffocate. Eating a piece of such a bag might cause an intestinal disorder.

A falling cat always lands on all fours, but because of its weak neck muscles it may hit its head on the ground and suffer serious injuries. Make sure that all windows and balconies are properly secured.

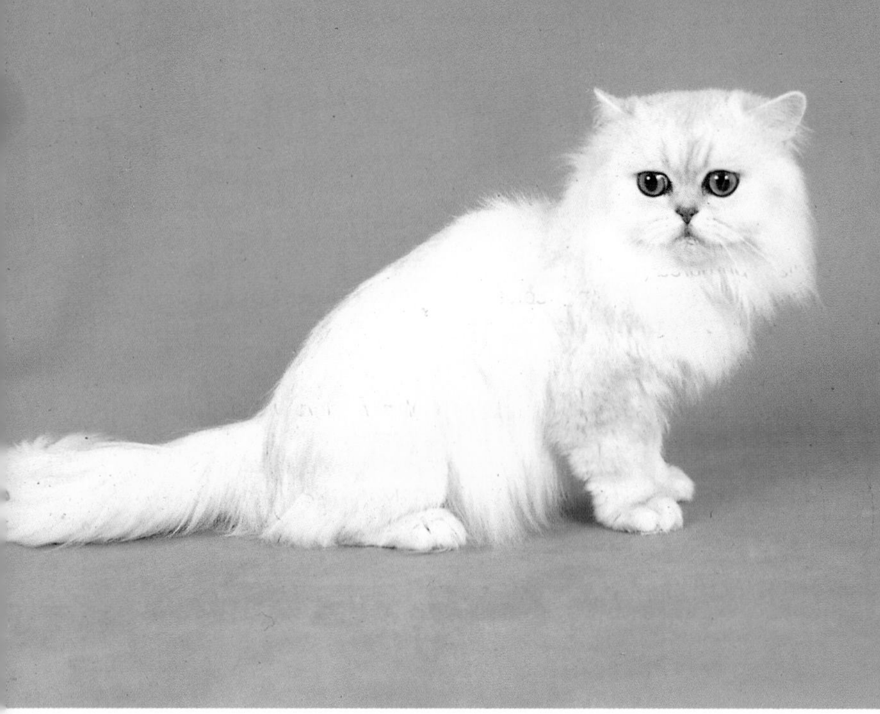

10 Plants Poisonous to Cats

Cats are more sensitive than humans or other animals to certain natural and synthetic substances. Cats that are kept indoors seem to lose some of their natural ability to distinguish between harmless and harmful plants, so it is important that you as a cat-owner know which these plants are.

•

The following plants are harmful to cats (and some of them are also harmful to human beings):

Aconitum napellus (monkshood)
Arum maculatum (cuckoo-pint, or lords-and-ladies)
Atropa belladonna (deadly nightshade)
Cheiranthus cheiri (wallflower)
Colchicum autumnale (autumn crocus)
Convallaria majalis (lily-of-the-valley)
Cyclamen persicum (cyclamen)
Cytisus labarnum (broom)
Daphne mezereum (mezereon)
Datura stramonium (Jimson weed)
Delphinium (delphinium, larkspur)
Dicentra spectabilis (bleeding heart)

◁ Persian Chinchilla.

Dieffenbachia seguina (dieffenbachia)
Digitalis purpurea (foxglove)
Euphorbia pulcherrima (poinsettia)
Fritillaria imperialis (crown imperial)
Hydrangea
Juniperus sabina (savin)
Monstera deliciosa
Narcissus papyraceus
Nerium oleander (oleander)
Philadelphus (mock orange)
Philodendron
Primula (primrose)
Pulsatilla vulgaris (pasque flower)
Ranunculus acris (common buttercup)
Ricinus communis (castor-oil plant)
Solanum nigrum (black nightshade)
Urginea maritima (sea squill)
Viscum album (mistletoe)
Zantedeschia aethiopica (arum lily)

Among the most common poisonous plants are: (1) *Dieffenbachia seguina,* (2) *Monstera deliciosa,* (3) *Euphorbia pulcherrima,* (4) *Convallaria majalis,* (5) *Cyclamen persicum,* (6) *Nerium oleander.*

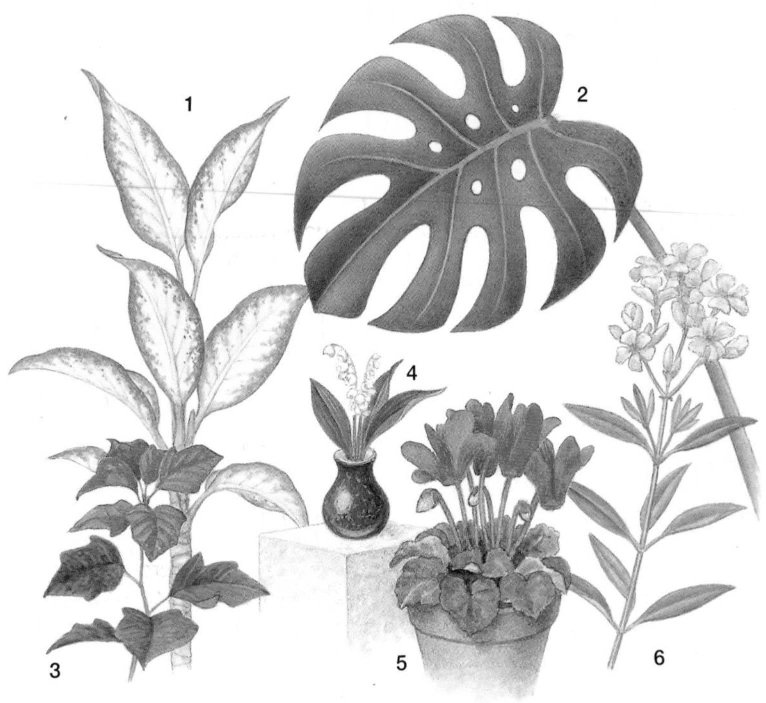

11 What is Cattery Breeding?

In breeding a large number of cats, breeders sometimes use a kennel-type system. In establishing a cattery one must respect the animals' need for a certain minimum living space without which they would be under constant stress and also possibly harmed physically by lack of movement. Cats bred in this way must have adequate heat and light; the cattery must be well ventilated and easy to clean. It is extremely important that each animal has frequent contact with human beings, otherwise they will become timid and distrustful.

A cattery for one animal consists of a small 'house' and an exercise area. A divided house can be used by more than one animal. The minimum house space for each animal should be 2.5 × 1.8m (8 $^1/_2$ × 6ft). The heating should be in this part of the cattery — and the heat must not dip below 8°C (46°F) for longhair or below 13°C (56°F) for shorthair cats. The cattery must contain everything a cat needs to live: bedding to sleep on, a litter tray, and bowls for food and water. The floor is usually covered with vinyl for easy cleaning. Attached to this living space is an ourdoor exercise area measuring at least 3.5 × 3m (12 × 10ft). The frame of this pen is constructed of

◁ One way to give your cat a run-out in an apartment block is to install a wire cage on the balcony.

hardwood or metal and covered with strong wire mesh on the sides and top. About half the pen is roofed and protected against draughts. The floor consists half of grass, and half of a good covering that can be cleaned (tiles, etc.). The pen should have a tree trunk or climbing pole with a number of wooden rest places. It should also have both sunny and shady spots. Non-poisonous climbing plants can be trained up the wire mesh to provide shade and visual interest. There must be entrances from the 'house' part and from the pen which are easily accessible.

Similar outdoor pens can be used as exercise areas for cats that are kept at home. Such pens usually have one side against a house wall containing either a window or a door in which a cat flap can be installed, so that the cat can go in and out whenever it wants. This is a very useful and practical way of solving a cat's exercise problem if you are raising an animal for breeding purposes.

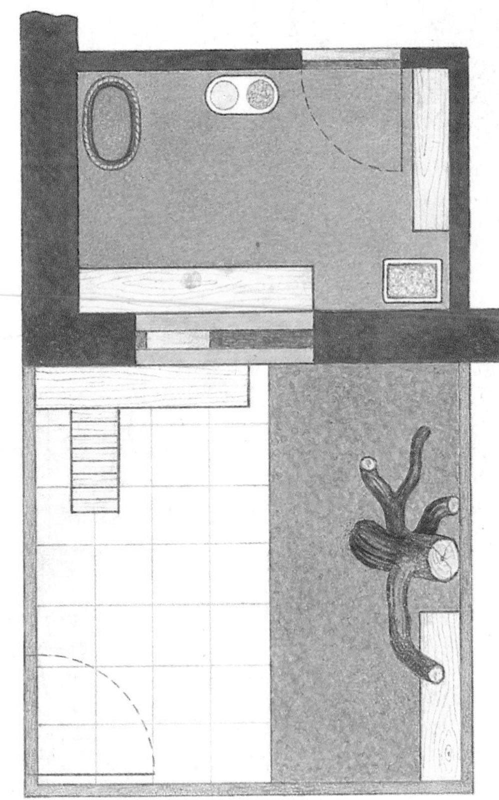

Basic equipment of a cattery.

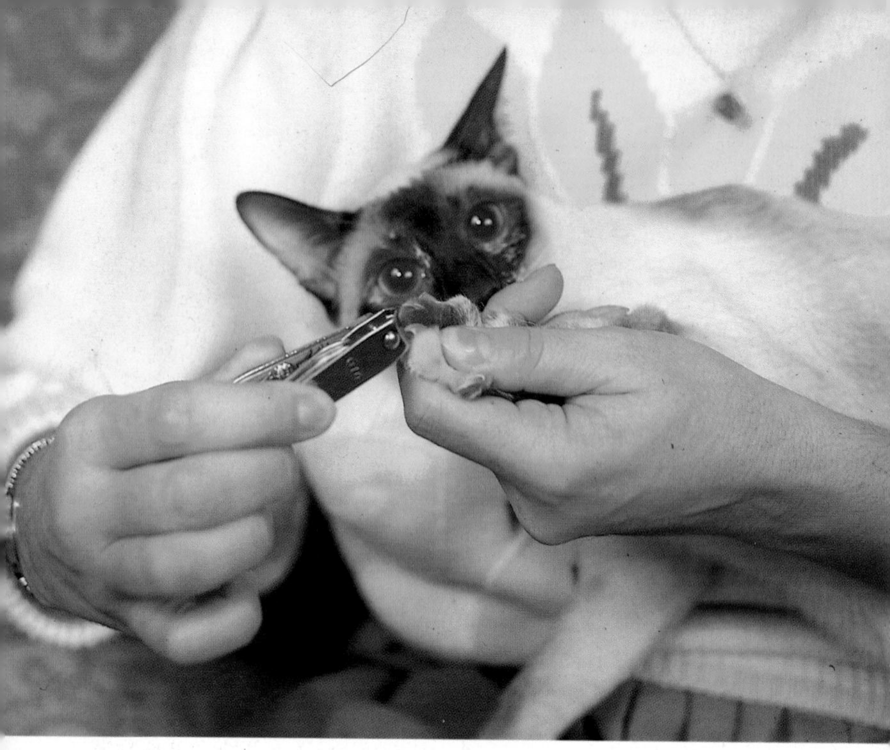

12 Cat Health and Hygiene

A healthy cat gives much attention to its own hygiene, but the owner should check periodically to see, for instance, whether too much wax has collected in the ears. Even in a healthy cat, if too much copper-coloured ear-wax forms it may lead to infection. Use an ear swab covered with cotton dipped in a baby oil or paraffin oil to clean it. Clean only the inner ear flaps; do not go deeper than you can see, or you may injure the ear-drum. Leave more thorough cleaning of the ears to the vet. A cat's ear should be examined about once a week.

Under normal conditions a cat's eyes are dry. If 'sleep' forms on the eyes, remove it with cotton-wool dipped in boiled water. Breeds with shortened face features, especially Persians, often produce an excessive amount of tears. If the area around the eyes of such breeds is not cleaned regularly, the coat tends to turn yellow or even brownish, giving it an unaesthetic appearance. These cats should have their eyes cleaned daily, and sometimes several times a day. Warm water should be used to wash away the yellowish discoloration in the coat.

Most cat owners do not trim their cat's claws, but there are instances when such a procedure cannot be avoided — for instance, when a limb has to be

◁ When trimming claws, the paw should be firmly fixed in place and the claw squeezed out by gentle pressure on the last toe segment.

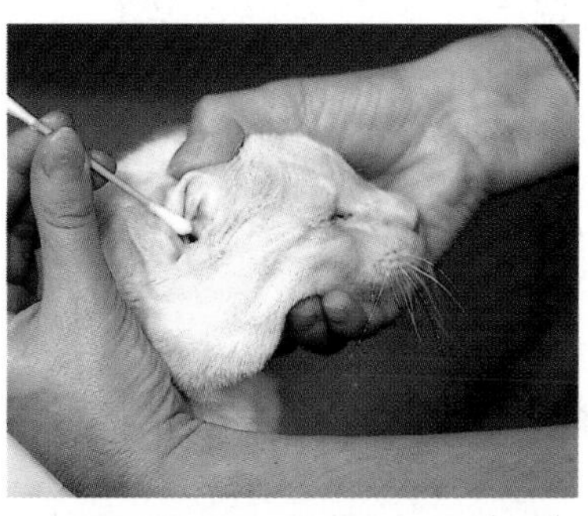

Regular cleaning of the inside of the ear flap with surgical spirit prevents accumulation of wax. Never attempt to clean the ear canal.

placed in a splint after being injured, or when the cat hasn't the strength to sharpen its claws, or when a kitten scratches the mother's teat while she is suckling it. Trim only the tip of the claw, and take care not to nick the sensitive fleshy part. Such wounds bleed profusely, are painful, and the claw may become infected. Use special scissors for trimming, or nail clippers used to cut toe-nails. Many owners, of course, prefer to leave claw-trimming to the vet.

Most cats have problems with tartar. Elderly cats suffer the most because tartar causes painful inflammation of the gums and loosens the teeth or even leads to tooth-loss. Such cats eat reluctantly, their gums bleed, and they have a bad breath. It is not easy to remove the tartar, so this is another job best left to the vet. But an owner can prevent the formation of tartar by not feeding the cat exclusively on minced food, occasionally giving it soft bones to chew on, or sometimes by brushing the cat's teeth. But this only removes the soft plaque, which by retaining mineral substances becomes tartar. It is therefore necessary to begin a regular brushing regime before tartar forms or after it is removed. Brush the teeth with your finger wrapped in a piece of rough cloth. You can put a few drops of lemon juice on the cloth, as this is good for engorged gums. The teeth should be closed tight since the tartar forms on the outer surface, where the saliva glands terminate.

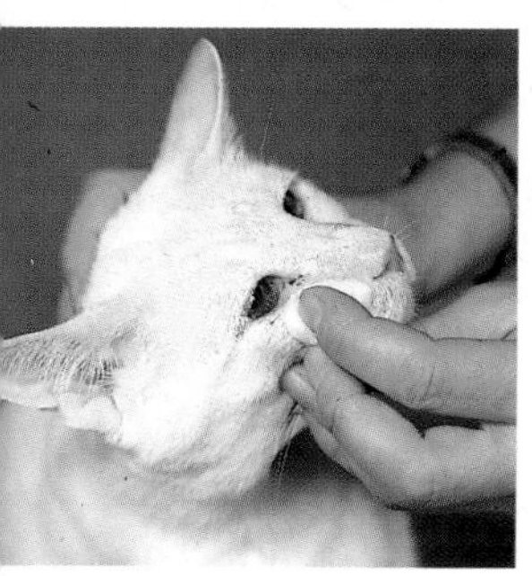

The eyes should be cleaned with a piece of cotton wool or gauze, soaked in warm but not hot water.

The best way to clean teeth is with a piece of gauze.

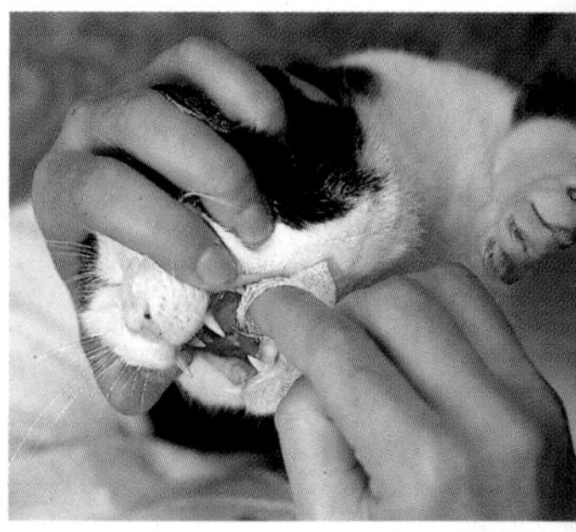

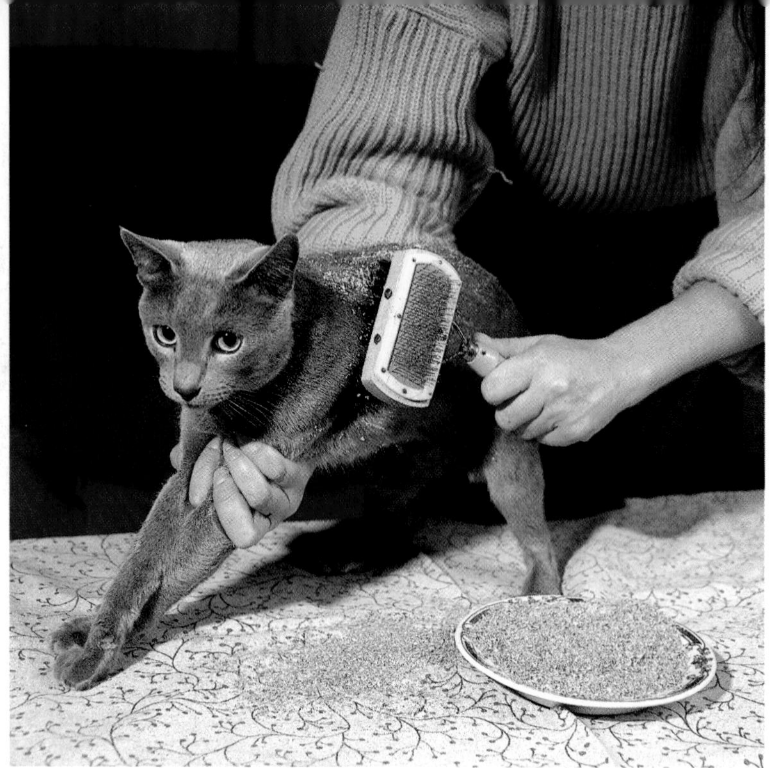

13 Grooming Your Cat's Coat

Methods of grooming a cat's coat include brushing, combing, bathing and powdering. Longhair Persian cats need careful attention every day. Shorthair coats are not so demanding, requiring only the occasional brushing. The coat of rexes is unusually soft, so grooming is confined to careful, brief brushing with a soft brush and smoothing down the coat with a piece of chamois. Generally speaking it is necessary to devote more care to the coats of neutered or spayed cats: such coats are thicker, they shed more hairs, and so the animals' own grooming activity leads more frequently to the formation of hair-balls in the stomach.

The coats of Persian cats have a tendency to become matted, and should be combed every day, especially the hair between the legs. Even a young kitten can become accustomed to being combed daily. Comb the entire body, except for the tail. Comb in the direction in which the hair grows; only the frill or 'ruff' (the long hair on the neck and chest) is combed in the opposite direction. For thorough grooming use a brush. The coat on the back, flanks and chest should be brushed upwards so that it is fluffy and stands out a little. It is best to use a metal comb with blunt teeth; for grooming use

◁ A water bath may be substituted by a bran 'bath'. Warmed-up bran is gently rubbed into the coat and then thoroughly brushed out.

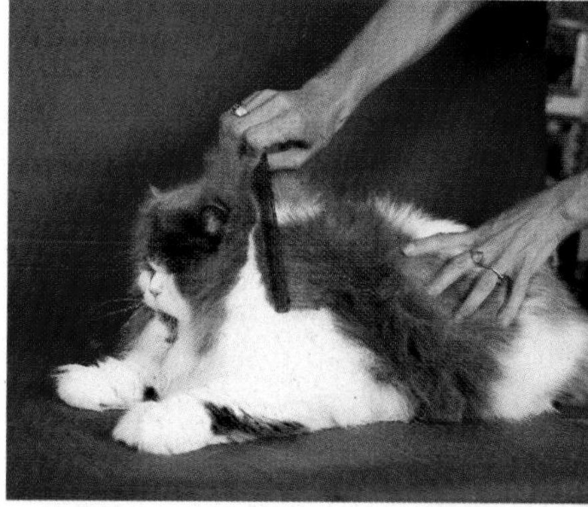

A Persian's neck hair (the 'collar') should be combed against the direction of growth.

a brush of natural or synthetic fibres. Use a toothbrush for the hairs on the face. Some breeders cut the Persian cat's coat short in summer. It should be trimmed evenly so that it grows evenly, but it will take several months to regain its normal length.

Use a thick comb or brush for shorthair cats, grooming the coat in the direction in which the hairs grow. After combing, smooth the coat down with chamois or silk cloth so that it has a high sheen. Adding a little oil, butter and yeast to the cat's food will give it a specially rich and glossy coat.

Powdering has the effect of removing superfluous oil from the coat. Longhair cats are usually powdered, but you can also use powder on cats with short hair. Powder only a coat that has been well combed and has no matted clumps of hair. Use special cat powder or very fine talcum powder, then brush the powder out of the coat. Be particularly careful when powdering cats with dark coats.

Bathing is a regular feature of looking after longhair cats, especially before a show. But too much bathing takes the oil off the coat. Do not bathe a cat immediately before a show but about five to seven days earlier. Put a rubber pad or towel in the tub and fill the tub with about 10cm (4in) of water at 38 to 39°C (100—102°F). Do not allow the water to get into the cat's eyes or ears. Use only special cat shampoo; other shampoos are too strong for its sensitive coat. After a thorough rinse, wipe the cat with a terrycloth towel, or use an electric hair drier; keep the animal warm the whole of the following day. It is better to have someone assist you when bathing the cat.

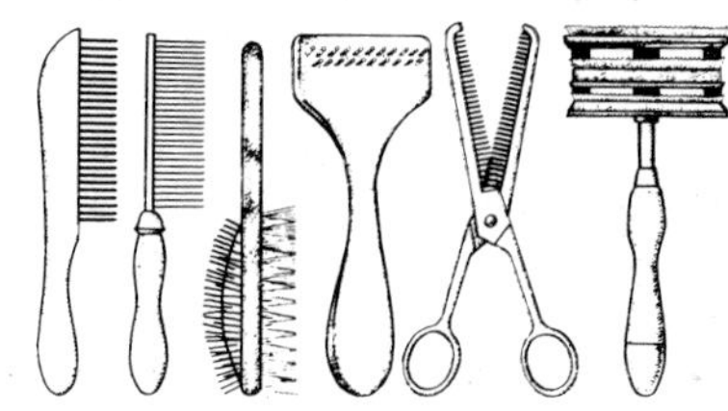

Hair care accessories.

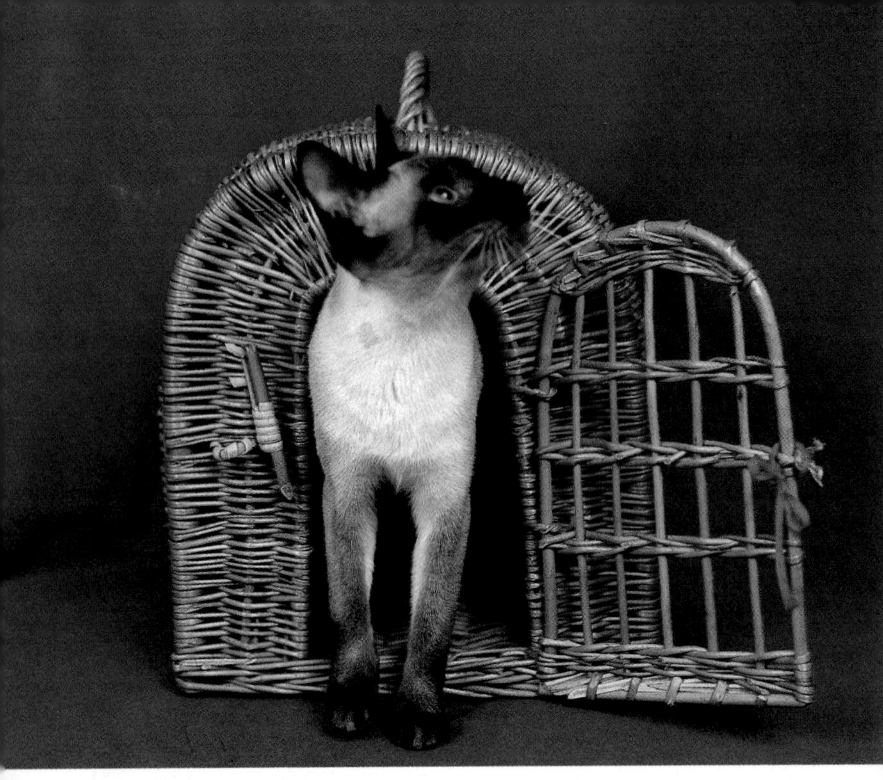

14 Travelling with a Cat

Most cats do not like to travel. A cat can be taught to tolerate travelling but it requires a great deal to patience on your part. If possible train your animal to become accustomed to travelling from an early age.

If you are planning a long journey, do not give the cat food or drink later than five to six hours before you set out. A day before the trip, do not feed it laxative foods. Easily digestible types of meat, for instance, or poultry, are suitable.

Purpose-built carrying containers are the best way to transport a cat. The most suitable are plastic baskets with steel mesh doors. The baskets are airy, secure, comfortable, easy to wash, and can be securely closed. You can also use a wicker basket, but it must have a good locking device so that the cat cannot get out. Line the container with a disposable pad and, for long journeys, add a small litter tray. The container must never stand in a draught or in direct sunlight. In winter put a warm coverlet in the carrier, or wrap the whole basket in a cover: remember that the cat cannot move around freely and might become cold. Check on the carrier from time to time, and if necessary change the pad; also, give the cat a little something to drink. If possible,

◁ Wicker carriers are well ventilated, and thus especially suitable for the summer months.

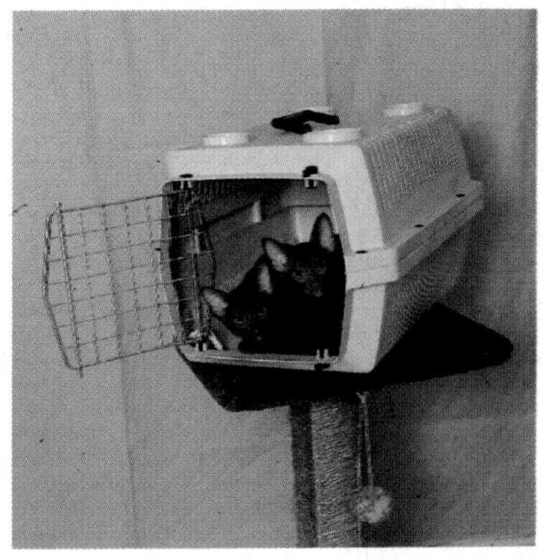

This plastic carrier with wire mesh opening is very practical. These Oriental Havana kittens feel fine in it.

let the cat out of the carrier for a little while (for instance, inside a closed car) and encourage it to urinate. To enable it to stretch its legs on a long trip, walk it on a lead. If you have to leave the cat for a little while alone in a parked car, try to find a parking space in the shade. In any event, it is essential to leave one or more windows partly open.

Never let a cat move about freely in the car when you are on the move. Even a calm animal can be frightened and threaten the safety of passengers. If you have a very calm cat, accustomed to travelling, you can keep it on the back seat in a harness tied by the lead to something firm, such as a safety belt. Even then it is better if someone sits in the back with the cat.

Cats that are poor travellers should be given a sedative or tranquiliser before setting out on the journey. Consult your vet about the most suitable kind and the dosage. Cats transported by plane are also given medication prior to the flight.

A placid cat can even be carried in a soft travel bag.

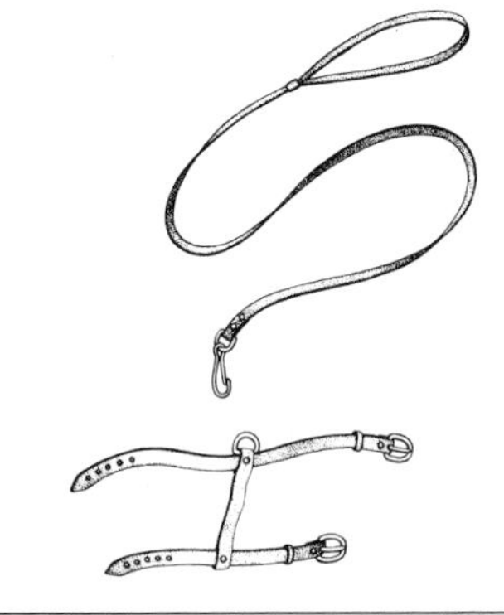

Cat harness.

15 Correct Feeding Methods

Proper and nourishing food for a cat is essential for successful breeding and the animal's health and happiness. A domestic cat's diet is different from that of a cat that depends entirely on hunting for food. Natural cat food consists of all the body parts of the captured prey — that is, not just the muscle tissues but also the internal organs, bones, hair or feathers, and so on. This ensures that the cat obtains all the components of a natural diet. But cats bred at home depend on us and we must offer them the kind of food they need.

Originally, cats were exclusively carnivorous and because of this they have a short intestine. Although under the influence of domestication a cat will accept, to a limited degree, other kinds of food (and, compared to its wild relatives, has a longer intestine), it remains essentially a meat eater and is unable to digest a number of other foods. Cats have a tendency to insist on their favourite food while rejecting other equally suitable kinds. The owner must not permit this to happen. He/she must give the cat the greatest possible variety of foods and insist that the animal eat them. But it is impossible to offer precise instructions as to the choice of food for cats because they are very individualistic in this respect. The food should always be served in

◁ The European Black Tiger cat is an undemanding and pleasant companion.

a suitably-shaped, clean bowl (see Hint 8). If the food is kept in a freezer, make sure it is thawed completely before offering it to the cat: meat that remains frozen inside can cause the cat great digestive difficulties.

Apart from food for elderly, sick cats and young kittens, do not mince meat but cut it up into 1—2cm ($^{1}/_{2}$in) cubes. Chewing helps, among other things, to prevent the formation of tartar on the teeth. Leave some of the gristle and membranes in the meat.

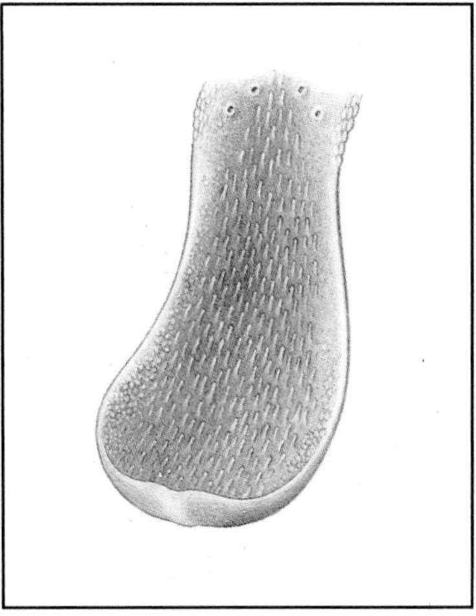

The cat's tongue surface is rough owing to the hook-shaped, backward-facing papillae in the centre of the surface. The taste buds are located at the front and sides of the tongue, and also near the root at the back.

Each cat should have its own bowl. When cats eat from a common dish you do not know how much each cat has had, and very often a slower eater does not get enough. A cat that eats poorly or slowly should be fed separately, in another room, where it is undisturbed. After it has finished eating, give the cat time to wash itself, rest and digest its food. The daily food intake varies from breed to breed and from animal to animal.

Providing suitable liquids is also part of proper nourishment. A cat should always have water available. Some cats also drink tea. Milk is both a liquid and a food; some cats like it, while it does not agree with others. Many of the tinned cat foods contain most of the moisture a cat needs, but always ensure that is also has a bowlful of its preferred drink. A proper intake of water helps prevent illnesses of the urinary tract which occur quite frequently among cats.

Feeding bowls must be shallow and accident-proof.

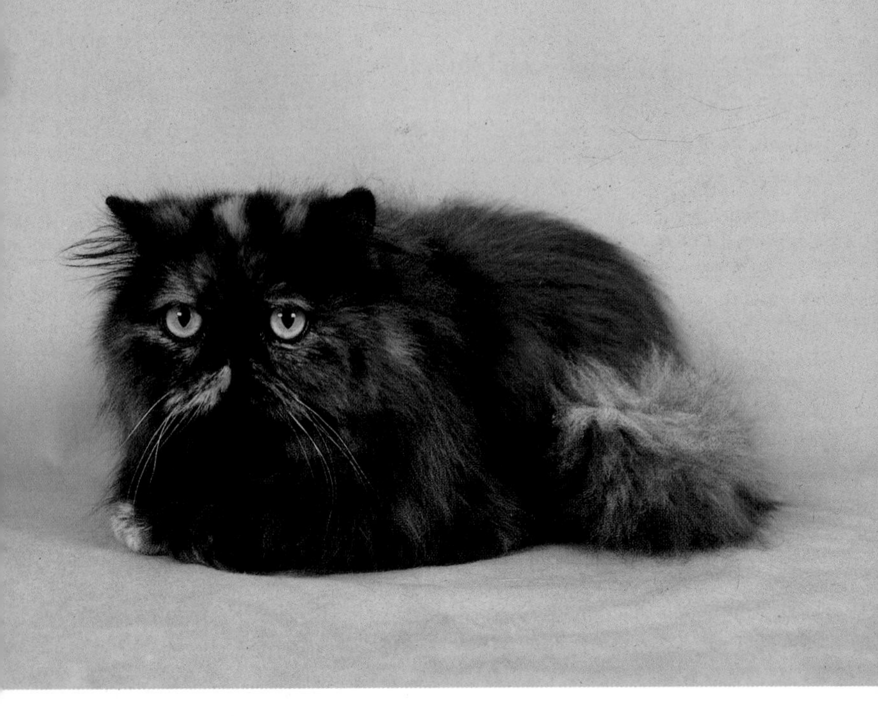

16 The Balanced Diet

The basic food for a cat is protein, which should make up not less than 40 per cent of its diet. The basic constituents of proteins are acids, which are essential for the development of muscle tissue, skin, coat, blood and reproductive organs. In nature, there are both animal and plant proteins. The decisive role in feeding a cat is played by the animal proteins found in meat, milk and eggs. A lack of proteins in food leads to a cat's inclination to infection and general ill health.

•

The main sources of proteins for domesticated cats are beef, veal, poultry, rabbit and fish, but you can also give your cat lean lamb, pork and game. All these are nowadays found in tinned cat foods. Offal does not have any great nutrient value, but it contains other important substances; do not serve it often and certainly not exclusively. Meat can be given either raw or cooked. Beef that has been frozen at —25°C (—77°F) or cooked to prevent infection can be offered; pork and game must always be cooked first. Meat should form two thirds of the daily intake.

◁ The Persian Tortoiseshell is popular for breeding because of the colour variety of the offspring.

Another important component of food is fat. Fats are the chief source of energy for mammals, and for meat-eating animals they are found in other animals or are derived from them – for instance, in the form of cream or butter. Fat should not exceed 25 per cent of a cat's diet. Another important source of energy are sugars, which belong to the group of foods known as carbohydrates that are found in cereals, potatoes, rice, pasta and legumes such as peas and beans. The amount of sugars in a cat's diet should not exceed 35 per cent of dry substances and should be in the form of a supplement mixed in with meat dishes. Suitable supplements are cooked oatmeal, rice and pasta.

●

Food should also include fibrous substances ('roughage'), such as cellulose which promote the activities of the digestive organs. Cellulose is found in vegetables and oatmeal, and both are served as supplements.

Some cats like vegetable food additives, such as grass or cereals, mixed in with their normal food. Such plants provide vitamins and roughage to help both digestion and regurgitation of hairballs.

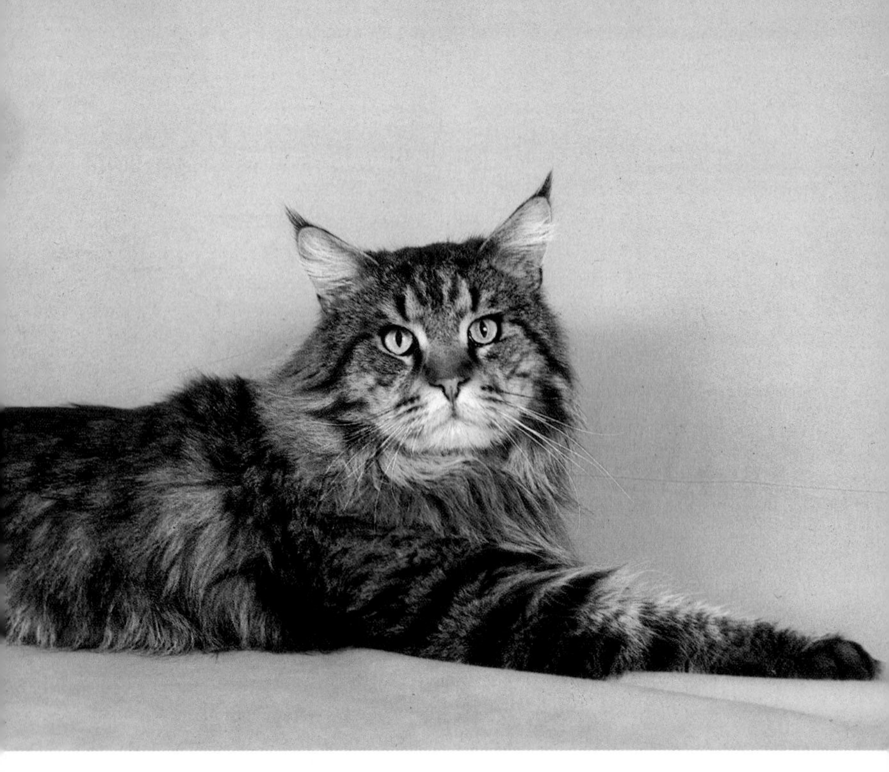

17 Minerals, Vitamins and Trace Elements in Cat Food

Mineral substances, in small quantities, are absolutely essential for the proper development and functioning of animal bodies. They regulate vital functions and the metabolism. The basic elements — potassium, sodium, magnesium and iron — help to maintain a balanced acid base. Potassium is important also for the functioning of the heart and to expel water from the organism. Magnesium is vital for creating enzymes, which help trigger many vital chemical reactions in the body. Iron is needed to produce red blood corpuscles. Calcium is essential for the formation of the bones and teeth, as is phosphorus. Sulphur is important for the liver and in forming proteins.

Trace elements are chemical substances that, although required only in minute quantities, are vital to physiological processes. They include iodine (for the thyroid gland), copper (for the production of red corpuscles), manganese for oxidation processes and activities of the reproductory glands, zinc for the metabolism, and a number of others, including cobalt and silicon.

We can ensure adequate provision of these substances by putting together a balanced diet. Sources of calcium include milk, yoghurt, cheese,

◁ The Maine Coon is currently the largest breed of cat.

and bones; phosphorus is found mainly in meat. The prime source of iodine is marine fish, which also contain a lot of phosphorus. Egg yolks abound in iron.

Vitamins also influence significantly the functioning of a number of organs, although a cat needs few of them. Lack of vitamins can come about by an unbalanced diet. Again, varied and good quality food is the best way to get vitamins into the body. According to solubility, vitamins are divided into those that dissolve in water (B, C, H) and those that dissolve in fats (A, D, E, K).

A balanced diet may be achieved only by giving your cat a varied diet.

Vitamin	Source	Signs of Insufficiency
A	liver, milk, butter, eggs	eyesight diseases, growth disorders, infections of the skin and mucous membranes
D	fish oil, seafood, liver	rickets
E	vegetable sprouts	fertility and growth defects
B	liver, eggs, oatmeal, yeast	nervous disorders, deficiency in growth, malfunctioning of the liver, eczemas and other skin ailments
H	liver, egg yolks, yeast	skin and mucous membrane infections
C	vegetables, green food	reduced defence against infections

18 A Cat's Changing Dietary Needs

Over the course of its life a cat's food needs, including the amount of nutrients and the total intake, are subject to change. Particularly important is the period of growth when erroneous feeding can cause irreparable damage. A growing organism places great demands on the intake of proteins, trace elements and vitamins. A kitten has a small stomach and must therefore receive its relatively big need for nutrients by means of small but frequent meals. Kittens less than four months old are fed five or six times a day; after the sixth month the frequency drops to three times a day, and after that to twice daily. You should begin to add solid food to the diet of a suckling kitten in the fourth week. At first, offer it liquid food (milk is best for kittens) and minced or scraped meat. Two weeks later, after the kitten has been weaned, start to give it a more varied diet. Gradually add small pieces of meat and, twice weekly, add half an egg yolk and various approved supplements. Check on the kitten's progress by weighing it regularly.

Feed adult cats twice a day. The morning portion is usually smaller; the main meal comes in the evening. Offer the food at regular times. Cats show the greatest interest in food at about six in the evening, which is in line with their natural daily rhythm. Leave the food in the bowl for about half an hour and take away what's left.

Elderly cats, who usually eat less eagerly, may be fed more than twice a day, but

◁ These ten-week-old Oriental and Siamese kittens are able to feed on their own.

A good indication of a sound diet is the quality of the coat. A well-fed cat's coat is glossy and elastic, without moulting or dandruff problems.

given smaller portions. You should limit the amount of offal and, as far as fresh (as opposed to tinned) meat is concerned give preference to white meat (poultry, rabbit), which is more easily digestible. Supply sufficient vitamins in a variety of foods. Salt the food of elderly cats a little in order to make them drink more: elderly cats have a tendency not to drink enough. For cats with missing teeth, mince the meat. Very cautiously increase the amount of food given to queens, although they have a big appetite. The embryo grows only in the second half of pregnancy and a queen that is overweight may have difficulty giving birth. Take careful note of the quality of the food, including how many mineral substances and vitamins it contains. The food is divided into three to four daily feedings.

A lactating queen has an enormous need for nutrients. You must give it food containing adequate calcium and lots of liquids. Lactating queens usually take to good-quality milk, and soups are good for them, too. Do not restrict the amount of food; give them sufficient amounts and as often as they demand it.

Daily energy expenditure (in Joules) of cats at various stages of life	
kitten up to 8 weeks	628
kitten up to 3 months	837
kitten up to 4 months	963
adult cat (weighing 3 kg)	1,005
adult cat (weighing 4 kg)	1,340
adult cat (weighing 5 kg)	1,465
queen cat (weighing from 2.5 to 4 kg)	1,600
lactating cat	up to 4,000

Energy value (in Joules) of certain foods per 100 grams	
lean beef	666
veal	628
lean pork	992
chicken	519
fowl (stewing hen)	1,264
liver	543
fish fillet	310
hard cheese	1,118
egg	812
2% low-fat milk	201
butter	3,002
rice	1,482
oatmeal	1,629

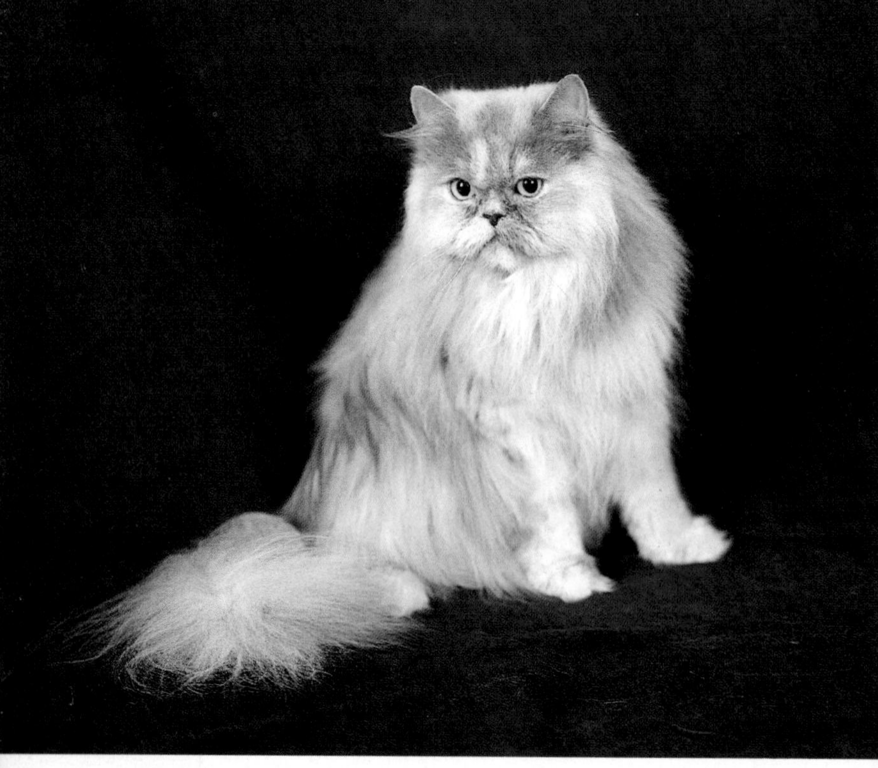

19 Varying Your Cat's Diet

Many different kinds of prepared cat foods are on the market. These products are put together according to special recipes and fully meet the cat's dietary needs. Besides basic nutrients they contain mineral substances and vitamins in balanced amounts so as to guarantee optimum nourishment.

•

Most owners alternate readymade and fresh food. Prepared foods come either in tins or in dry form, such as biscuits. Dried food is mostly given as the morning meal. It is important to remember that the cat must drink while eating dried food, so it should be served in a bowl next to one with water; or you might try dunking it in water or milk.

•

Another sometimes welcome and suitable supplement for cats is green food. Cats like to eat cereal or grass sprouts. The main reason it eats grass is to help it regurgitate hair balls. Grains or grass can be planted in a box or cul-

◁ Persian Blue Cream.

tivated hydroponically. This will protect your house plants, which the cat may otherwise nibble. Regurgitation after eating grass is quite normal; in other words it is not a sign of anything gone wrong. If you decide to allow a cat to chew on a houseplant, first wash the plant well with water to remove any trace of fertilizer or pesticides.

If the natural amount of all necessary minerals and vitamins are not contained in the cat's food, supply them in the form of various types of commercially available dietary supplements available as tablets, pastes, etc. Many are flavoured so that the cat enjoys eating them. Always follow the instructions on the label, as you may harm your cat if you exceed the recommended dose.

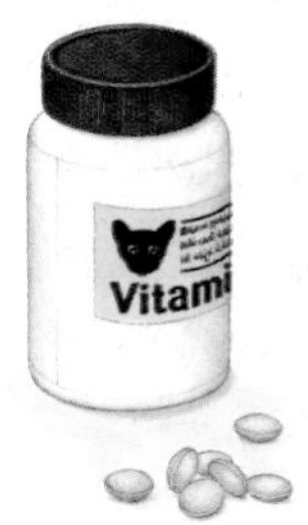

Vitamin tablets are a useful food additive.

Cats are able to get the green food on their own in the garden run-out. But there is a danger of poisoning if the lawn has been treated recently with fertilizers or pesticides. In such cases, prevent your cat from eating the grass until the effects of the chemical agents are over. The same applies to sprays used on vegetables or fruit trees.

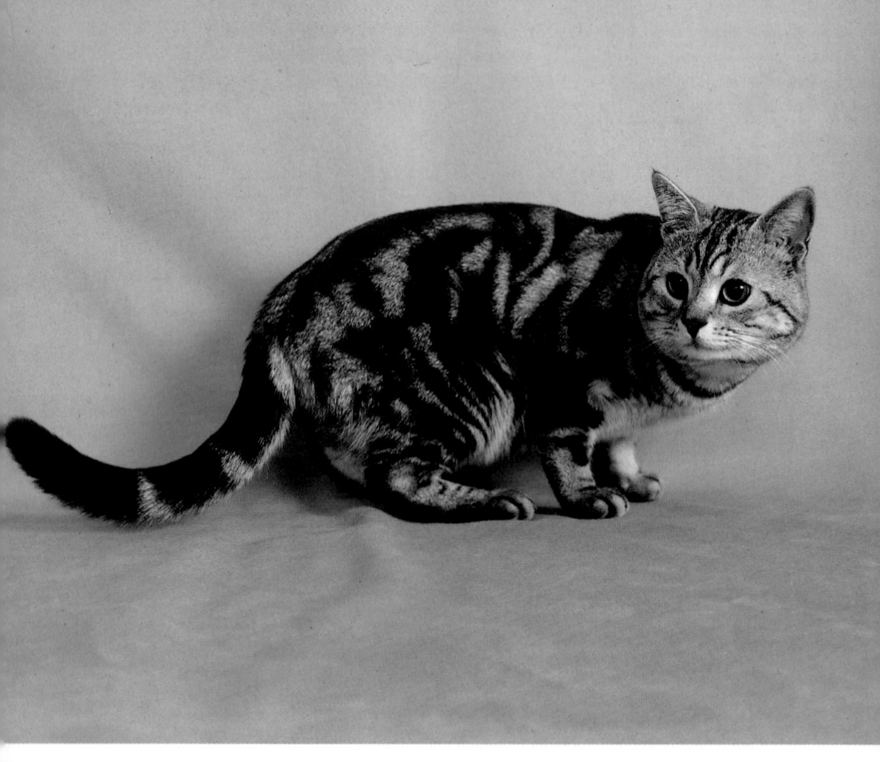

20 Common Errors in Feeding Your Cat

Perhaps the most frequent mistake in feeding a cat is to give it an unbalanced diet. Cats have an inclination to like one food, usually certain kinds of meat, and they stubbornly refuse to eat other things. Habit plays a big part in this. You should try to teach a young kitten to accept a variety of foods from the outset — though not, of course, at the expense of quality. Sea fish, which most cats love to eat, contain a large amount of phosphorus, but too much sea fish may cause the formation of stones in the urinary tract, especially in neutered males. Freshwater fish contain thiamine, an enzyme that destroys vitamin B1; but this problem is eliminated if you cook the fish.

•

Liver, which contains a large amount of vitamin A, should not be served too often because this can lead to decreased fertility and illnesses or cause growths to form on the vertebrae. These press on the spinal column nerves, causing the cat pain and preventing it from moving freely. In certain instances the animal can be completely incapacitated.

◁ British Silvery Black Marbled.

Overeating in cats, as in humans, is damaging to health. Keep your cat's needs in mind and adapt its diet to this. Cats become obese if they are overfed. Obesity can cause a variety of health problems, including reduced fertility. Obesity results mainly from overfeeding of sugars and fats.

●

It is impermissible to restrict a cat only to leftovers from the family table, and cats fed in this way inevitably suffer from malnutrition. A lack of good-quality proteins can mean growth deficiencies, a skinny look, and a matted and 'spiky' coat; the cat will be listless and succumb easily to infectious diseases. Proteins in food cannot be replaced by fats or carbohydrates, and cats fed this way suffer: despite being obese, such animals are in fact undernourished.

This well-fed British cat is strong and well muscled but not obese.

Dry food must always be served with sufficient water, preferably in a two-compartment bowl.

21 The Origins and Ancestors of the Domestic Cat

The question of the forebears of the domestic cat is still a subject of discussion. Most specialists today are agreed that the common ancestor of most, and probably all, breeds of domestic cat is the African wild cat (*Felis libyca*). Possibly the European wild cat (*F. silvestris*) played a part in the emergence of the domestic cat; its coat typically resembles that of a dark tabby. It has been suggested that the Siamese cat is descended from the leopard cat, or Bengal cat (*Felis bengalensis*), which, like the Siamese, is native to South-East Asia. Somewhat unclear is the role of Pallas's cat or manul (*F. manul*), of central Asia, which was once believed to have contributed to the development of longhaired cats. It has a round head, big eyes, a powerfully built body and long hair. But it is not yet known whether, if mated with a domestic cat, it can produce oddspring capable of further reproduction.

The domestic cat (*Felis catus*), according to zoological division, belongs to the order of flesh-eating mammals (Carnivora), the family of cats (Felidae), and the genus of small cats (*Felis*).

Feline beasts of prey are divided into three subgroups — the small cats (Felinae), the large cats (Pantherinae) and the cheetah (Acinony). The individual members of the sub-group Felinae differ considerably in size and appearance. The largest cat of

◁ One of the close relatives of the domestic cat is the Bengal cat (*Felis bengalensis*).

The cheetah, the fastest mammal known, is also a distant relative of our cat.

the Felis genus is the puma or mountain lion (*Felis concolor*) of the Americas, which weighs 45 to 60kg (100—130lb). One of the smallest is the blackfooted cat (*F. nigripes*), weighing only 1–2 kg (2 $^{1}/_{4}$—4 $^{1}/_{2}$lb). Other members of this genus include the caracal (*F. caracal*), the mountain cat (*F. jacobita*), the lynx (*F. lynx*), the ocelot (*F. pardalis*), the bobcat (*F. rufus*), the serval (*F. serval*), the tiger cat (*F. tigrina*), and the fishing cat (*F. viverrina*).

The African wild cat (*Felis libyca*), which is also found in some Mediterranean islands and in the Middle East, is probably a direct ancestor of the domestic cat.

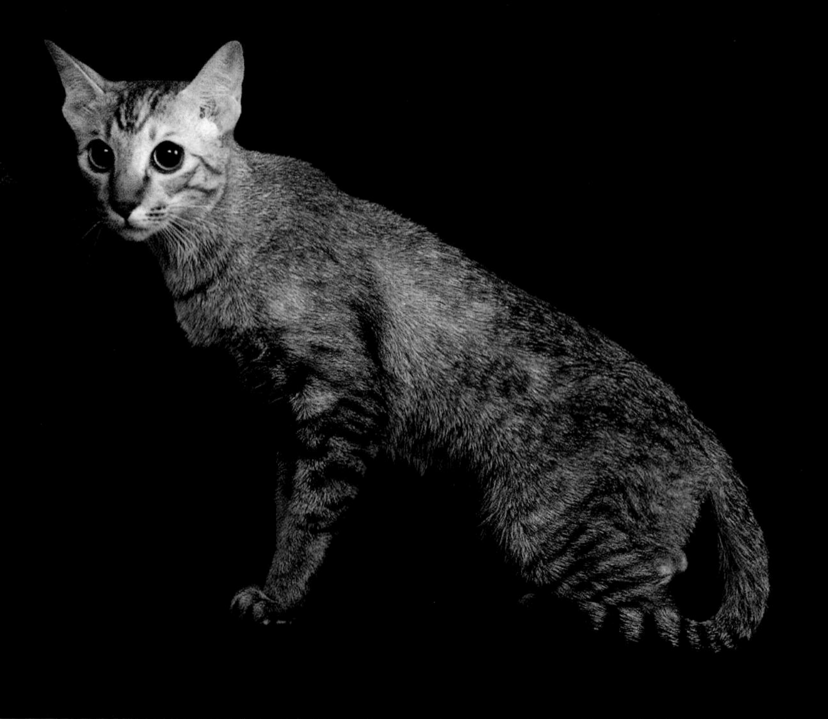

22 Feline Anatomy

The anatomy of the domestic cat differs hardly at all from that of its wild consins. On the other hand, while the wild species differ considerably in size, most of the breeds of domestic cats vary little in size and in the proportions of the individual parts of the body. All the cats are blessed with a physique that gives them great mobility combined with graceful elegance. The skeleton of a cat consists of 244 bones. Thanks to certain anatomical peculiarities (for instance the absence of a collarbone) the cat is an excellent jumper. The cat's silent stalking is due to the fact that it does not walk on the soles of its foot but on its toes. The powerful muscle insertion on the skeleton, especially the hind leg bones, gives the cat the energy to pounce, the essential condition for a successful hunt. The great mobility of the cervical spine makes it easier for the hunter cat to find its bearings quickly in new surroundings. The cat's claws are ingenious and an important weapon. The cat draws them by using minor muscles attached to the last bone of the toe. Of all the body parts, the skull is the most variable among domestic breeds, and it contains many features by which the breeds can be distinguished. Only among a few breeds are other parts of the skeleton different; an exception is the 'tailless' Manx and the Japanese Bobtail, a cat with a short tail.

◁ Oriental Chocolate Spotted Tortoise.

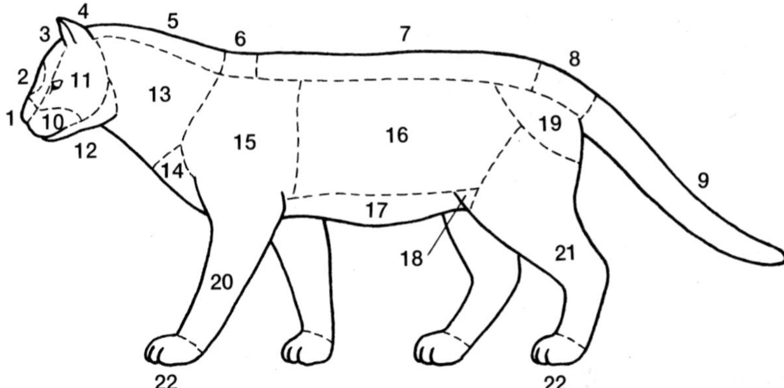

The main parts of the cat's body: (1) muzzle, (2) nose, (3) forehead, (4) ear, (5) neck, (6) comb, (7) back, (8) tail root, (9) tail, (10) upper jaw, (11) face, (12) lower jaw, (13) neck, (14) chest, (15) shoulder, (16) side, (17) abdomen, (18) flank, (19) behind, (20) fore legs, (21) hind legs, (22) paws.

The cat's principle bones: (1) skull, (2) lower jaw, (3) neck vertebrae, (4) chest vertebrae, (5) shoulder blade, (6) upper leg bone, (7) leg joint bone, (8) wrist, (9) wrist bones, (10) toes, (11) ribs, (12) spine, (13) loin vertebrae, (14) tail vertebrae, (15) hip bone, (16) patella, (17) shin and calf bones, (18) heel bone, (19) rear toe bones, (20) toes.

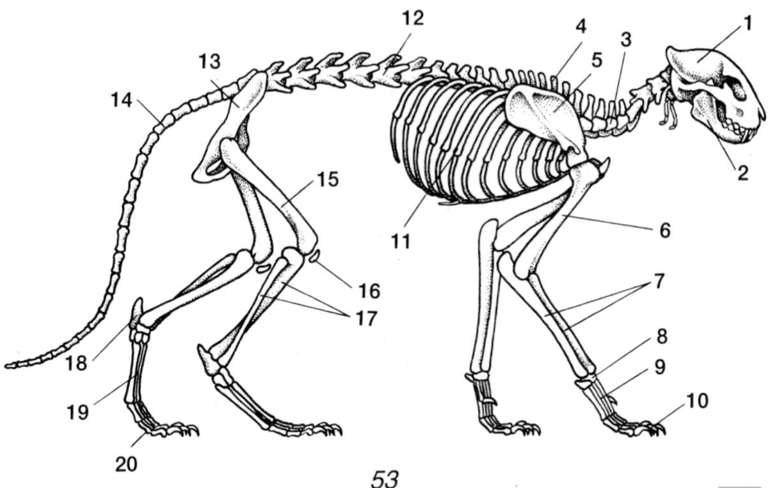

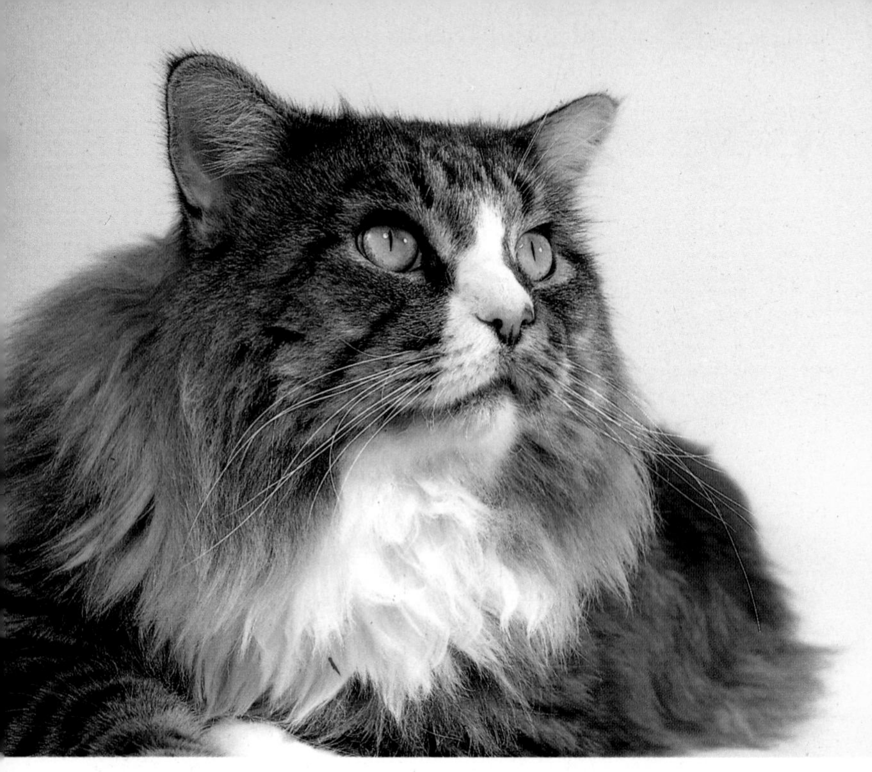

23 Feline Physiology

The structure and function of the cat's body does not differ markedly from those of other mammals, and they have a number of similarities to the human body. The circulatory system consists of a network of arteries and veins, the blood is pumped through the body by a two-chamber heart. In term of the size of the body, the cat's heart is relatively small. This means the cat does not have the stamina to run long distances. It can run fast, but only for short distances. Its pulse is 100 to 140 heartbeats per minute, that of kittens as much as 300 per minute. The cat's circulatory system contains about a quarter of a litre of blood. Cat's blood coagulates faster than human blood. It contains a higher concentration of red and white corpuscles, which significantly aid the organism's defence against infections.

When at rest, a cat breathes 30 to 50 times a minute. The breathing system plays a big part in regulating the body temperature. When it is hot, cats — like dogs — breathe faster and with their mouth open, thus helping to cool the blood flowing along the walls of the respiratory organs. A cat perspires only imperceptibly and it has almost no effect on the regulation of its body temperature (see Hint 24). A cat's normal body temperature is 38°C to 39°C (100—102°F) and its temperature is always taken in the rectum (younger cats have slightly higher body temperature).

◁ The Maine Coon: black tiger-striped and white variety.

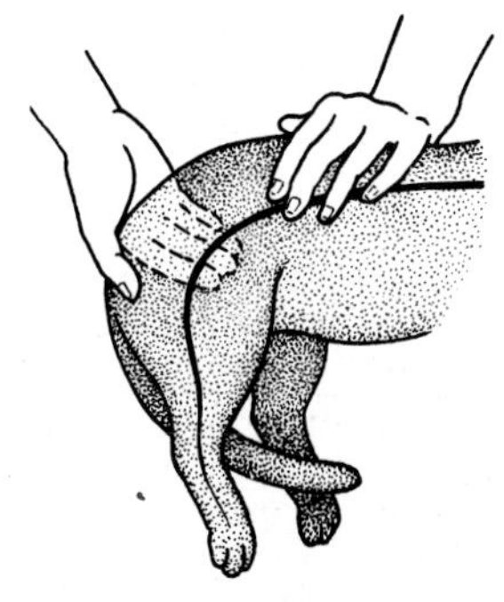

The pulse is best taken by feeling the hip artery located on the inner thigh.

The digestion of food begins in the mouth. After it is swallowed food reaches the stomach through the gullet (oesophagus). The cat's gastric juices are very effective, as they are among all wild beasts who eat virtually all the body parts of their prey. The intestines are relatively short, corresponding to the structure of the digestive system among carnivorous animals. Undigested food passes into the last part of the digestive system, the large intestine, where it is absorbed with water; then it thickens, becomes semi-solid waste matter, and is expelled as faeces through the rectum. Among domestically bred cats it is considered quite normal if the cat has a bowel movement only every two or three days. Cats that are kept more or less permanently indoors tend to become constipated owing to lack of exercise.

The urinary organs consist of paired kidneys, the urinary duct, the urinary bladder and the urethra. Waste material leaves the body in the urine. Owing to the anatomical structure of male cats (especially those neutered early in life), including the length and narrowness of the urethra, an infection of the urinary tract and kidneys known as the feline urological syndrome (FUS) is fairly common. That is why you should observe closely the urination of male cats, noting its frequency and colour. A warning signal is the discovery of blood in the urine, or pain, or an inability to urinate freely. A cat normally urinates twice or three times a day; the total amount passed is 100 to 200ml (3.5 to 7fl.oz).

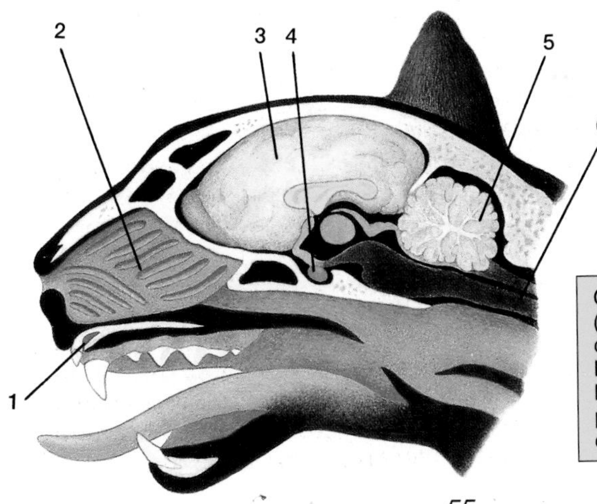

Cross-section of head: (1) Jacobson's organ, (2) olfactory mucous membrane in nasal cavity, (3) brain, (4) cerebellum, (5) pituitary gland, (6) spinal cord extension.

24 Your Cat's Coat

The skin and coat are important organs that chiefly have a protective function. They protect the body against outside influences and influence body temperature. Feline skin has a rather complex structure. Its inner layer, the dermis, contains nerve fibres registering pressure, pain and cold, and hair follicles and sebaceous glands. The sweat glands of a cat occur only on its paw pads and around the nose. They are of importance only in identifying smells and play no role in regulating body temperature. The outer layer of the skin, the epidermis, has a primarily protective function. This outer layer hardens. Most cats are covered with hair. Hairless places include paw pads, the nose, a small area around the anus, and the teats. The hair grows from hair follicles located deep in the skin. We distinguish between three types of hair: guard hairs, which are the longest and the strongest; the somewhat thinner awn hairs; and the very fine down hairs. A knowledge of the hair structure allows us to understand some of the special features of hair structure among different breeds, for which these deviations from the usual type of hairs are characteristic.

In terms of coat length, cats fall into one of two broad categories: longhairs and shorthairs. Within these categories, however, there are various further divisions. In the shorthair coats the primary or guard hairs are as much as 4.5cm (2in) long and

◁ Somali Ruddy.

the down hairs are well developed. The shorthair Russian Blue has down hair that is even more developed, creating the appearance of a so-called double-haired cat. The shorthair Siamese, on the other hand, should not have an undercoat: its presence is considered a flaw.

In longhaired coats the guard hairs are 12 to 13 cm (5—5 $^1/_2$in) long. Persian cats have a greatly developed undercoat: the awn hairs are nearly as long as the down hairs. Furthermore, all their types of hairs are very fine.

Semi-longhair breeds, genetically speaking, also have long hairs but the individual breeds have differently developed undercoats. The coat of a Turkish Angora, for instance, has almost no down hair, while that of the Norwegian Forest is well developed; moreover, it has modified guard hairs that are particularly strong, long and oily, making its coat efficiently water repellent. The hair of the Rex types is of a special kind: it is curly; and one, the Cornish Rex, is totally without bristles. The American wirehair has another type of curly coat. It contains all types of hairs, and each is strong and irregularly curly. There are also cats without hair. The Sphinx breed has only very fine down instead of hair.

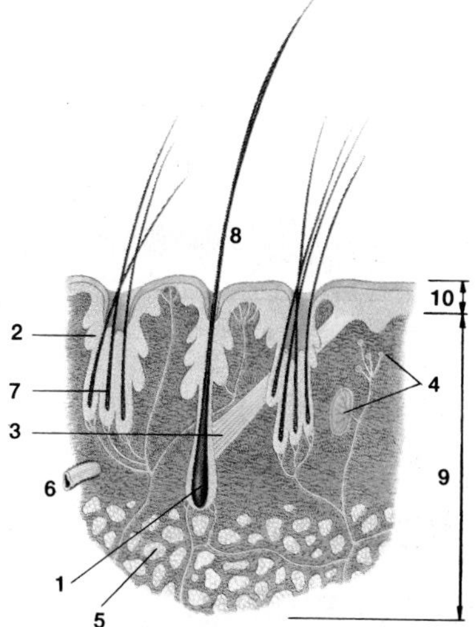

Cross-section of the skin: (1) hair follicle, (2) sebaceous gland, (3) muscle, (4) nerve receptor, (5) fat tissue, (6) vein, (7) down hair, (8) outer coat hair, (9) dermis, (10) epidermis.

Hair types: (a) outer coat hair, (b) bristles, (c) down hair.

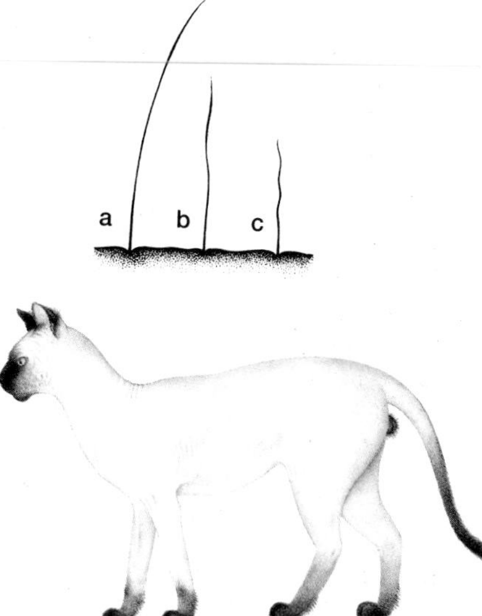

The hairless Sphinx breed's coat consists of light fuzz.

25 Mouth and Teeth

The cat's mouth cavity is structured like that of a typical predator, with long, powerful canine teeth that are used to kill its prey. Teeth are vitally important for the hunter-cat. The teeth are in dental sockets in an alveolate (honeycomb-like) jawbone: the animal has a protruding jaw covered by thick gums. An adult cat has 30 teeth consisting of incisors, canines, premolars and molars. The dental formula for one side of its face shows the number and kind of teeth. For an adult cat the formula is 3131 over 3121, which means that on one side of the face the animal has three incisors, one canine, three premolars in the upper jaw (but two in the lower) and one molar.

A kitten has milk teeth which appear between the fifteenth and thirtieth day of life. There are 26 such teeth: the molars are missing. The dental formula is 3130 over 3120. Between the fifth and seventh month the milk teeth are replaced by permanent teeth. In this period the kitten's gums are painful and tender and it eats poorly, so you should mince its food, or at least cut it into very small pieces.

In judging cats at shows, stress is laid not only on the correct number of teeth and their condition, but also on the position of the teeth and the jaws. Missing teeth are not as common among cats as among dogs, but anomalies

◁ Persian: tortoise and white.

do occur. Physiologically, cats should have a 'pincer' bite, in which the tips of the incisors come together. If the lower incisors jut out in front of the upper incisors, it is called an overbite, and if the upper incisors come out over the lower ones it is called an underbite. These defects can be caused either by faulty position of the teeth or asymmetrical growth of the jaws. Most cats with an overbite are found among breeds with shortened face parts, for instance the Persian cats. An overbite up to 2mm (0.08in) is tolerated. If the overbite is larger, it disrupts the harmony of the head; moreover, the teeth may strike against the soft tissues, so that the cat has trouble eating and cannot fully close the mouth. In these cases the overbite is regarded as degenerative and such animals are unsuitable for further breeding. Sometimes it is necessary for defective teeth to be filed down or even extracted because the cat is in constant pain.

A cat's teeth should be given regular attention. It is important to remove tartar in time, and to feed the animal solid food to limit the amount of tartar that forms. Cats often suffer from gum infections, which can lead to the teeth becoming loose or even falling out.

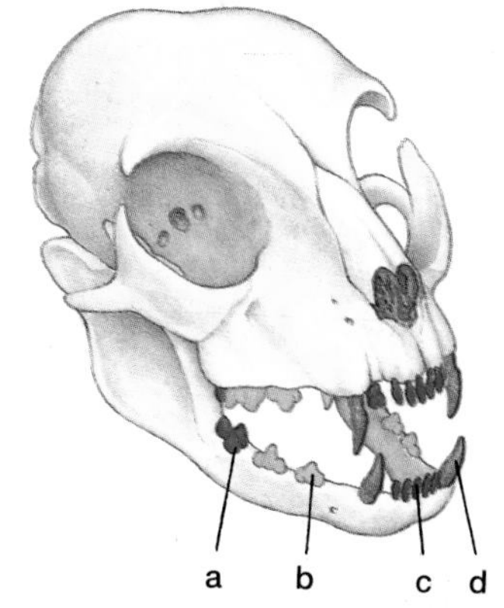

Teeth location diagram: (a) incisors, (b) fangs, (c) premolars, (d) molars.

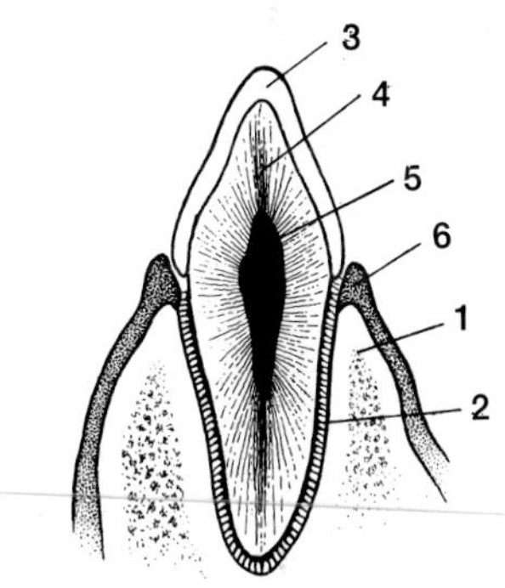

Tooth cross-section: (1) bone tooth base, (2) periodontium, (3) tooth enamel, (4) dentine ivory, (5) dental core, (6) gum.

Bite types: (a) overbite, (b) physiological bite, (c) underbite.

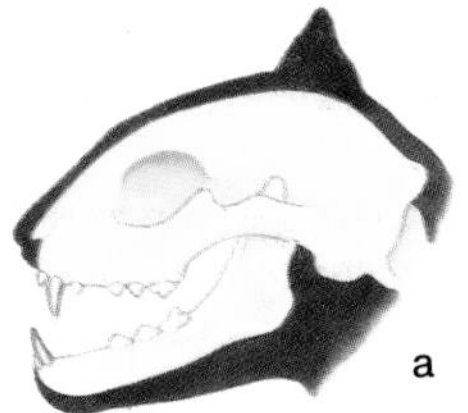

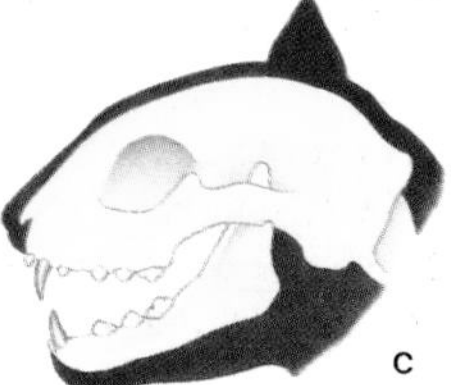

26 The Cat's Keen Eyesight

The most highly developed sense organ of a cat is its vision. As a hunter and, originally, a nocturnal animal, the cat needs excellent vision to find prey. Recent investigations have proved that a cat distinguishes colours (earlier it was thought that this is not so). Many breeders agree that their cats most of all like white covers and blankets for sleeping.

The position of the cat's eyes, set forward on the head, enable it to have binocular vision. This is important in estimating size, distance and height in jumping and hunting. Thanks to the curvature of the cornea, the cat has a wide field of view. Indeed, very little escapes a cat's vision, but from birth cats are somewhat far-sighted: they see things best at a distance of 2—6 m (6 $^{1}/_{2}$—20 ft), while close-up stationary objects appear somewhat blurred.

•

The ability of cats to see in dim light is well-known. The cat's pupil is able to expand or contract according to the amount of light; in dim light the pupil is large and round, in bright light it narrows to a slit; a reflecting layer behind the

◁ Blue Point Burmese.

retina of the eye helps it to see better in dim light. The pupil is an opening in the iris of the eye, the iris functioning as a lens. In complete darkness not even a cat can see.

●

Cat-breeders are particularly interested in the colour of the iris, which determines the colour of the eyes. In fact, eye colour is one of the important features of individual breeds and greatly influences the success or failure of a show cat and its breeding value. The colour of the iris depends on the amount and location of the pigment. An iris of copper and orange has the most pigment; blue irises have the least. No pigment at all is in the iris of albinos. They are pink because the blood vessels at the back of the retina show through the colourless iris. For breeding purposes it is not easy to influence the colour of the eyes, especially their shades. One must use the method of selection in breeding and consistently choose only cats with suitable eye colour.

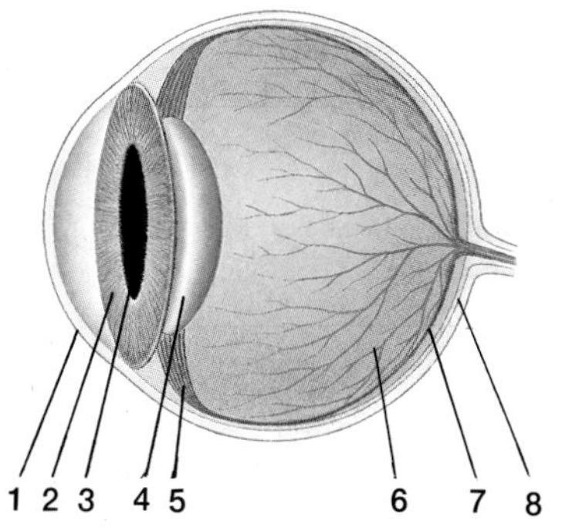

Cat's eye diagram: (1) cornea, (2) iris, (3) pupil, (4) lens, (5) vitreous body, (6) pupil-controlling muscles, (7) retina, (8) choriodea.

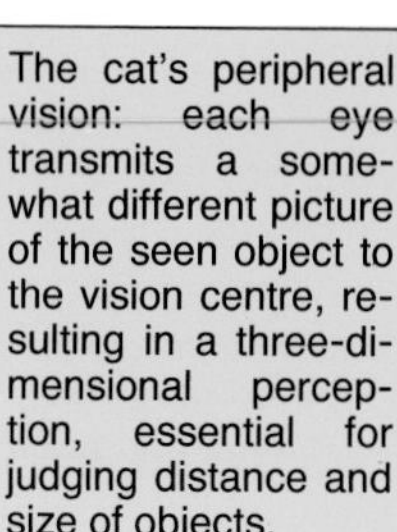

The cat's peripheral vision: each eye transmits a somewhat different picture of the seen object to the vision centre, resulting in a three-dimensional perception, essential for judging distance and size of objects.

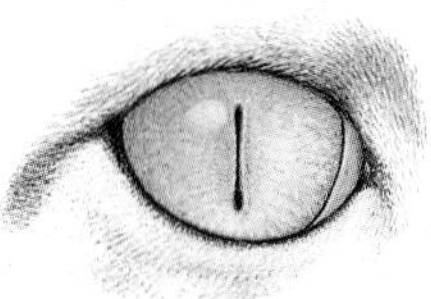

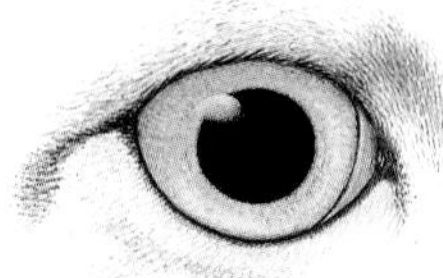

The cat's pupil functions as a perfect light filter, its size regulated by the light available.

27 Other Cat Senses

All the cat's senses are well developed, and in some cases are superior to those of human beings. Hence the rise of legends about cats' magical abilities.

The sense least developed in the cat is that of taste. Many breeders might dispute this, bearing in mind cats' finicky eating behaviour. It was long believed that cats could not recognize a sweet taste, but more recent study has shown that it can.

The second most developed sense a cat possesses, after sight, is hearing. It is said that a car hears sounds having an oscillation frequency of from 30 Hz (low sounds) up to as high as 65 kHz, which is getting on for two octaves above that capable of being heard by the human ear and is also beyond the perception of dogs. This sensitivity to high-pitched sounds may explain a well-travelled cat's nervousness in a car travelling at high speed.

Some cats are born deaf. Deafness is most common in white cats, especially those with blue eyes. Although breeding rules are not hard and fast on this score (one need not exclude a deaf animal from breeding), the number of cats with such an impairment should not be increased.

◁ Black-coloured Oriental.

The cat's sense of balance is well-known. Its perfectly functioning sensory organ is located in the inner ear. A cat does not suffer from vertigo, and if it falls from a height it always lands on its feet. But do not assume that this ability can always save it from severe injury in a fall.

The sense of smell is well developed in cats. They also have a related, chemical sense which is partly smell and partly taste and is activated by a receptor in the roof of the mouth. The receptor is stimulated by certain pungent odours, such as that of urine of females on heat. These odours are trapped by the tongue and are transferred to the receptor when the cat presses its tongue against the roof of the mouth. When the receptor is thus stimulated, the cat makes a unique facial movement known as the flehmen reaction. Some cats also react in this way to the smell of catnip (*Nepeta cataria*).

The sense of touch is located in sensory receptors in deep folds of the skin, and through the vibrissae, commonly known as whiskers, which are at least twice as thick as the guard hairs. If the vibrissae are cut off, the animal becomes extremely unsteady. A queen often bites them off its kittens, evidently to keep them close to home. The vibrissae probably also help in its perception of changes in atmospheric pressure.

Whiskers – tactile hairs – are important sensory organs. Their position changes according to the cat's mood: (a) at rest, (b) cat examines an unfamiliar object, (c) expression of anger.

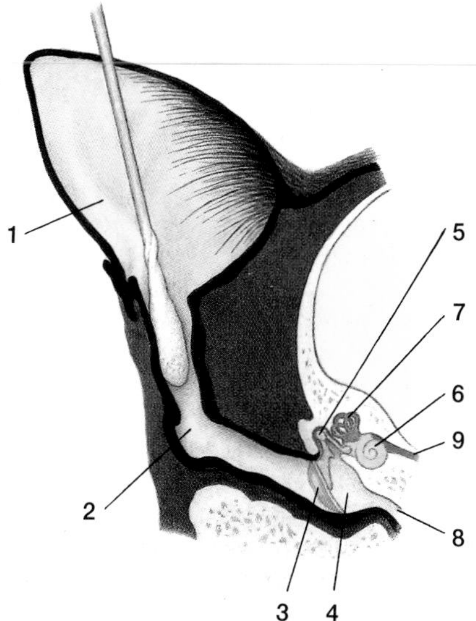

A cat's middle and inner ear: (1) earlobe, (2) outer auditory canal, (3) ear-drum, (4) middle ear, (5) ear ossicles: malleus, incus, stapes, (6) cochlea, (7) equilibrium tract, (8) eustachian tube, (9) statuacoustic nerve. Only the opening of the auditory canal should be cleaned, otherwise a painful injury may occur.

28 The Feline Voice

Cats produce various sounds. Some cats are quiet, while others are noisy. The Siamese is particularly known for this, and has been called the 'talkative' breed.

The cat's vocal apparatus is somewhat different from man's. Besides vocal cords it has two folds of membrane known as false vocal cords. Unlike humans, cats can make sounds while inhaling as well as exhaling. The sound is produced by the construction of the laryngeal muscles and the force with which the air is driven through the vocal cords. Sounds are modulated by changing the shape of the mouth.

•

Cats are capable of creating a variety of sounds when they mew. Cats also know how to purr, to produce the characteristic low vibratory drone. There is a whole range of cooing sounds produced by the queen when she is 'talking' to her kittens. Hissing and spitting are part of the fighting and threatening vocabulary. A total of 16 sounds has so far been distinguished by which cats communicate vocally among themselves or with a human.

◁ Persian Silvery Blue Tiger Tortoise-shell.

The cat uses vocal sounds for various purposes — to ask for things, for instance, or to express surprise or pleasure. Most cats have their own little vocabulary through which they communicate basic desires: I want to go out, I'm hungry, I need help, and so on.

Probably for us the loveliest vocal expression of a cat is purring. Cats do not purr only when they are satisfied. They may also purr if they are nervous or even in pain. To this day it is not known how the cat produces this sound. Several theories have been put forward. According to one, the sound is produced by the false vocal cords. Another theory explains purring in a rather complicated way, as vibrations produced through various structures, even coming from the vena cava (the main vein that returns the blood from the body to the heart). The sound is said to be produced from turbulence of the blood in the vena cava, causing the diaphragm to vibrate. The diaphragm in turn causes vibrations in the chest, which are then transmitted upward through the windpipe to the sinus cavities in the skull. The combination of these vibrations emerges as purring.

This posture of the cat is often accompanied by noisy calls.

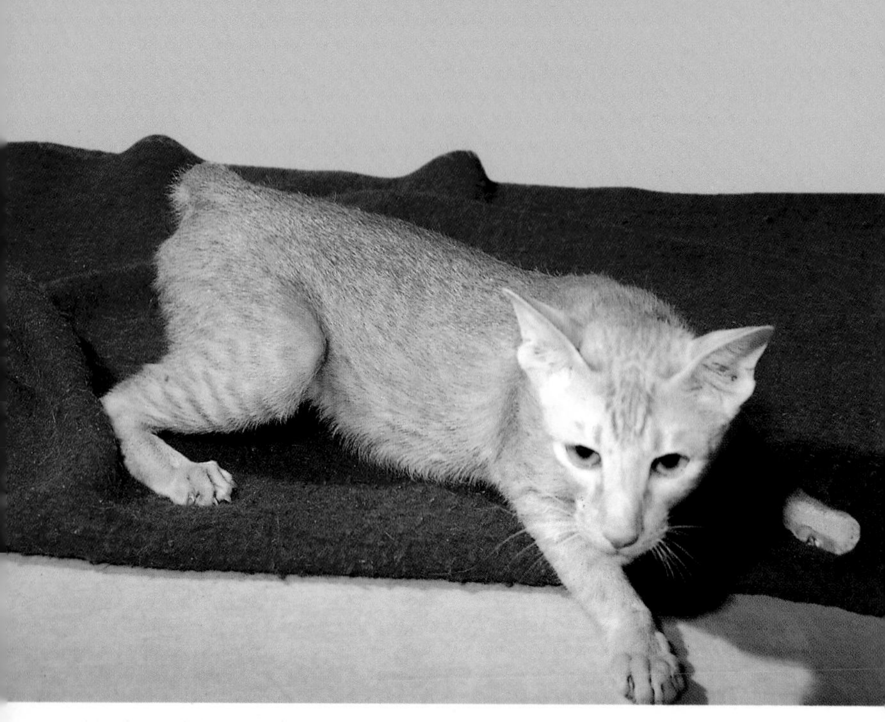

29 The Mating Season

Adult female cats (queens) come into oestrus, or 'on heat', and are sexually receptive to males, in cycles that occur several times a year, mainly in late winter/early spring and late spring/early summer. The female sex hormones, oestrogens, produced by the ovaries, are responsible for the external and internal manifestations of oestrus, during which the queen is at her most fertile and is most attractive to tom cats.

•

The duration and intensity of oestrus varies between breeds and may also vary somewhat between individual queens of the same breed. Females generally mature at between three and nine months, and males somewhat later. In general, the slimmer breeds, such as Siamese and Burmese, mature earlier and undergo a more intense oestrus than heavier breeds such as Persian and British cats.

◁ Typical posture of a queen in oestrus.

While in heat queens are more affectionate, more restless, eat less and urinate more often, and mew loudly and monotonously for long periods. A queen in heat shows her readiness to mate by crouching low, kneeding the ground with her front paws, raising her rump and deflecting her tail to one side. This posture is known as 'lordosis' and is infallibly attractive to entire (unneutered) adult toms.

For some queens, frequent and intensive oestrus is debilitating. If such a cat is not intended for breeding, it may be advisable to treat her with a hormonal preparation or have her spayed. At the other extreme are queens whose oestrus is so low key that they exhibit few of the usual physical symptoms, and because they are unreptive to toms, are unsatisfactory from the point of view of breeding.

•

Oestrus normally lasts up to 10 days (less if mating occurs and the queen ovulates). Then follows an infertile (anoestrus) period while the body readies itself for the next onset of oestrus. The intervals between oestrus are highly individual and differ both between breeds of cats and also between individuals of the same breed. In cats housed indoors, the influence of artificial light, relatively high temperatures and better food can bring about oestrus at any time of the year. As a rule, home-bred cats also mature earlier than those living mainly outdoors. Even so, cats should not be allowed to produce litters until they are a year old.

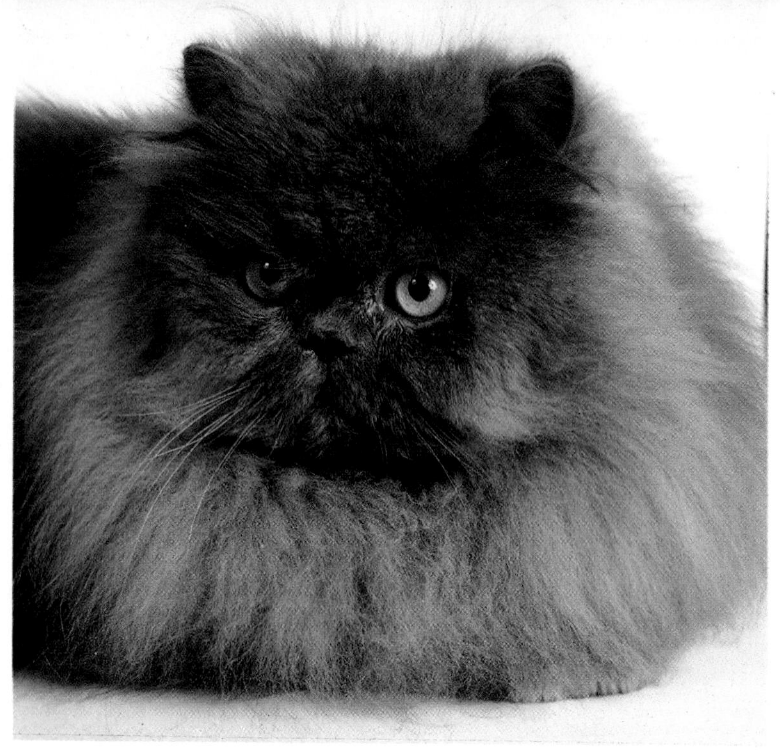

30 Looking After an Older Cat

The average life-span of a cat is 14 to 15 years, though many cats live beyond their twentieth year. It is often claimed that Burmese and Siamese cats live to an exceptional age, but there are no available statistics to support this.

Neutered/spayed cats usually live the longest, while unneutered male cats have the shortest life expectancy. But much depends on the conditions in which the cat lives, on its use in breeding and the diseases it has suffered during its lifetime. Animals that are the products of inbreeding usually have a shorter life expectancy.

Signs of ageing in cats appear at about the eleventh to twelfth year. They are most pronounced in cats used for breeding. Oestrus is less intense and less frequent. The litters are smaller; and, by the age of 11 or 12, despite successful mating, queens fail to produce kittens. Most breeders no longer mate elderly queens and have them spayed before this. The potency of male cats lasts a long time: it is not unusual for a 15-year-old male cat to father offspring.

Older cats sleep more and look for warm places; most also eat less food. They should be fed more often but with smaller portions. Sometimes, if there

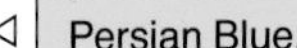

Persian Blue.

is teeth trouble, they may need to be given minced food. Except for overfed animals, older cats are usually slimmer than in their youth, and sometimes even outright skinny. The subcutaneous fat disappears, the skin seems to be too big for the body, they have sunken cheeks and the bones of the spine stick out. The coats of elderly cats tend to turn grey, especially on the face.

Elderly cats hear less well and some go completely deaf. This must be taken into consideration when communicating with them, since their deafness may be interpreted as disobedience. Eyesight also becomes less acute. If you have a blind or semi-blind cat at home, avoid re-arranging the furniture as the cat might otherwise hurt itself by jumping into it.

In old age cats often suffer from constipation. They must be given foods that encourage bowel movement, and, on advice from your vet, perhaps a mild laxative. Because elderly cats are inclined to drink little, salt their food slightly to encourage them to take in more liquids.

One sees evidence of the loss of strength and suppleness in an old cat in the poorer state of their coats. You should brush an older cat more frequently and also wipe it occasionally with a damp cloth. The nails on the claws should be cut carefully. Veterinarians recommend that an elderly animal be given a medical check-up every year. Any disease caught at an early stage can be treated far more successfully than one that is more advanced.

Elderly cats invariably prefer warm places, and will often appreciate an electric blanket at a low setting.

One year in the adult cat's life is equivalent to seven in a human being. But a kitten's development it much faster: its first year equates to the the first 15 of a child. The ratio decreases as cats get older: for those between the age of 10 and 15 it falls to a 3:1 ratio.

Cat	1	2	6	10	14	20	25	30
Human	15	25	45	60	72	90	105	120

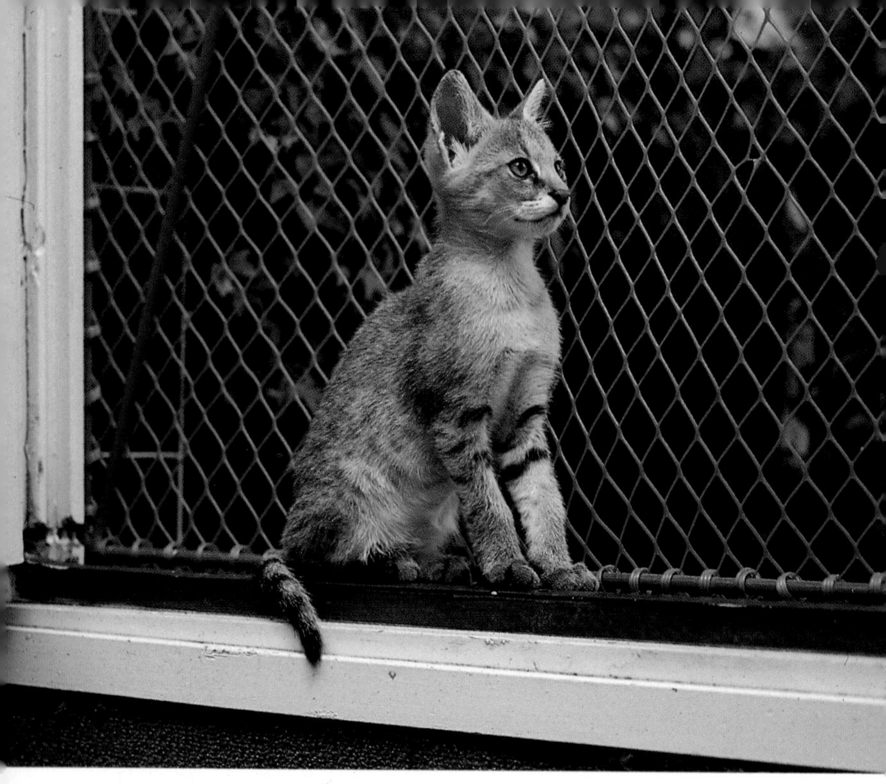

31 Keeping Your Cat Healthy

Most true cat lovers can tell immediately when their cat is not well: they can detect even the smallest changes in their pet's appearance or behaviour. This is important because it means that any health problems can be treated early. You should examine your cat carefully and systematically at least once a month. Have a good look at the eyes, ears, mouth, coat and anus. The most obvious signs are discharges from the eyes and ears. When something itches, the cat shakes its head, 'closes' its ears and scratches them. Tartar may form on the teeth, and may combine with an infection that makes the gums red and liable to bleed. Many cats suffer from swollen subcutaneous glands around the rectum, which can easily be seen. A cat will sometimes rub its rectum on the ground, dragging itself forward with its front paws.

When you examine your cat's coat you may find not only fleas and various parasites, but also some bald spots. You should consult your vet about these: skin diseases, even with correct treatment, tend to be persistent and it is important to treat them as soon as symptoms appear. Veterinarians recommend regular general medical check-ups; as noted already, elderly cats should have one at least once a year.

◁ Kittens of the jungle cat often like human dwellings and may be at least partially tamed.

To prevent illnesses vaccinations are an absolute necessity. Present-day vaccines are reliable and are free of side effects. All cats, without exception, should be vaccinated, whether they are allowed outdoors or confined to the house. Those entered in shows will certainly be required to have been vaccinated. Cats trained for shows and those allowed to roam outdoors, if only in your garden, obviously run a greater risk of infection. On the other hand, cats kept indoors build up less resistance to diseases because of their isolation and they can have a nasty time of it when ill. The first vaccination should be between the eighth and eleventh week of the kitten's life. The basic vaccinations include those against panleukopaenia, rhinotracheitis and calicivirus infections. There are acombined vaccines that protect the animal against all these infections.

A kitten can be vaccinated against leukosis from the ninth week. A cat or a kitten is always examined before immunization: it goes with saying that only a healthy animal can be vaccinated. All vaccinations, including the annual booster, are recorded on a special certificate.

Another preventive measure is de-worming. The first such procedure is carried out in the fourth week, the next in the seventh week of life, before the first vaccination. It is recommended that cats should be de-wormed twice a year. Another recommendation is to have the cat's faeces examined regularly for parasites. The right medicine and dosage is prescribed by the vet. Today there is a whole series of medicaments that cause cats no difficulty. De-worming treatment, for instance, is nowadays administered by injection.

Dental plaque resulting in an inflammation of the gums.

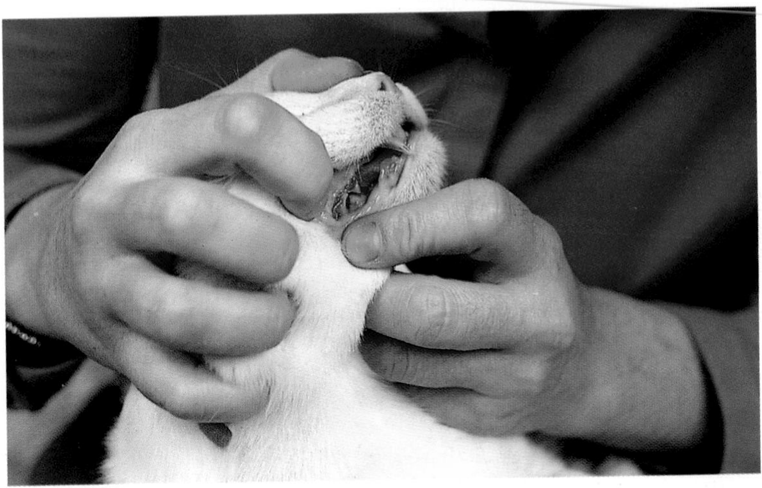

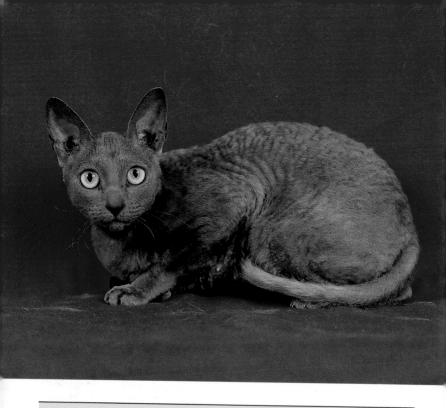

32 Signs of Health and Illness

A healthy cat likes its food and eats with appetite, looks after its coat and grooms itself. Its coat is sleek and flat, the cat has a clear look in its eyes, is curious and behaves in a normal way. It responds to its owner's care. Every change in behaviour, such as seeking out dark corners, crawling under the furniture or sitting listlessly, can mean that something is wrong.

Typical posture of a sick cat: sitting apathetically, with a 'staring' coat and seemingly unfocussed expression.

◁ Blue Cornish Rex.

Even before there are any typical symptoms of illness, it is possible to tell from the cat's appearance that it is out of sorts. Obvious signs are a fluffed up, matted coat, appearance of the nictitating membrane (the so-called third eyelid), a loss of appetite, listlessness and so on. Observe the cat carefully at such a time so that you do not miss any symptoms. If such a change in the animal's condition does not disappear entirely within 24 hours, consult your vet. An experienced cat breeder recognizes many seemingly minor but important changes and by explaining everything in great detail to the veterinarian he or she can effectively help towards the correct diagnosis.

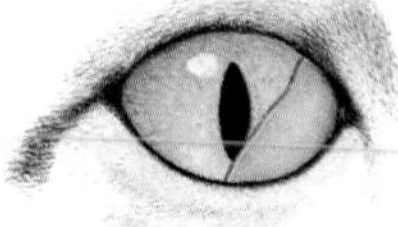

A common sign of illness is an enlarged third eyelid.

A firm but not hurtful grip on the cat is essential when making a thorough physical examination. The cat should be calmed by talking to it and petting it (a, b). A restless cat should be held by the scruff of the neck with one hand, while the other takes a firm grasp of the hind legs (c). Often a second pair of hands is needed.

33 Looking After a Sick Cat

The first thing to provide for a sick cat is quiet and warmth. Let the animal lie on an electric blanket set at the lowest temperature. If possible, allow it to stay in its favourite spot in the house. If you have more than one cat, keep the sick one away from the others but check on it often and speak to it. Cats with infectious diseases must of course be isolated. When a sick cat begins to get well, allow it to be with the others. There must be water and, if appropriate, food as well as a litter tray near the cat's corner so it doesn't have far to go. Sick cats prefer a shady place to a brightly lit one.

•

Your vet will specify treatment of the sick cat and will explain in detail about the medicine and how often and how much must be given. During the first few days, medicine may be given by injection, which means visiting the veterinarian's surgery. In some instances a cat is put on a diet. It is often very difficult to make a cat accept such food. Many powder medicines, however, are nowadays highly palatable to cats. Sick cats sometimes have to have minced food or food given in very tiny pieces, or even be fed a liquid diet using syringes. Always follow the vet's instructions. If the cat is seriously ill to

◁ Persian Tortoiseshell and Persian Black and White.

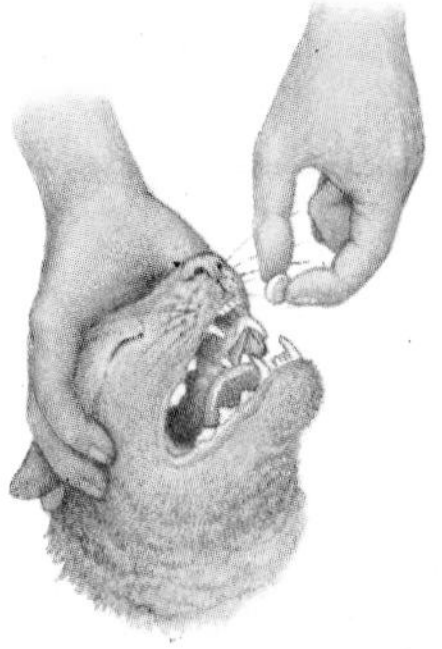

When a cat is to be given a pill the neck should be slightly pushed back and the jaw joint gently squeezed to make it open its mouth. The fingers of the other hand should press down on the lower incisors in order to open the mouth even further. The pill is placed as far back on the tongue as possible and the mouth held closed. Gentle stroking of the front of the throat will help the cat to swallow it. If the cat resists, another person should be summoned for assistance. It may help to wrap the cat's legs and body in a towel.

When applying medication in the form of drops or during forced feeding of liquid, a plastic syringe is used. The neck and the chest of the cat should be wrapped with a towel in case of spillage.

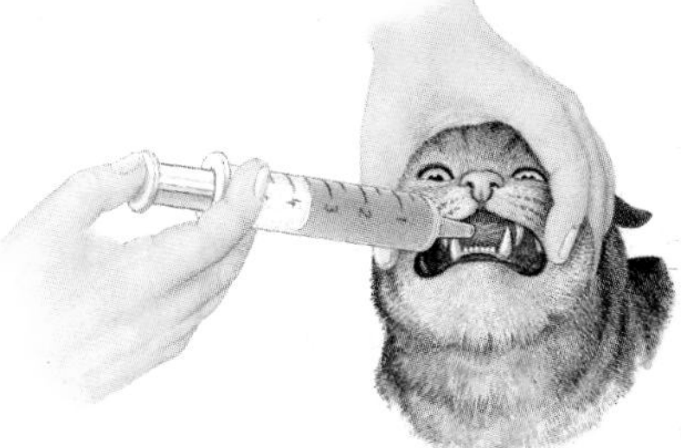

the point where it does not take care of its coat, wipe the coat with a moist terrycloth towel wherever it is unclean. If you are looking after a temporarily immobilised cat, you must change the soiled and wet litter tray regularly. The vet may recommend gentle massage of the cat's muscles to help blood circulation, regeneration of any damaged nerves and the animal's mental condition.

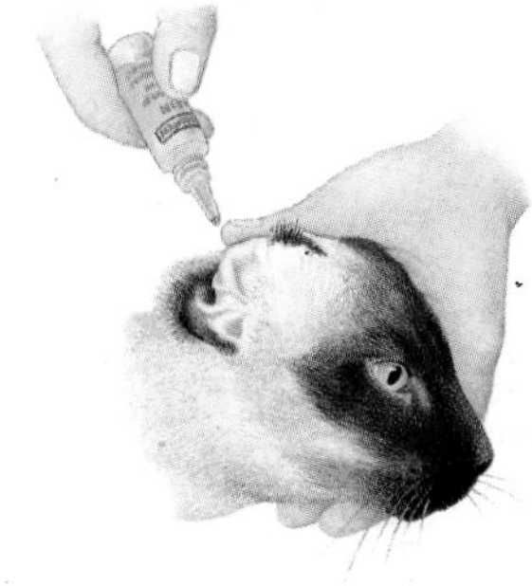

After applying ear drops, which should be warmed to room temperature, the ear flap is temporarily closed with a finger and the ear lobe gently rubbed at the back.

A second person should hold the cat still when eye drops are being applied. Eye discharges should be wiped away with gauze dipped in boiled water before the drops are applied.

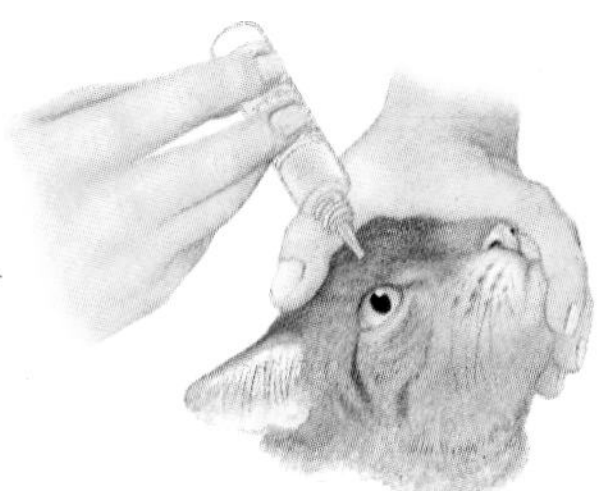

34 A Cat's First-Aid Kit

The cat owner should always have a basic first-aid kit available so he or she can treat a cat in the event of an emergency. The medicine chest should include:

- cotton bandages 2.5 and 5 cm (1 and 2 in) wide
- cotton wool
- cotton swabs
- curved, blunt-edged scissors
- blunt tweezers
- a thermometer
- petroleum jelly
- medicinal liquid paraffin
- hydrogen peroxide 3%
- boric acid
- feline surgical collar
- eye dropper
- activated charcoal
- antiseptic powder
- antiseptic solution (non-toxic)

Remember that drugs do not last indefinitely, so check on their use-by date from time to time and replace as necessary. Keep all the instruments clean so that you can use them immediately if need be. The medicine chest should always be kept in a certain place. It could also contain a list of vets' addresses and emergency phone numbers.

◁ Somali Blue.

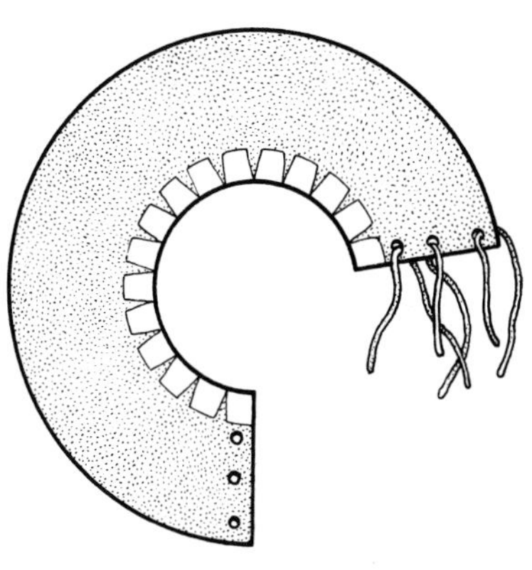

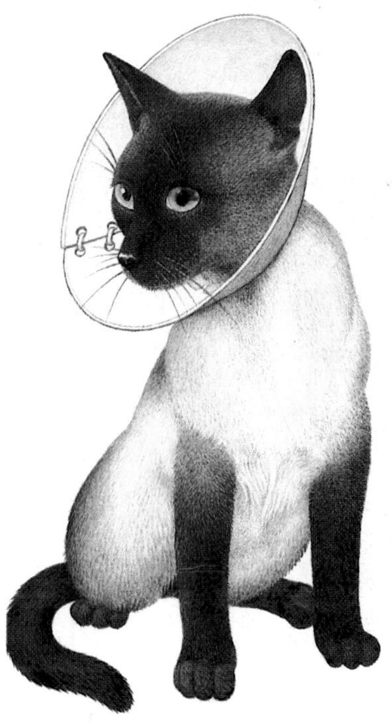

This veterinary, or Elizabethan, collar prevents the cat from licking open wounds on the skin or removing surgical stitches. Collars may easily be home-made out of a cardboard disk about 30 cm (12 in) in diameter. A hole of about 10 cm (4 in) is cut out of the centre of the disk. One quarter of the disk is removed and laces are tied to one end and eyelets are made in the other end. Adhesive tape should be attached around the inner diameter of the collar so that the edge of the cardboard does not cut the animal's neck.

Most cats adjust to the collar quite easily provided it is not too tight.

A cat's temperature is taken by inserting the thermometer about 3 cm ($1\,^1/_4$ in) into the rectum. The thermometer should be coated with vaseline or edible oil and inserted by a gentle rotating movement. Another person should assist in the procedure. Fast-speed thermometers take 20 seconds for a measurement; the traditional kinds take two to three minutes. The procedure should be practised occasionally on a healthy cat; this will enable it to get used to the operation.

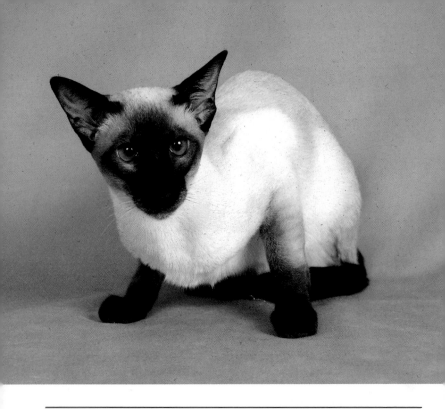

35 Dealing with Cat Injuries

Always act gently and cautiously with an injured cat. Before picking it up, wrap it in something warm (a sweater, or jacket). Place it in a roomy carrier, be sure it is warm, and get it to the vet as quickly as possible. An injury may bring on shock — the failure or collapse of the circulatory system caused by a drop in blood pressure. The symptoms of shock are collapse, rapid and shallow breathing, rapid and weak pulse, cold limbs and a delayed reaction of the pupils to light. Without further treatment a state of shock usually leads to death. Place the injured animal in a position where its head is lower than its body (to encourage blood to flow to the brain) and cover it warmly (illustration 1). Carefully pick up the cat, laying it gently on its side, supporting it with spread fingers under the chest and hips and transfer it to a firmer pad (a newspaper or magazine). Avoid bending or pulling of any part of the body (illustration 2). An injured cat that is not unconscious or is not lying down should

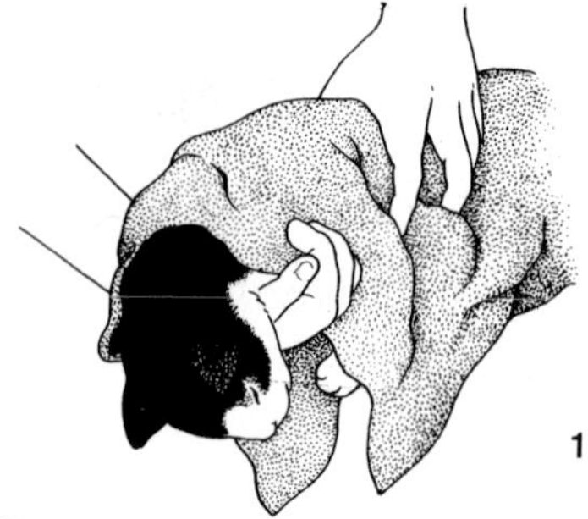

◁ Seal-Point Dark Brown Siamese.

be grasped by the skin on the back and its hind quarters supported. The weight of the body is thus transferred to the skin, thereby lessening the pressure on the injured internal organs. This is also a way to protect yourself, because an injured cat may bite.

If the cat is no longer breathing, try artificial respiration. Put the animal on its side on a firm surface (a table or a bench),

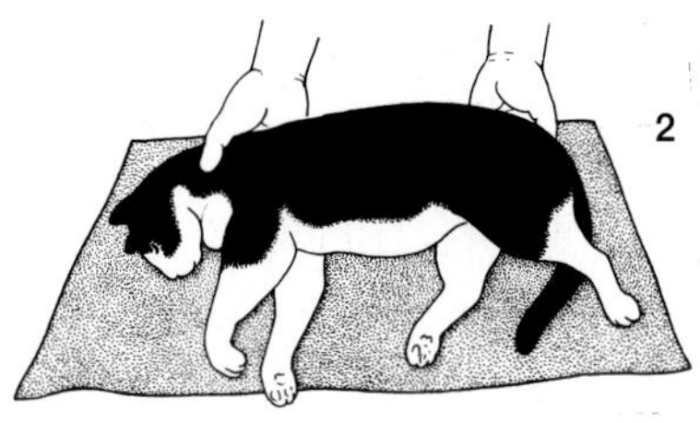
2

open its mouth and pull out its tongue. Remove any traces of vomit or blood from the mouth. Press the chest 20 times per minute using just enough strength so as not to fracture the ribs (illustration 3). Tilt the head slightly backward to open the airway. Another method of artificial respiration is mouth-to-mouth resuscitation. One must take into consideration, of course, the size of the cat's body and regulate the pressure that forces the air into the lungs. The movement of the cat's

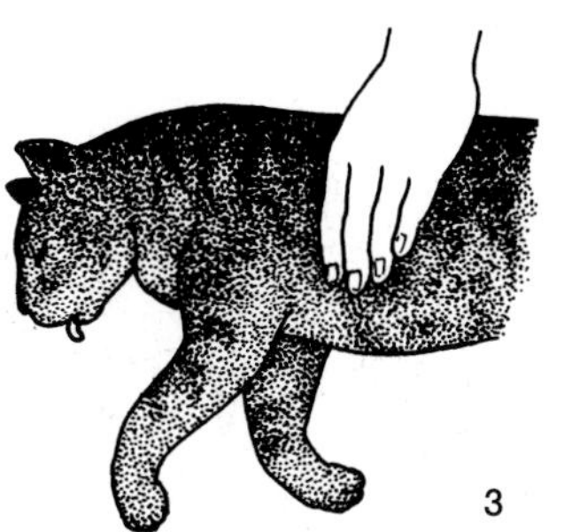
3

4

chest tells you if you are doing it successfully. If necessary, massage the heart (Hint 36) at the same time.

If the animal is bleeding make sure there is no foreign body in the injury. Try to remove small objects (for instance a thorn). Larger objects should be left to the vet to remove. If the wound is small it is enough to apply finger pressure briefly to stop the bleeding. For a bigger wound

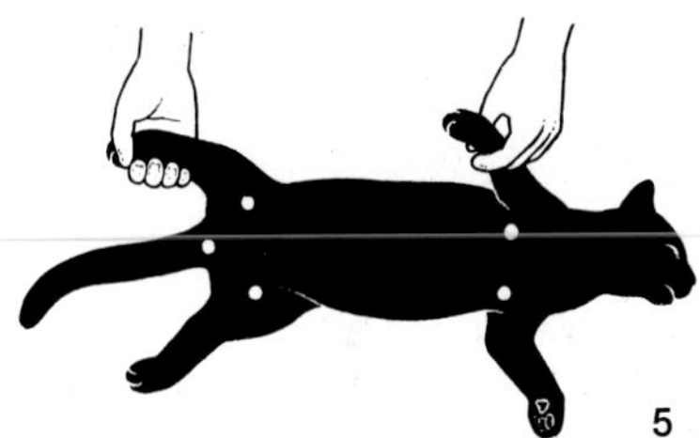
5

apply a piece of gauze, adding cold compresses. For more serious injuries apply a tourniquet, encircling the limb or the tail. Use a handkerchief for this purpose, inserting a pencil or small stick in the knot to tighten the bandage (illustration 4). Get the cat to the vet immediately. On the way loosen the tourniquet every quarter of an hour so as not to stop the blood circulation. For injuries to which a bandage cannot be applied, firmly press the artery in the places indicated (illustration 5).

36 Coping with Other Crises

If your cat gets too hot, say in a closed car, it may start to vomit, show symptoms of shock, or even lose consciousness. Carry the cat outside and sprinkle it with cool water, or place a wet pack around it. Cool down its entire body, especially the head, where you can also place ice packs. Once it has cooled, dry the cat. Burns should be similarly treated. First wash the wound with clean, cold water and immediately take the animal to a veterinary surgeon (illustration 1). In the event of an electric shock, remove the plug of the offending appliance before handling the cat. Check whether its heart is functioning and if necessary institute artificial respiration (see Hint 35). When massaging the heart place the animal on its left side on a firm base. Press the chest 120

◁ Persian Blue Cream.

times a minute, i.e. twice a second; use your fingers to press a place close behind the front limbs (illustration 2). You can feel the pulse if you place your palm over the cat's heart or by touching the artery on the inside of the top of the hind leg.

An alarming symptom is if the animal tries to vomit on an empty stomach: this indicates that the cat is choking. You will need the help of another person to help discover the cause. Often it is due to

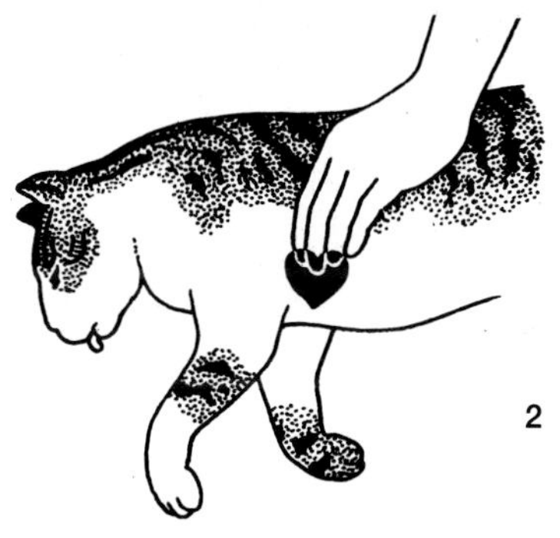

2

a bone stuck in the throat. If the bone is accessible, carefully remove it with a pair of tweezers. If not, get the cat to your vet immediately (illustration 3).

When pulling from the water a drowning cat which has ceased to breathe for only a minute or two, it may be worth trying to resuscitate it. Take it by the hind limbs and turn it with the stomach facing you. Stand with your legs apart and swing the cat backwards and forwards between your legs all the way to a horizontal position. Repeat this several times before trying another resuscitation procedure (illustration 4). In this way it may be possible also to remove any foreign object from the respiratory organs.

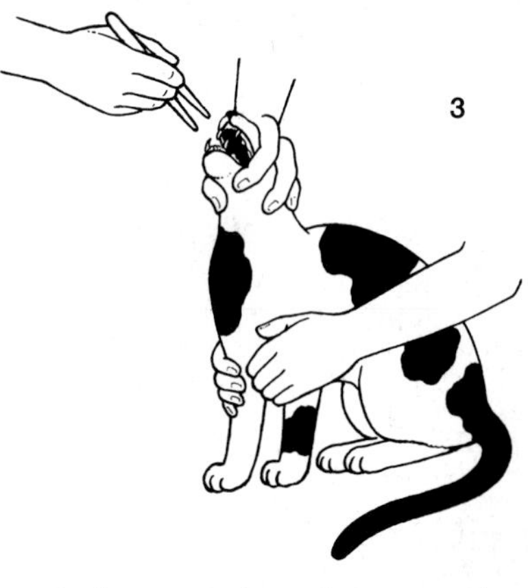

3

In the event of a poisonous snakebite it is essential to see a veterinary surgeon within two hours at the most. The bitten spot is generally swollen, and the cat vomits and reveals the first symptoms of shock. Place the animal in a position of rest to make sure the poison does not spread throughout the body, put a rubber bandage on the affected place as well as cold compresses to slow down the blood circulation.

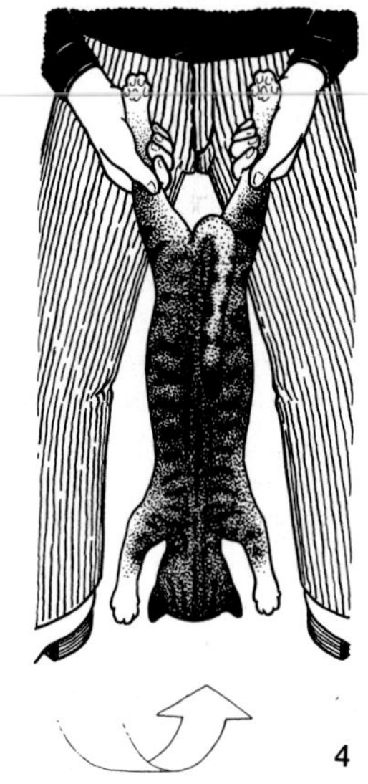

4

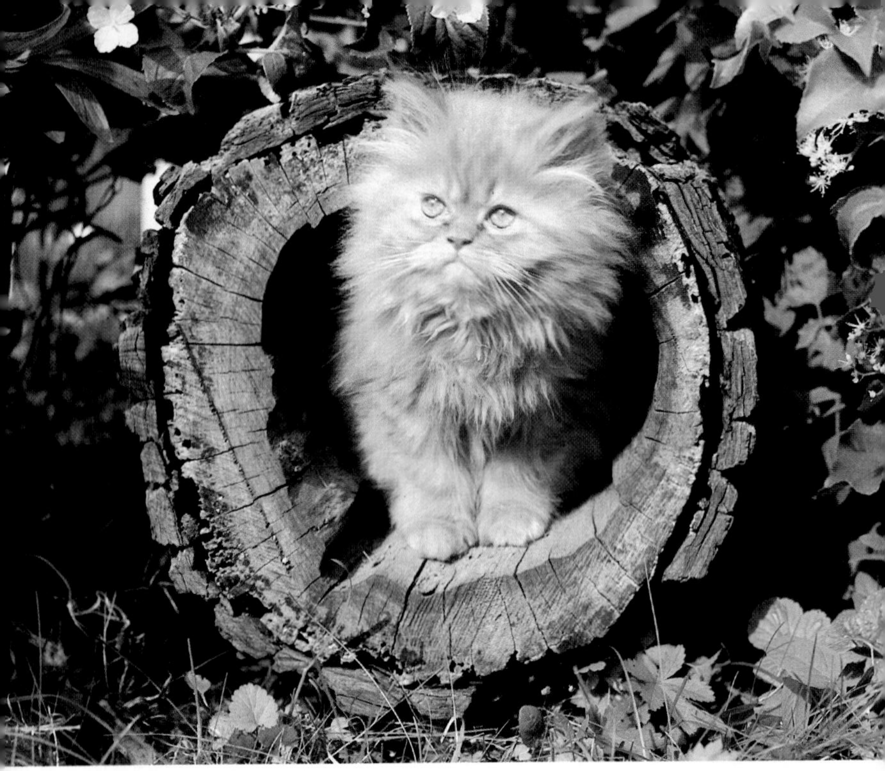

37 Urgent Cases for the Vet

Conditions which require an immediate visit to the vet naturally include all the health disorders we mentioned in the last few hints. But there are also many other situations when the owner is virtually unable to offer the animal any help. Always remember that every sickness requires the help of a specialist, and do not attempt to administer any course of treatment without expert advice.

•

Feline urological syndrome (FUS) is a serious complaint caused by the cat failing to drink sufficient liquid. This can make the urine too concentrated and cause various salts in the urine to form into stones. FUS prevents normal urination and will be fatal unless treated immediately. Tell-tale signs are the cat repeatedly trying to urinate while not fully settling into its usual position on the litter tray. It may whimper, and might even vomit. Yet urine does not appear, or only in a small quantity mixed with blood; you may even spot a drop of blood on the end of the urethra. This complaint is most common among

◁ Persian Red kitten.

males. The cat requires immediate treatment to free the obstruction of stones in the urinary tract. Initial treatment is followed by a long-term cure and an adjustment in the diet (dry foods are sometimes a contributory factor). Successful treatment is ensured by giving the animal a sufficient quantity of liquid food and special medication.

Poisoning is another instance requiring immediate assistance. If the cat has swallowed a suspect liquid or solid, take the remnants of the packaging to show the veterinary surgeon. If no acids have been swallowed, give the cat spoonfuls of dissolved cooking salt or soda to act as a retching agent. Never give a cat salicylic acid (aspirin) — it is poisonous for the animal — nor use common domestic disinfectants, which are equally harmful. Bear in mind that a cat can poison itself merely by licking a toxic substance that has soiled its coat or paws.

●

Expansion of the stomach may be a symptom of a serious complaint. An innocuous cause of bloating can be a faulty diet, but it could also be due to an intestinal obstruction. The latter may be caused by constipation, extremely hard faeces, an invasion of parasitic thread-worms, ingestion of foreign objects (such as a plastic bag), volvulus (twisting of the intestine) and so on. In the initial stage you will note no more than constipation. This may be followed by vomiting, a bloated stomach, pains, whining and a progressive state of shock. Unless immediate help is provided the animal will die in great pain. Never attempt to administer an enema or any other treatment: **seek specialised assistance without delay.**

Difficulties may also arise when a queen is giving birth to kittens. We deal with this in greater detail in Hint 48 but, generally speaking, it can be said that if a cat has strong labour pains for more than two hours and no kitten has yet been born it is essential to seek the help of a vet.

Normal urination posture (a), a typical position indicating closure of the urethral tract (b).

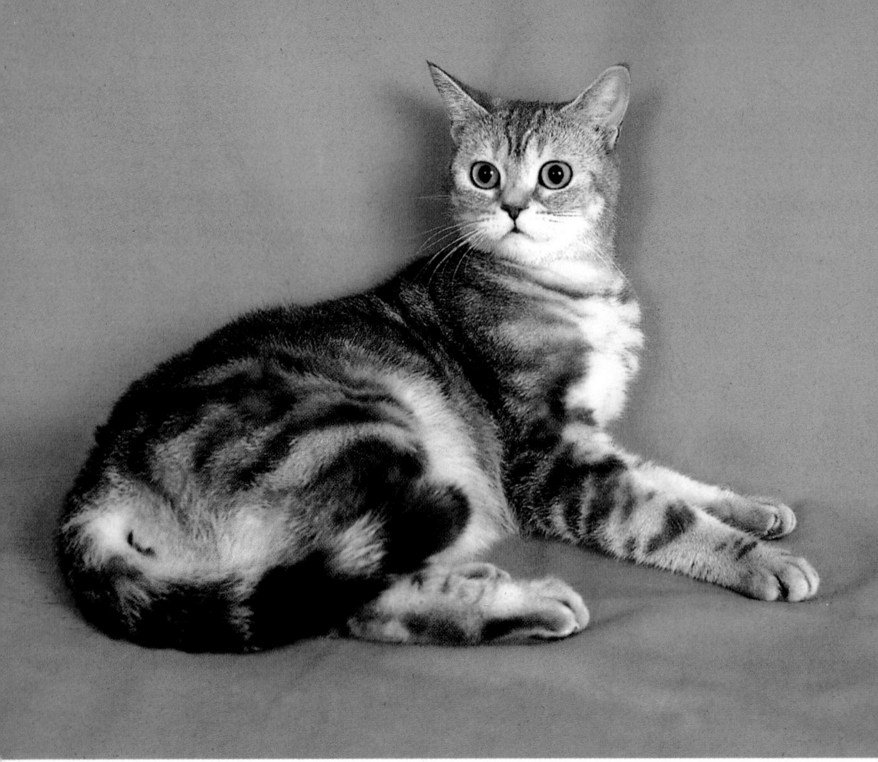

38 Infectious Diseases of Cats

One of the most dangerous diseases of cats is feline infectious enteritis (FIE), also known as feline panleukopaenia (FPL), which is caused by a virus of the parvovirus group. It is spread mostly in the air and its incubation period is between 2 and 10 days. The disease causes sever inflammation of the mucous membrane, stomach and intestines. If it takes an acute course, the cat may die within 24 hours. The predominant symptoms are violent, sometimes bloody diarrhoea, when the intestinal mucous membrane is peeling off (you may detect membrane particles in the faeces). Diarrhoea leads to rapid dehydration of the organism and to disintegration of the internal organs. The disease is frequently fatal, especially among young cats. The treatment consists in the administration of antibiotics at a very early stage and administering copious quantities of intravenous fluids. But the main defence against the disease is annual vaccinations from the age of 12 to 16 weeks.

The feline disease causing greatest anxiety nowadays is leukosis, produced by a virus of the retroviral group known as feline leukaemia virus (FeLV). The virus penetrates the chromosome cells where it may rest for months or even years without revealing any signs. Later, when the organism is weakened, the disease appears. It causes cancer of the white blood cells and malignant tumours elsewhere in the body,

◁ British Silvery Blue Marbled.

and its other effects include anaemia and a reduced resistance to diseases. Animals thus affected can then die of even the most trivial infection. The virus is in the blood, saliva, faeces and urine of the sick animal and is passed on by direct contact or from the mother to the embryo. The presence of antitoxins in the blood, indicating that the cat has already encountered the infection, can be ascertained by a blood test. Such animals are excluded from breeding and from mass events such as cat shows. Cats can be vaccinated against leukosis but if this is to be effective they must have a negative blood reaction to antitoxin against FeLV. There is no cure once the disease takes hold, in which case the vet will usually advise that the cat be put down.

The virus of feline viral rhinotracheitis (FVR) causes the so-called cat cold or cat influenza. It is a disease of the upper respiratory tract which may at times lead to pneumonia and ultimately death. Sometimes it affects the cornea of the eyes, which discharges mucus and develops ulceration, leading to total blindness. FVR is spread by droplet infection (as from coughs and sneezes) and has an incubation period of 2 to 10 days. The main symptoms are sneezing, a cold and cough. There is an effective vaccine against FVR which is frequently combined with the vaccine against FPL. Inflammation of the upper respiratory tract could be caused by feline calicivirus (FCV), which is accompanied by open sores or ulcers in the mouth. The vaccine against this disease is also usually combined with that against FVR.

Feline infectious peritonitis (FIP) is another serious disease. It causes inflammation of the peritoneum, the membrane lining the abdomen and its organs. A typical symptom is the build up of liquid in the abdominal cavity, giving rise to a bloated stomach. The disease progresses slowly among adult cats, whereas among kittens it takes a swift course and leads to death. Antitoxins against FIP can be ascertained by a blood test; vaccines are still in a stage of clinical testing. Cats with a positive FIP reaction cannot be used for breeding nor exhibited at shows.

The immune-deficiency syndrome among cats is produced by the FIV virus specific to cats. The symptoms of infection vary a great deal and are due to the organism's reduced defence against infections. The presence of antitoxins can be discovered by a blood test, but an effective vaccine is still in a stage of clinical research.

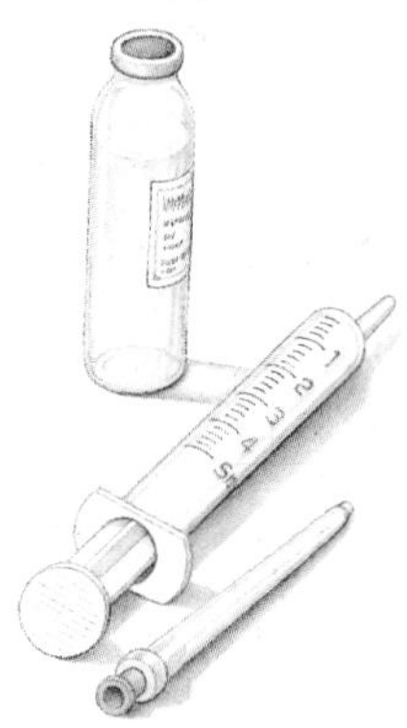

39 Fleas and Other External Pests

The most common external parasite is the flea. A cat can be infected by the cat flea (*Ctenocephalides felis*), the dog flea (*Ctenocephalides canis*), the common flea (*Pulex irritans*) and others. The life span of a flea is up to two years and during its life it lays a huge number of eggs. The eggs are laid not only in the cat's coat but also in its bed, on carpets, and in any dusty corner of the house. This parasite not only gives the cat a great deal of discomfort but its bite can infect it with tapeworm (the flea is an inter-host of the dog tapeworm).

A cat with fleas is nervous, it frequently scratches itself, and its skin twitches. Small kittens with an excessive number of fleas even show signs of anaemia. Fleas are best treated with insecticidal liquid or powder, shampoos or special collars impregnated with insecticide. The cat's bed must also be thoroughly cleaned, possibly treated with an insecticidal spray, as must all carpets, which should be painstakingly vacuum

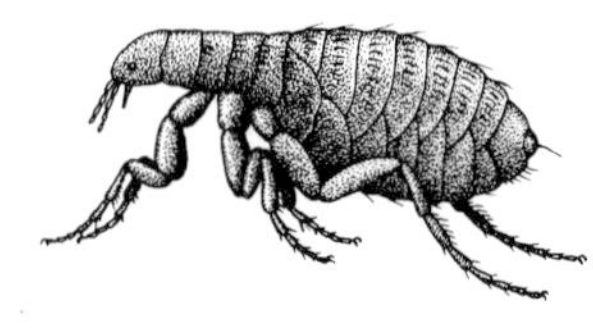

Cat flea.

◁ Ruddy Abyssinian.

cleaned before spraying. Bear in mind that your cat may be infected with a tapeworm, so a vermicide injection should be administered by your vet as a precaution.

Ear mite (*Otodectes cynotis*) infection of cats is one of the main causes of an inflammation of the outer auditory canal. The mite irritates the skin of the auditory canal and leads to the ear producing a greater quantity of ear wax. The wax forms typical brown lumps and the ear gives the impression of being dirty. The cat scratches and its ear is turned down. Frequent scratching causes a bacterial infection in the ear and a discharge. The accompanying inflammation, if neglected, may penetrate the middle and inner ear and damage both the hearing and the equilibrium mechanisms. Treatment must begin promptly and the complaint must be totally cured.

It is generally difficult to detect notoedric mange, or feline scabies, in cats. The females of the head mite (*Notoedres cati*) bury themselves under the skin, where they lay their eggs. Severe itching makes the cat scratch, thus causing a secondary infection in the skin. The skin is then covered with crusts and scales and its hair begins to fall out. The place most frequently affected is the skin on the head between the ears, from where the infection spreads to the chest and the whole body. The cat becomes infected by direct contact with a sick animal, but a dog as well as a human being may catch the infection as well. You must isolate a sick cat and give it proper treatment. Since the cat's skin itches, an operation collar is used to prevent it scratching and make sure it does not lick off the medication that has been applied. The cat's bed must be disinfected and everything must be done to boost the cat's general condition. Notoedric mange as a rule affects cats whose general fitness is below par.

Ticks (*Ixodes*) are among the commonest feline parasites. When removing a tick from the cat, you must ensure that the insect does not leave its barbed mouth-parts in the skin; this could cause an abscess. The best way to prevent this is to apply a drop of alcohol or ether to the tick. This will make it let go of the skin and you can pick it off with tweezers.

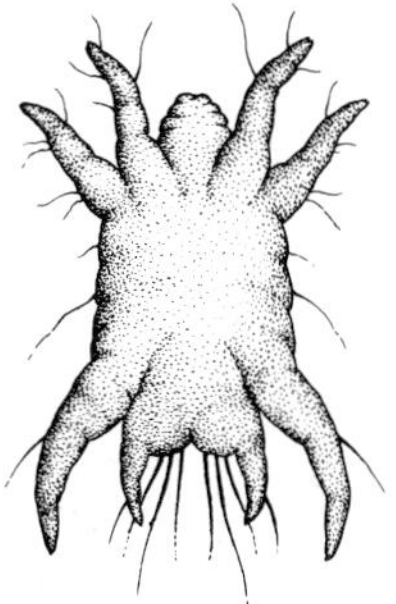

Ear mite.

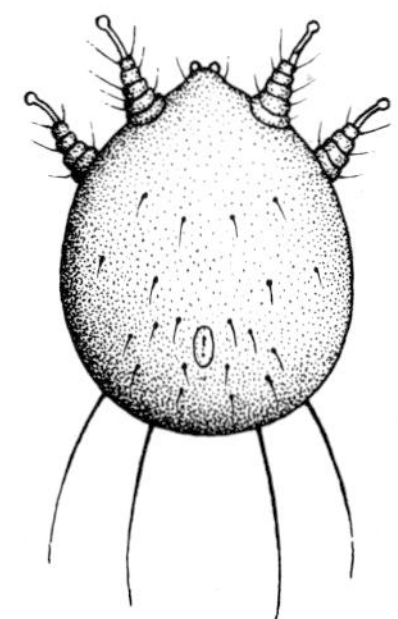

Head mite.

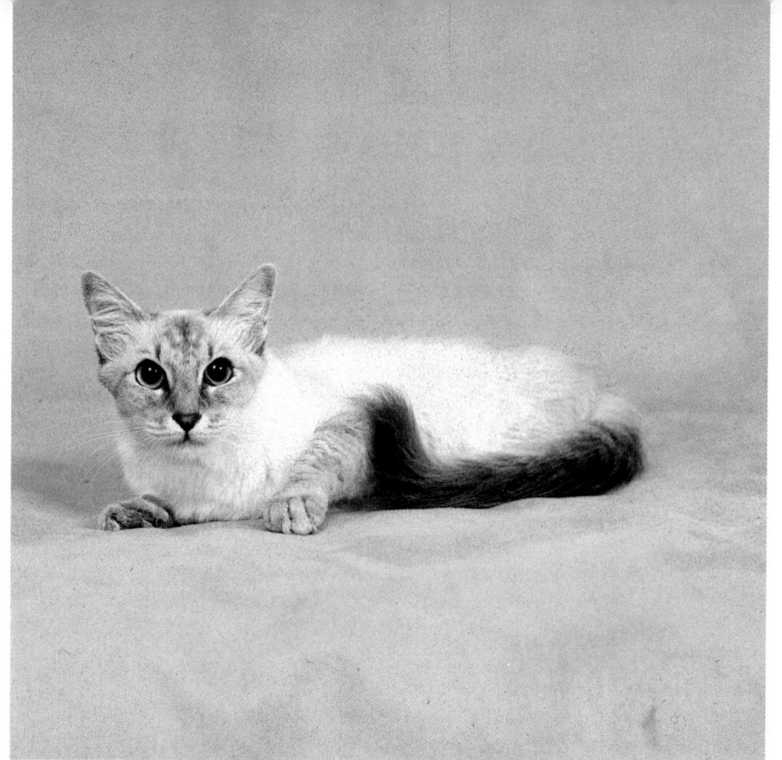

40 Internal Parasites

The roundworm (*Toxocara cati*), one of the ascarids, affects about 20 per cent of the cat population and can be highly dangerous. Roundworms are thick white worms, up to 10 cm (4 in) long, which are found in the excrement or vomit of an affected cat. If a small kitten is badly affected by roundworms it is deprived of many of its nutrients, and becomes weak, anaemic and undernourished. The roundworm may totally block the intestine and cause an intestinal perforation. Thread-worm in a pregnant cat may damage the foetus or even cause their death. Cats are infected by contact with the faeces of a sick cat or by contact with a mouse, rat or insects that have eaten the eggs of the worm. Roundworms cab be dealt with by administering tablets or powders containing piperazine. It is vitally important that your vet positively identifies the pest as roundworms and that only the prescribed dosage of the preparation is given: exceeding the dosage, or using it to deal with something other than roundworms, is highly dangerous; and it should not be given to very young cats.

A cat may be affected by several types of tapeworms, mainly *Dipylidium caninum,* which is present in some lice and fleas, or *Taenia taeniaeformis,*

◁ The Balinese (longhair Siamese) with blue markings.

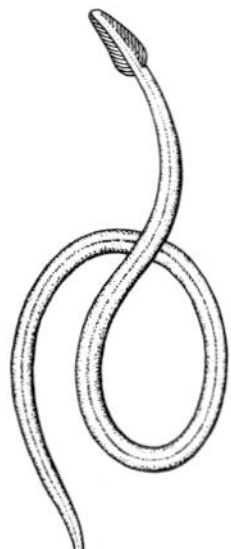

Canine roundworm.

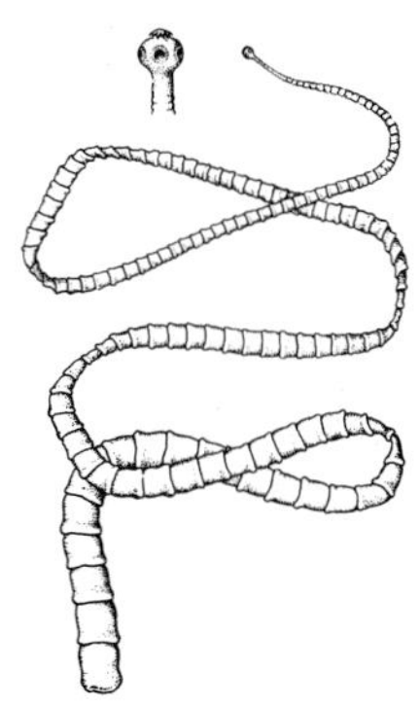

Canine tapeworm.

which is found in prey such as mice. These are ribbon-like intestinal worms with an articulated body up to 1m ($3^1/_4$ft) long. A cat affected by a tapeworm retains a healthy appetite, yet loses weight, its coat becomes lacklustre and segments of tapeworm may appear in its faeces. The cat's rectum begins to itch and the animal uses a peculiar movement to rub it against the ground. De-worming with the appropriate medication should be prescribed only by your veterinary surgeon. The best method of prevention is thorough cleanliness of the animal, anti-flea treatment, and allowing the cat to eat meat only in cooked form.

Among protozoan (single-celled) parasites, the most serious is *Toxoplasma gondii* because it affects all mammals, including human beings. However, only cats can spread the infection, known as toxoplasmosis, which is achieved via cysts that are shed in their faeces. Your cat may be infected by a sick cat or after eating raw meat or eggs. The disease generally has no visible symptoms (in either the cat or human beings), though kittens may appear to be suffering from pneumonia. The disease in a pregnant woman can have serious effects on her unborn child. The infection can be dealt with by certain drugs, and can be prevented by offering your cat only heat-processed cat foods and well-cooked fresh meat, while observing the strictest standards of hygiene.

'Sledging' of the cat caused by parasite infestation or by an itching rectum due to clogged rectal sebaceous glands. Examination of the faeces is the only way to make a diagnosis.

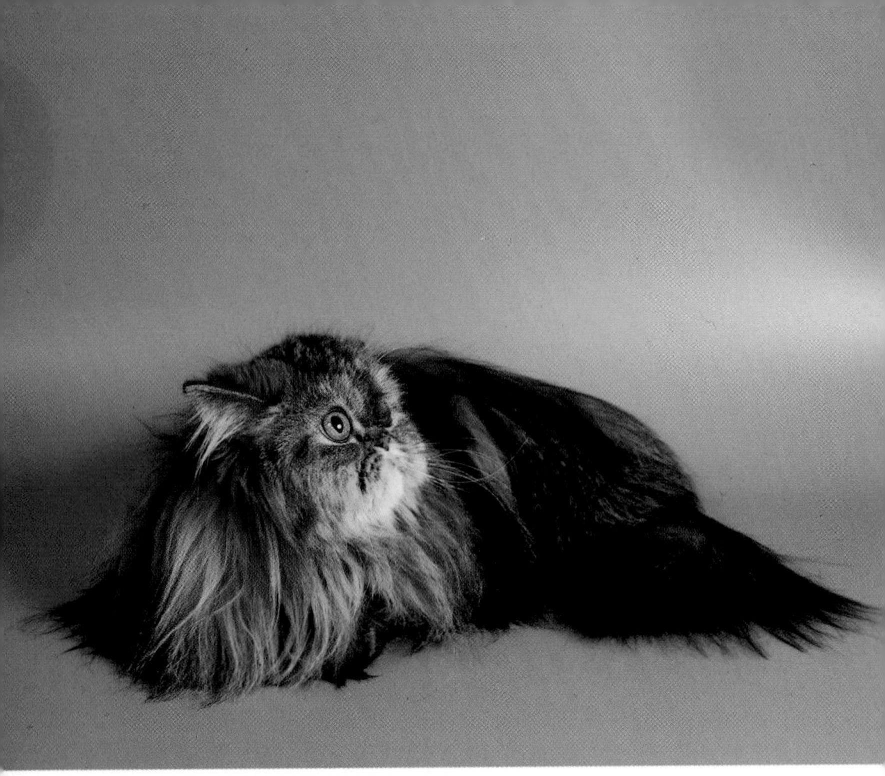

41 Breeding and Show Organizations

Cat breeders are organized in various associations and clubs. The clubs generally have one or more governing organizations or associations that keep a register of pedigree cats and regulate cat shows. Thanks to the pedigree register there is a complete record of the number and types of animals being bred, and the authenticity of pedigrees is ensured. Various national associations make up the international federations.

•

One of the biggest international federations is the FIFe (Fédération Internationale Féline), founded by Mme Rave in France in 1949. Today it includes more than 30 European and non-European associations. The international federation issues mandatory regulations, especially standards governing the breeds of cats, including detailed descriptions of their appearance. The standards of each breed are binding on all national associations, for judges at shows and, of course, for all breeders. The international federation recognizes new breeds, and registers and assesses the work of judges. It issues

◁ Persian Black Marbled.

an annual list of judges as well as of all shows. It gives permission for shows to be held within certain time limits and at venues so that they do not interfere with each other.

Each national association has two authorized breed registers — the main breed register and an experimental breed register. There are detailed and accurate regulations governing entries of the birth of kittens as well as of imports of cats in keeping with specific conditions. National associations, furthermore, issue mandatory regulations for the breeding of cats, shows, the training of judges and so forth. Such associations may issue their own specific regulations (which are the sole responsibility of these associations) but these must not conflict with the overall concepts of the international federation. The international federation provides for fruitful collaboration among breeders in various countries, promoting the cause of cat breeding and high-quality shows all over the world.

The Norwegian Forest breed was recognized by FIFe in 1981. It is popular mainly in Scandinavia.

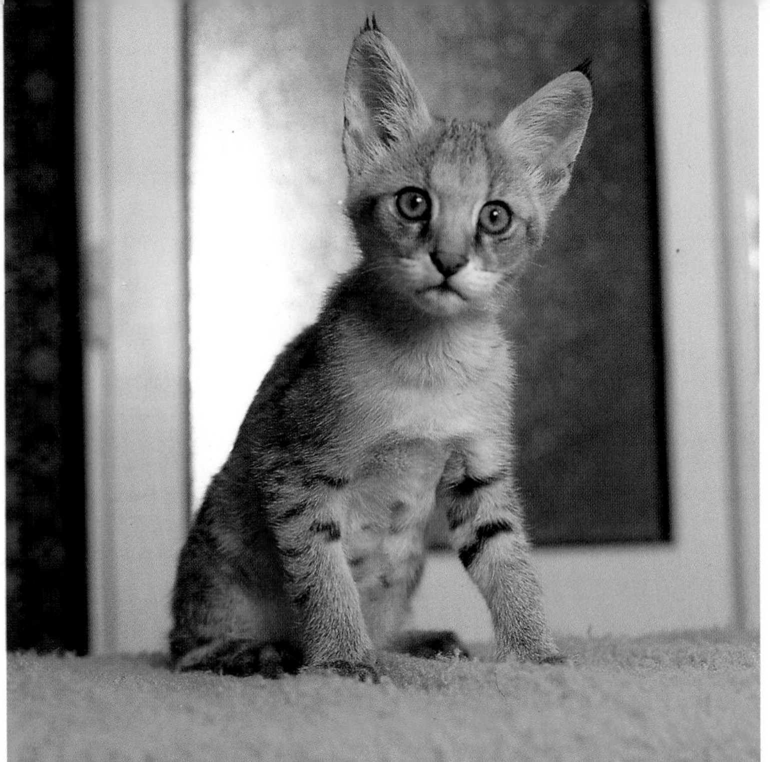

42 The Pedigree Document

The pedigree is a document about a cat's origin, issued by the secretariat of the breed register. It contains the name of the animal, consisting of the 'Christian' name, and the name of the breeder's establishment. The latter is a registered name used by a breeder for all his breeds, i.e. for all kittens born to their cats. If the breeder keeps dogs as well, the same name is used also for his or her puppies. The pedigree also contains the date of the kitten's birth and the number of the entry in the breed register.

The kitten may be entered either in the main or in the experimental breed register. The main register contains only offspring of mating by normal admissible methods which are at variance neither with genetic principles nor with breeding regulations. The experimental register contains data on kittens produced by unusual methods (for example, an inbreeding cross) in order to develop a new colour variety or a new breed. Entries in the breed registers are governed by precise regulations which must be strictly observed to avoid degrading the genetic integrity of the population of pure-bred cats and, consequently, degrading individual breeds. The pedigree further contains the name of the breed and the colour variety of the kitten. This is stated in words as well as in a specific code. The international federation has issued a system of colour coding to make sure that the description is uniform, unambiguous and

One of the domestic cat's close relatives: the jungle cat (*Felis chaus*).

brief. The FIFe nowadays uses the so-called EMS (Easy Minde System), which derived its name from its Norwegian inventor, Mme Minde (see page 186). Each code is made up of a three-letter abbreviation for each breed (e.g. PER for Persian). Another code specifies the colour of the coat in lower-case letters (e.g. 'd' for red). If the animal has other specific external signs (e.g. white patches, or a mottled coat) a numerical code is used: each external trait has its own permanent code (e.g. 22 signifies marble). The EMS system contains further codes for all types of colours of the coat, the eyes, and for deviations from the normal physical shape (e.g. tailless cats). Codes of breeds and varieties contain only the absolutely essential identification information. Characteristics typical for a breed are automatically omitted from the indicator.

•

The pedigree also gives the name and address of the breeder. This information is followed by details of four generations of ancestors — their names, colour varieties and, in the case of the first and second generation, the number of their entry in the breeder register. This means that the pedigree contains information about 30 ancestors of the animal. The pedigree is an official document, issued on the pertinent form, and authenticated by an official responsible for the breed register, including his signature and rubber stamp. Entries in the pedigree document may be made solely by the secretariat of the breed register. See also page 187.

The pedigree provides information on the cat's 30 immediate ancestors.

THE SIAMESE CAT SOCIETY of the BRITISH EMPIRE

Pedigree of: TRESEAN LILAC GEMINI

G.C.C.F. Reg. No. NS 105173

Breed No. 24C
Colour LILAC POINT
Breeder MRS M R BAKER
Address 2, ARCHERY
SCHOOL LANE BURGHFIELD COMMON
Tel: BURGHFIELD COMMON 2900 (073 529)
NR READING
BERKS. RG7 3ES

Date of Birth 27.2.78
Sex FEMALE
Owner MRS ZORKA SOBLOVA
Address BĚLOCERKEVSKÁ 32
101 00 PRAHA 10-VINOHRADY
Tel: 73 42 52 / VEČER

Parents	Grand-Parents	Great Grand-Parents	Great Great Grand-Parent	Br. No.
SIRE Reg. No. NS 8402 SEPIA SOURIRE Breed No. 24 Colour. SEAL POINT	Sire Reg. No. 213308 CH. CASUARINA SATURN Breed No. 24 Colour. SEAL POINT	Sire Reg. No. 194837 CH UBON ORION Breed No. 24 S.P.	Sire CH FAIRVALE ROSCOE	24
			Dam KINGSPLAY NANON	24
		Dam Reg. No. 108867 PI-DEN CAPRI Breed No. 24 S.P	Sire CH STARSHINE BANDIDO	24
			Dam DONERAILE ROSA	24
	Dam Reg. No. 210070 CARMELLA TANSY Breed No. 24 Colour. SEAL POINT	Sire Reg. No. 176060 CH. PI-DEN CUPID Breed No. 24B CH.P	Sire ROUNDWAY OURISIA	24 B
			Dam WINCEBY HOLENA	24 C
		Dam Reg. No. 209015 AURUM LILY Breed No. 24A B.P	Sire BABUSHKA TERRAMY JASON	24
			Dam SANDLE PEARL CONCERTO	24
DAM Reg. No. NS 16059 TRESEAN TINA Breed No. 24C Colour. LILAC POINT	Sire Reg. No. 252110 CRAIGIEHILLOCH LILAC LASER Breed No. 24C Colour. LILAC POINT	Sire Reg. No. 142186 BEAUVALLET Breed No. 24B CH.P.	Sire CH. BATHGATE YIPPEE	24 B
			Dam IVOBINE	24
		Dam Reg. No. 225247 DRUIDES MAREE Breed No. 24B CH.P	Sire CH. BATHGATE YIPPEE	24 B
			Dam CH DRUIDES APRILA GEM	24 B
	Dam Reg. No. NS 15470 TANDI LASS Breed No. 24C Colour. LILAC POINT	Sire Reg. No. 237100 MINTON LILAC GANNYBOY 2CCS Breed No. 24C L.P	Sire CH TAMRUAT LILAC DOMINO	24 C
			Dam NOEMI ARABELLA	24 A
		Dam Reg. No. 199408 QUINTRAL FROLICKING MISS Breed No. 24C L.P	Sire CH PHYSALIS CHULA LONGKORN	24 C
			Dam PIMPERNEL POOH-BAH	24 A

REMARKS:

I certify that this Pedigree is correct to the best of my knowledge.

Signed. [illegible] Date. 11 APRIL 1978

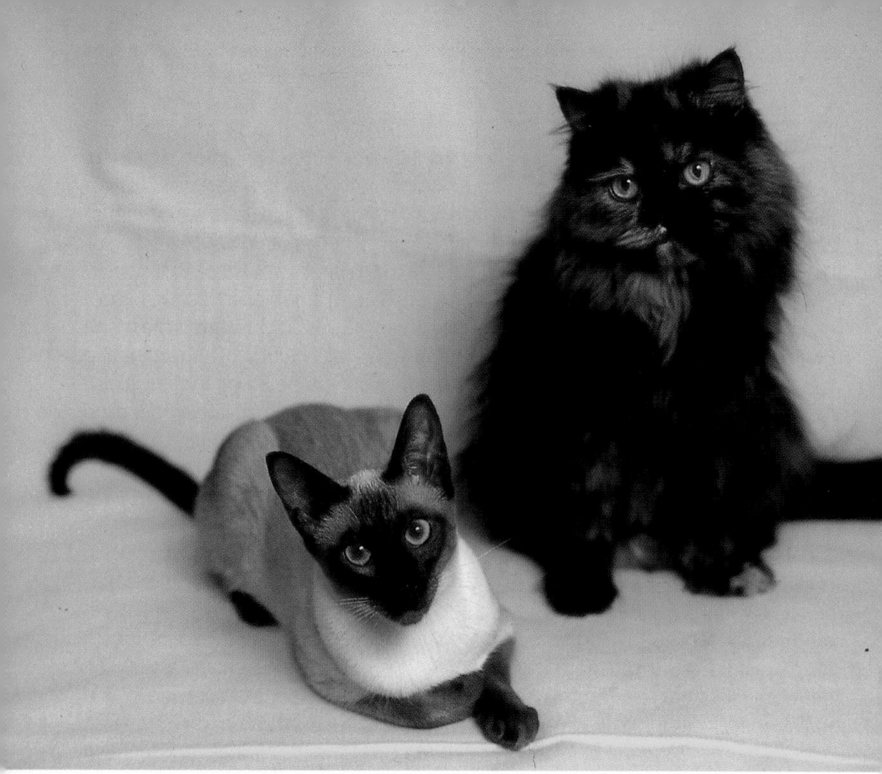

43 Choosing a Cat for Breeding

If an owner decides to breed kittens with a pedigree, cats chosen for breeding purposes must fulfil certain criteria. Breeding suitability is related to the specific requirements which are issued by each national association in the form of breeding regulations. One of these is generally an honour awarded at a show, mostly the 'excellent' mark, possibly the 'very good' mark. The requirements vary from country to country. As a rule, animals aged one year or over are chosen for breeding provided they show no sign of degeneration and are in good health.

Recently a new problem has arisen. Some breeders try to breed animals of the most extreme types regardless their health and physiological suitability. For example, the extremely shortened face part in Persian cats often results in a narrowing of the nostrils and causes breathing difficulties. Cats with a large overbite have trouble eating and this will handicap the animals throughout their life. Breeders must be aware of the need to strike a balance between physiology and aesthetics. Deliberate emphasis of unhealthy features is ethically unacceptable.

The choice of a suitable male partner for the female is made by the breeder

◁ Two opposites: a Persian and a Siamese can live together in harmony.

himself, or with advice from another, more experienced breeder, possibly together with a breeding counsellor or judge. The selection of a breeding pair is determined after a thorough scrutiny of the pedigree of both animals. All their appearance qualities are taken into consideration as well as their advantages and shortcomings, their character and colour varieties as well as those of their ancestors, and the breeding line in their pedigree. When considering the colour variety combination, certain rules must be observed since not all colours can be combined. If these tested and genetically sound rules are not observed the quality of the offspring will be disappointing.

The possible relationship between the pair must be considered: sometimes it might be advantageous, on other occasions not; so must the choice of related breeds. The character of the parents is an aspect which is frequently neglected. Apart from excellent appearance, bred animals should also have an equable temperament, neither unduly agressive nor timid. Such characteristics can be mitigated to some extent by considering the temperaments of the two partners to be mated.

The best way to become acquainted with animals of a specific breed is to visit a cat show. The catalogue will usually have information about the parents of the animal, from which you will be able to follow the results of the combination of breeding lines. More profound knowledge, however, is acquired by long-term study of the bred animals and their offspring.

44 Arrangements for Mating

The mating of the female must be agreed well in advance with the owner of the selected male. Most owners of breeding males require the selected queen to be vaccinated against infectious diseases and tested for leukosis; many require a veterinary certificate confirming that the cat is in good health. The two breeders agree in advance on the mating fee and the date when it is to be paid as well as the procedure to adopt if the mating is not successful; some breeders insist on a written agreement.

Generally the female is brought to the male, who is in a better position in his domestic environment and mating is generally more successful. But the breeders may also make other arrangements. It is certainly wrong for the owner of a breeding male to lend his cat regularly to cat breeders; a simple change of environment can create problems for the male. The best scenario is when the female cat is brought to the male at the height of her oestrus, i.e. on the second, third or fourth day after coming on heat. After arriving at the male's home the cat should be placed for a while in a position for the male to see and smell her but remain separated from her, by, for example, some wire mesh. After such an initial introduction the female is allowed to join the male and the ritual of getting to know each other commences. This ritual is always the same but may take a short or long time. Sometimes it may take several minutes; on

◁ The Norwegian Forest is one of the most handsome 'natural' breeds.

other occasions, one or two days. Everything depends on the experience of the two partners, on the intensity of the oestrus as well as on mutual attraction. Sometimes, for no obvious reason, mating does not take place at all. (This may also happen at times with large cats in captivity — for example, among cheetahs, where the female actually chooses her partner but mating is totally unsuccessful.)

Certain owners of males require the cat's claws to be cut back since, when the animals are getting to know each other and in the actual mating process, there is no shortage of hissing or ear boxing. The female generally remains with the male for two or three days. Mating should take place at least three times because females have a so-called provoked ovulation, which means that the egg comes up from the ovary only after the penis has excited the vaginal wall during mating.

After successful mating, oestrus may continue for another one or two days. During that period the queen should not be exposed to unnecessary stress which might have an adverse effect on the settling of fertilized eggs in the uterus. The journey home should be as gentle and quick as possible. The breeder must make a note of the exact mating date, e.g. the beginning and the end.

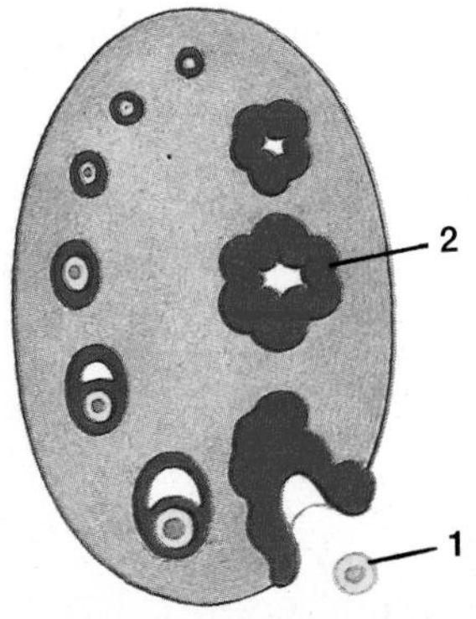

The release of eggs from the ovary takes place only after mating; this is the so-called provoked ovulation: (1) a mature egg expelled into the fallopian tube; (2) a yellow corpuscle with a hormonal function.

Spines on the tip of the male's penis intensely stimulate the queen's vaginal membrane; this, in turn, triggers ovulation.

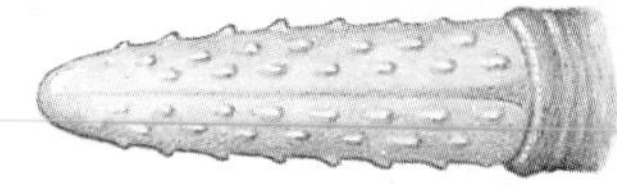

The position of the testes outside the abdominal cavity helps the sperm to mature: (a) testicle and epididymis, (b) seminal duct. An undropped testicle is an inborn defect, and males thus affected are not suitable for breeding purposes.

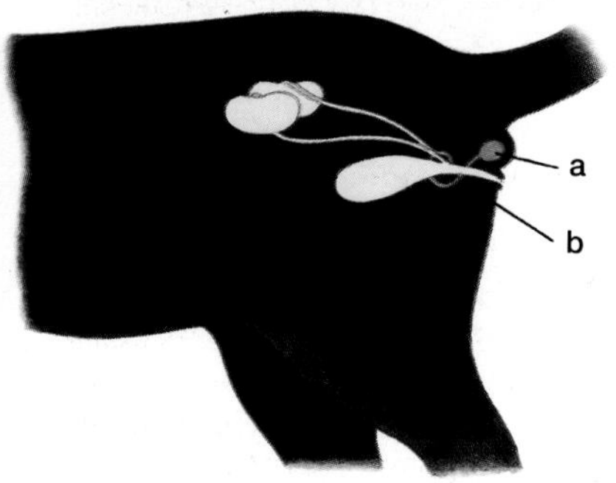

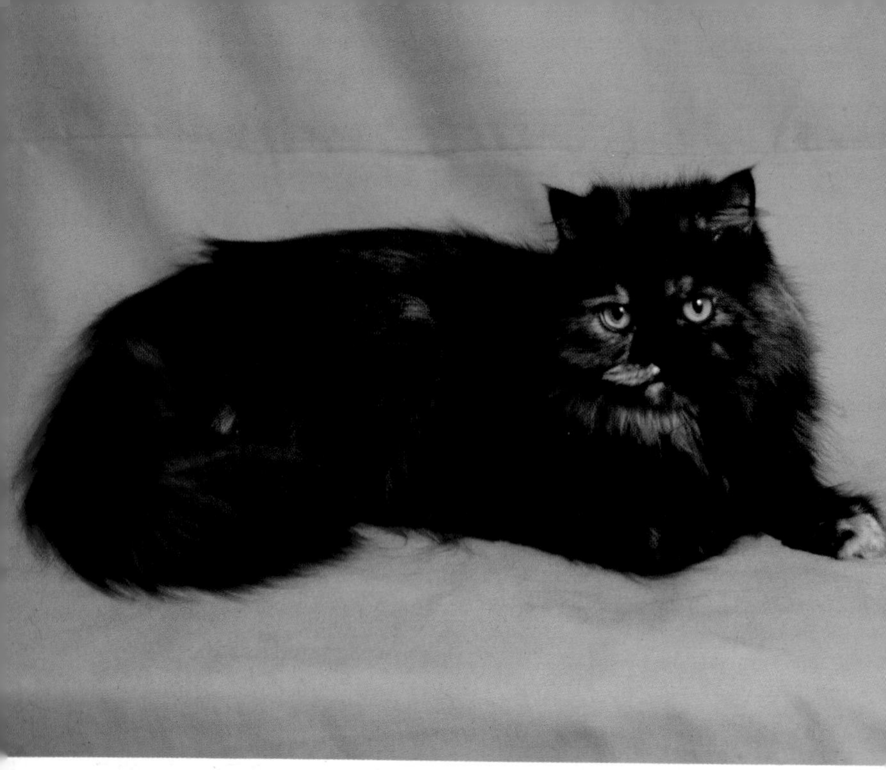

45 Signs of Pregnancy

After successful mating some females sleep more during the first few days and have a greater appetite; others, by contrast, may vomit. Neither of these symptoms, however, is an entirely reliable guide to whether the queen is pregnant.

If the mating was successful, the queen's teats and nipples will begin to turn pink after three weeks. The female begins to put on weight. Over the entire pregnancy the cat may put on between 1 and 1.5 kg (2.2 and 3.3 lb), depending on the breed, on the number of foetuses as well as on the individual queen. The belly begins to grow approximately in the fifth week of pregnancy. The swelling of the abdomen of queens pregnant for the first time is less conspicuous than of cats who have already had several litters. The size of the belly also depends, of course, on the number of foetuses. During the first half of pregnancy the weight increase is due almost entirely to the growth of the placenta and the foetus cover; the foetuses grow most rapidly during the last two weeks of pregnancy.

The most appropriate time to verify pregnancy is between the fifth and sixth weeks, when the veterinary surgeon is able to feel the growing foe-

◁ Persian Tortoiseshell.

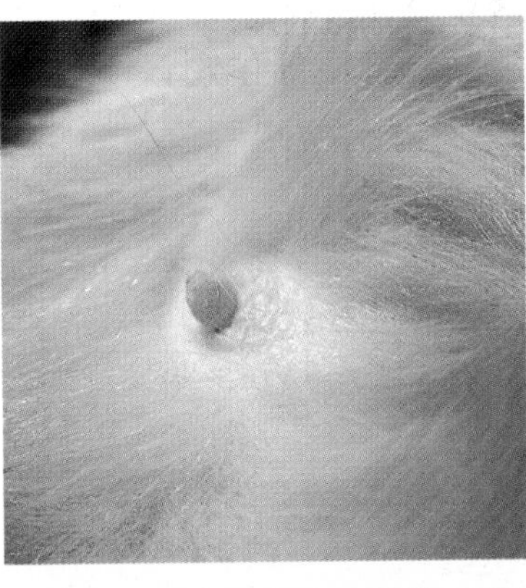

Enlarged dark pink teat of a pregnant cat.

tuses. At that point the foetuses are about the size of a walnut. Incidentally, never examine the cat in this way yourself or you may harm the queen or her foetuses. The veterinary surgeon can also use ultrasound to examine the cat. The kittens can be felt moving in the belly from the seventh week; the best way to do this is to place your palm on the side of the cat's abdomen.

Sometimes a queen has what is called a false pregnancy. It is a condition caused by hormones which convincingly imitates genuine pregnancy, with all its concomitant symptoms. At times the female cat may even show signs of lactation. False pregnancy generally ends during oestrus, which occurs roughly at the time of the anticipated birth. False pregnancy is not a serious disorder and during the next mating the cat may become pregnant quite normally. Changes in the female's appearance, however, including enlarged abdomen and lactose glands, may create difficulties for owners preparing for a show.

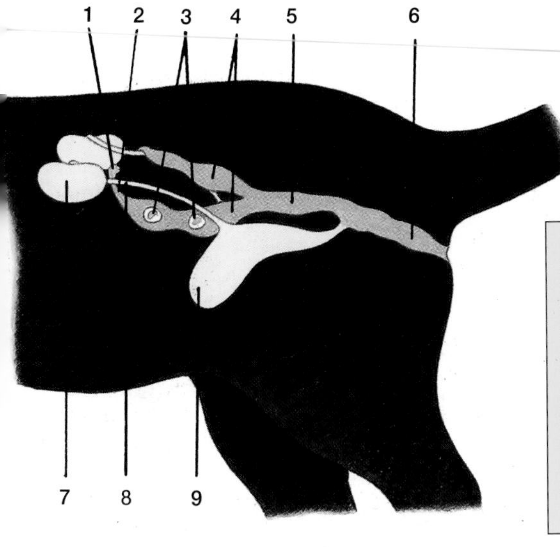

The feline uterus is in the shape of the letter Y; the foetus develops in its long uteral cornu. The diagram shows closeness of the sex organs to the urinary tract: (1) ovaries, (2) fallopian tube, (3) uteral cornu, (4) uterus, (5) vulva, (6) kidneys, (7) urethra, (8) bladder, (9) foetuses developing in the uteral cornu.

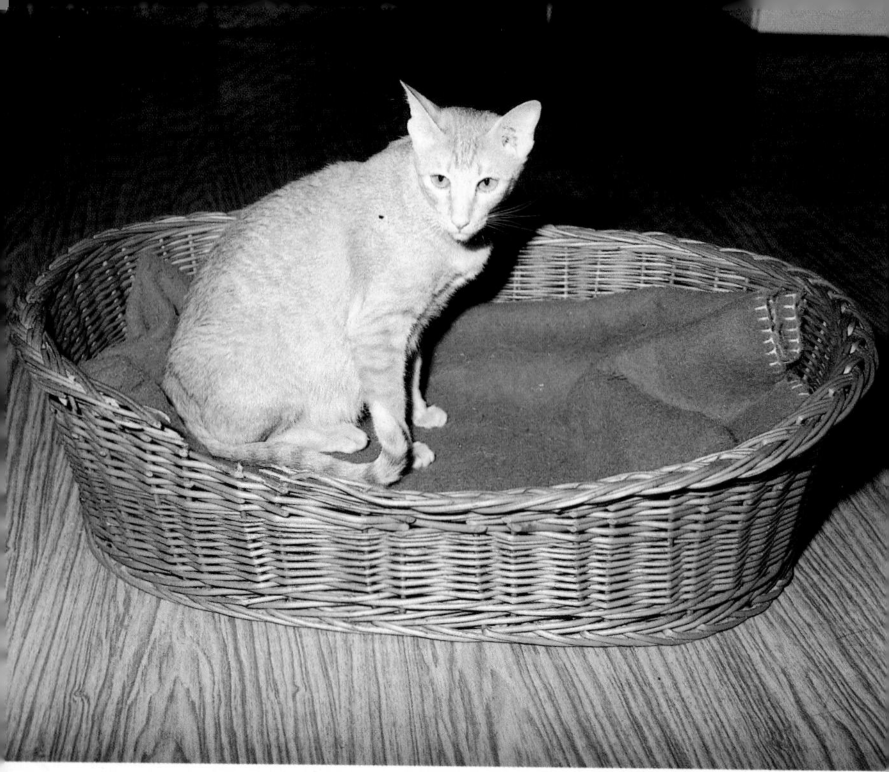

46 Caring for the Pregnant Queen

A pregnant cat sleeps more and needs more food, but apart from that her life carries on much as usual. The owner should not restrict her in any way, but he or she should not expose the female to unnecessary tension or the possibility of catching an infection. That is why pregnant cats must not take part in shows nor, unless it is absolutely essential, be moved from one place to another. A pregnant cat should be given medication only if it is essential and, even then, only at the direction of the vet.

•

Special attention must be given to the female's food, which must be highly nutritious. The food is divided into three or four daily portions. A pregnant cat needs about 50—60 per cent more calories than an ordinary adult female. In the final stages of pregnancy queens usually suffer from constipation which you should try to alleviate with a suitable diet: in most cases milk, a pat of butter or a spoonful of oil will do the trick.

A pregnant cat must be lifted with utmost care, supporting the rear part of its body. Never force it to jump, for instance from the table, and make sure never to knock its belly inadvertently.

In the later stages of pregnancy the queen rests a great deal. She should start getting accustomed to the place where she will give birth to her kittens.

Since in the last phase of pregnancy the swollen belly prevents the cat from cleaning her coat, you should wipe the places she cannot reach with a damp cloth. That is also how you clean her nipples a few days prior to confinement. In the case of long-haired cats it is advisable to trim the coat around the teats.

Work out the anticipated date of confinement. The average duration of a cat's pregnancy is 65 days, plus or minus four days, depending on the breed and the individual animal. It is well known that Siamese cats give birth somewhat later, usually after 66 or 67 days, whereas European cats give birth sooner. As a rule the duration of a queen's pregnancies is the same every time, which helps in working out the date of confinement with considerable accuracy.

A table for calculating the date of birth. It also includes the time when the teats begin to turn pink.

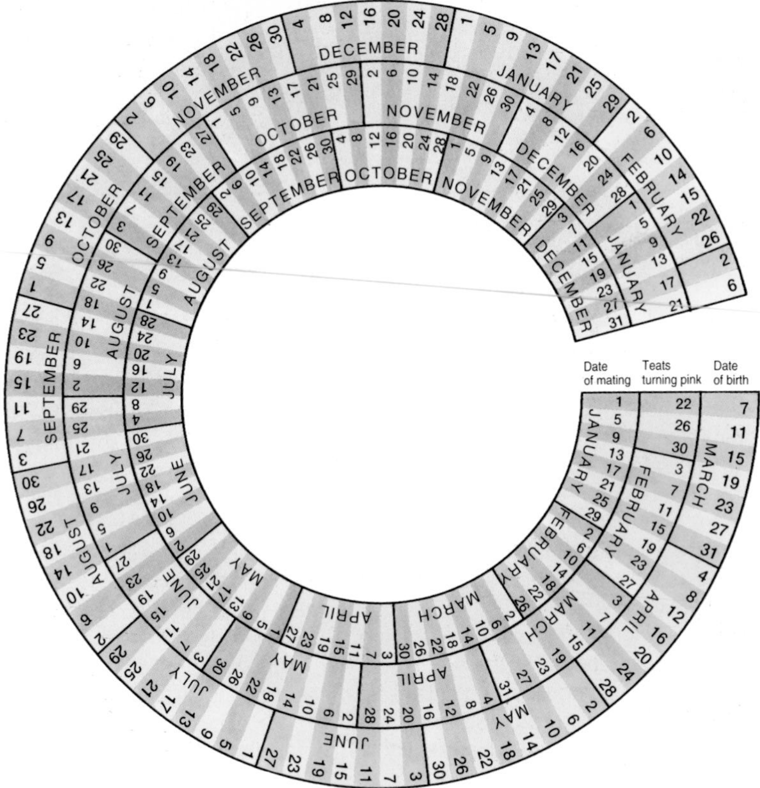

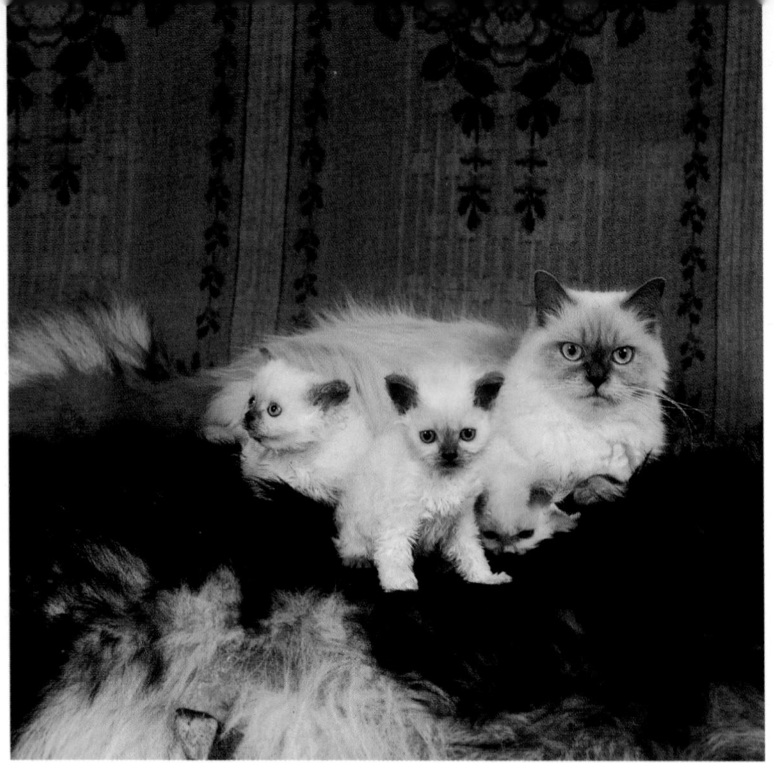

47 Preparing for the Queen's Confinement

About two weeks prior to the anticipated confinement you should prepare the 'maternity ward'. This may be a wooden or plastic box or even a carton. It must be comfortable, and about 60 × 50 cm (24 × 20 in) and 50 cm (20 in) high. It should have a spacious entrance on one side, with a sill about 10 cm (4 in) high. At least part of the box should be covered by a lid so that the cat will feel safe and protected, and also that there is not too much light inside. The lid must be removable to enable you to clean the box properly. Place clean, washable material inside the box and position the box in a quiet draught-free place. The queen often selects her own place of confinement. Try to accommodate her requirements and position the box in such a place. After the cat has had her box for a time she gets used to it and will not feel like having her kittens elsewhere. Although most cats — with the exception of some having kittens for the first time — are capable of looking after their newborn, the breeder should always be present during birth to observe the progress and to provide assistance in the event of complications.

It is also advisable and useful to inform the vet about the date of the anticipated confinement in advance to be sure that he is available if need be.

◁ Persian with blue markings and her litter.

Prior to the confinement, prepare the following items on a small tray: a harmless disinfectant for cats; pure alcohol; clean cotton wool; scissors with a rounded edge; a thermometer; a heating bottle; a baby's suction device; at least six small, clean and ironed rags the size of a handkerchief; several clean and ironed 'sheets' for the box; and thread to tie the umbilical cords. All instruments should be sterilized in boiling water.

The physiological span of the pregnancy is between 61 and 70 days. Until that time there is no need for concern, unless warning symptoms emerge, such as high temperature or bleeding. If the cat is accustomed to going outside the house freely, do not allow it to leave the house after the 61st day, so that it will not give birth in some hidden place. If you want to ascertain the exact day of the birth, take its temperature daily after the 61st day. If the temperature drops by one full degree against normal — i.e. to roughly 37.6°C (99.6°F) — you can expect that it will give birth within 18 hours.

Another sign of the approaching confinement is production of milk. The behaviour of cats also changes just before giving birth. The animal becomes fidgety, passes water frequently, digs in its litter pan and in the 'maternity ward'; most queens, moreover, like to be close to their owner. One day before the birth, movement of the foetuses is intense. Some cats refuse their last meal prior to confinement, others eat normally.

A suitable box for the queen's confinement.

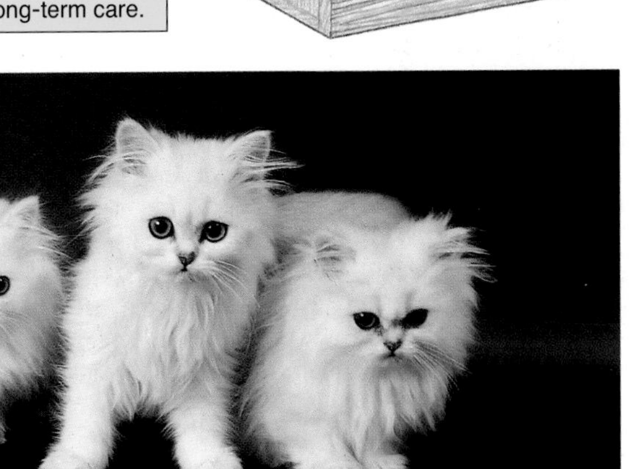

The birth of healthy kittens is the result of the breeder's long-term care.

48 Helping with the Confinement

As the cat goes into labour she generally remains in the box, purrs and is by and large calm. Make sure the room temperature remains at a minimum of 22°C (72°F) and from time to time take a look at the cat. The second phase of labour begins with contractions, which gradually become stronger and more frequent. This phase rarely lasts longer than two hours. It is followed by the foetus being pushed out, and this can last between 15 and 20 minutes. Most kittens are born head first, which is the most suitable position. Other position are less favourable but in most cases the kittens emerge safely.

Any assistance by the breeder must be given with maximum cleanliness and with great care and gentleness. If the female is exhausted by the act of giving birth, especially if this is her first litter, she may ignore the newborn kittens. If she neglects to start cleaning them within one minute, you must do the job for her. Break the foetus cover just above the nose and muzzle and clean the kitten's face. The kitten now should start to breathe. After this, take a firm hold of the umbilical cord, press it with your fingers at least 4 cm ($^1/_2$in) from the belly, cut it, and tie it off. Hold the umbilical cord firmly for a little while longer to make sure it does not bleed, then tie it off, too. Be care-

◁ Kittens may also be reared by a surrogate mother.

ful not to pull the cord or you may stretch the queen's abdominal wall. Place the kitten on a small rug and massage it. Hold it head downwards for a few moments so that all the amniotic fluid drains out of the respiratory organs. If the kitten shakes, hisses, or fails to breathe, use a suction pump to suck the amniotic fluid out of its nostrils as well as from the muzzle. If the kitten still fails to breathe, repeat the manoeuvre of its head downwards and the suction. You can also attempt gentle mouth-to-mouth breathing, but always taking into consideration the tiny body of the kitten. The moment the kitten begins to breathe and to squeal, place it near the queen's teats, whereupon the mother generally begins to show interest in it.

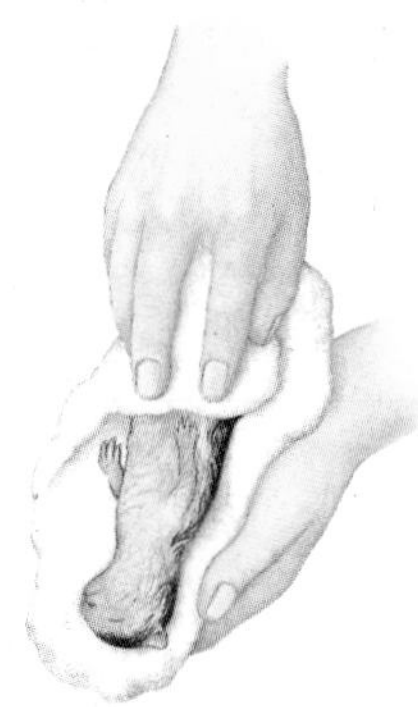

Resuscitating a newborn kitten, head down and massaging it.

Observe carefully whether each kitten in the litter is followed by the afterbirth. An exception to this is the case of twins, which have only one afterbirth with two umbilical cords.

Unless it is absolutely necessary, you should not interfere with the birth. Do not prevent the cat from eating the placentas. While she is in labour, offer the queen a drink and food; if she is exhausted, give her liquid food (an egg yolk in milk).

On occasions the last kitten in a litter is not born till 12 hours after the seemingly completed confinement. If it is alive, the queen is in no danger, but if it is stillborn, you must seek the advice of a vet. Generally, kittens are born at 15-minute intervals, but even one-hour intervals are quite common: there is no hard and fast rule as to the duration of the confinement. In the following situations, however, it is essential to call the vet without delay: 1 If intense contractions last for two hours yet no kitten has been born. 2 If the cat is unable to push out a kitten which has already partly emerged from the womb. 3 If contractions fade though it is evident that more kittens remain in the womb.

A swift intervention by the vet, including a caesarian section, is more considerate for the cat than a lengthy and excessively exhausting labour. During confinement try to calm the cat. Tension in the owner is easily picked up by the animal, especially by a female with strong ties to the owner.

The umbilical cord must be cut well away from the newborn kittens' abdomen to prevent infections.

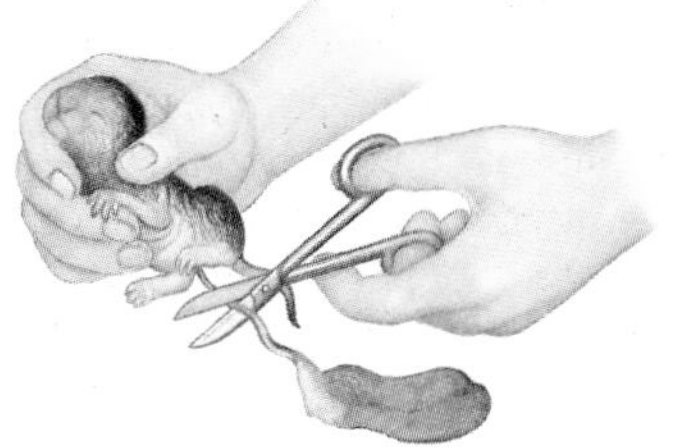

49 Caring for the Cat and Newborn Kittens

Having given birth, the queen attends to her own hygiene. If she is exhausted, help her by wiping with damp cotton wool around the genitals. Change the blood-stained and damp mat (possible several times during confinement). Give her something to drink as well as food. Make sure the kittens are sucking the teats. If the kittens are getting sufficient milk, everything is generally quiet in the bed. Hungry kittens squeal and are restless. If this is the case, check the production of colostrum (the initial milk secreted after parturition; it is rich in antibodies) by pressing the milk gland with two fingers towards the teats, from which a thin stream will spout. If no milk is secreted, call the veterinary surgeon.

•

For a few days after giving birth the queen cleans herself and has a mild blood-stained discharge. If the discharge becomes suppurated, is intense or smells unpleasantly, call the veterinary surgeon. Aversion to food, listlessness or a raised temperature are all warning symptoms (the temperature

◁ An Oriental Chocolate Tortoiseshell with five-week-old kittens; this is the age when kittens become interested in independent feeding and discover the litterbox.

must be taken, not guessed). Be alert to the possibility of eclampsia (so-called puerperal fever), which may appear during breast-feeding. It is a complaint caused by acute calcium deficiency endangering the animal's life. It starts with twitching, an unsteady walk and muscle spasms. Unless the cat receives immediate medical attention, this is followed by cramps, a high temperature and unconsciousness. The complaint can be put right by an intravenous calcium injection provided it is administered in time. To prevent calcium deficiency give the nursing cat food rich in calcium, including various calcium additives.

After the first few days after birth the kittens gain about 15 g ($^1/_2$oz) a day. Their eyes open between the fifth and tenth days. If you notice a discharge and the kitten's eyelids stick, ask the vet for a disinfectant fluid and treat the eyes. It is difficult to treat neglected inflammations at a later stage. If one of the kittens hurts the mother's nipples with its large claws, ask the vet to clip them. Weigh the kittens regularly to find out whether their mother has sufficient milk. If the litter includes a kitten with a serious defect, such as a split palate, it is better to have it put down painlessly.

Give the queen as much food as normal because of its huge consumption of nutrients (see Hint 18). The food must be of good quality and include a large amount of liquid.

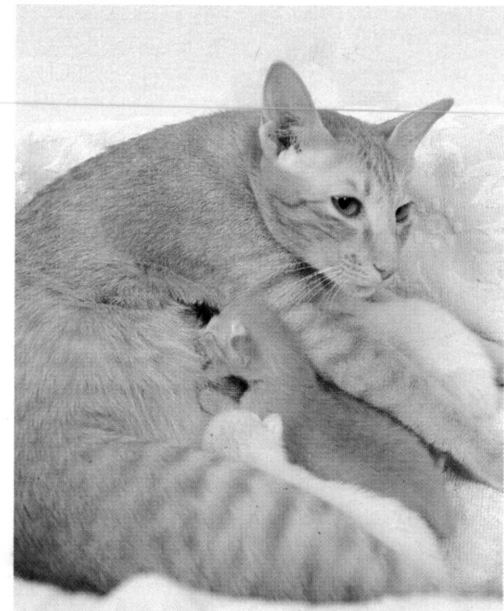

The first weeks after the birth of kittens are usually peaceful fot the queen as well as for the breeder. This Spotted Red Oriental with her litter seems to be in the best of health.

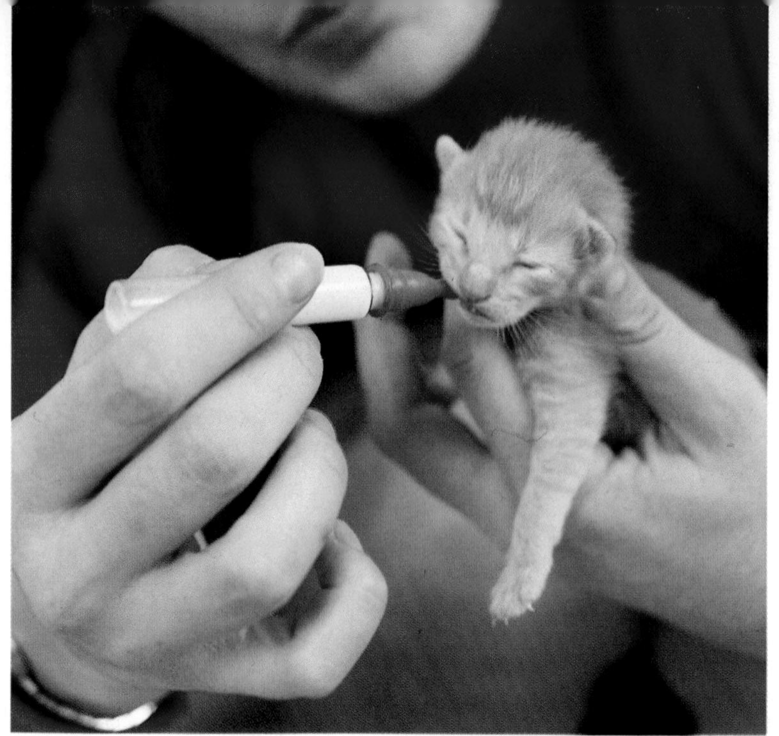

50 Raising Motherless Kittens

If the queen dies or becomes seriously ill while giving birth you must decide whether to rear the kittens by artificial means. Artificial rearing is exceedingly demanding. By far the best solution is to have a 'wet nurse', i.e. another queen which has either lost her kittens or is about to wean her litter. A nursing cat almost always accepts another cat's kittens, but if the 'wet nurse' has had a large litter herself it is better to use two surrogate mothers.

If you decide to rear the kittens on your own you must feed them from a bottle in the first few days; they must be fed every two hours during the day and night. After one week you can omit one night feed, and continue this regime until the end of the kittens' third week. After that you introduce a six-hour break during the night, while during the day they are fed every three hours. From the end of the fourth week they are fed six times a day. As to quantity, during the first week each kitten is given about 5 ml (1 teaspoonful) of milk per feed, during the second week 7 ml (1 $^1/_2$ teaspoonsful) and in the third week about 10 ml (2 teaspoonsful).

For this type of feeding you use special milk corresponding closely to that of the mother. Cow's milk is quite different from cat's milk, which has a higher concentration of proteins; use cow's milk only in an emergency. On the vet's advice you can add various vitamins to the milk.

◁ A kitten should be held with its abdomen down while bottle feeding.

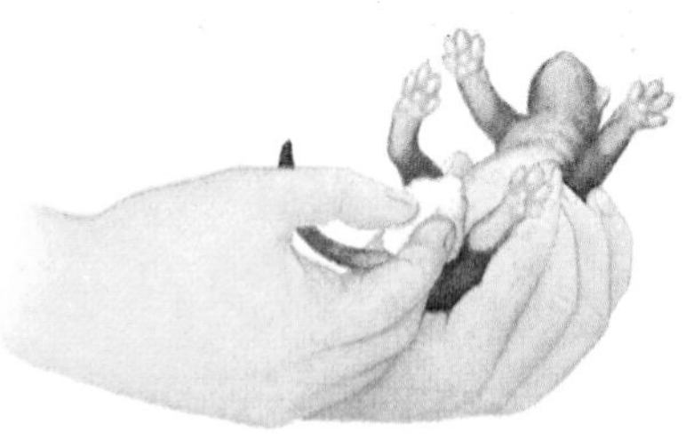

A gentle abdominal massage after each feeding substitutes for the mother's natural method of encouraging the kitten's bowel movement.

Prepare the milk specially for each feed. All utensils used must be sterilized. Throw away any left-over milk: kittens are extremely susceptible to diarrhoea. Always use a special baby bottle or plastic syringe; during the first few days a dropper is also suitable. Feed the kitten gently and slowly, so as not to flood its mouth, and always hold it belly downwards. Push the teat carefully into its mouth and raise the bottle so that the kitten does not swallow air. The temperature of the milk should be about 30°C (100.4°F), the same as that of the mother.

After each feed gently massage the kittens' bellies to encourage bowel movement. The massaging should be done with your fingers, anti-clockwise. A piece of cotton wool or cloth is also used to gently massage the end of the urethra and rectum. In this way we take over the massaging done by the mother, and without which the kittens will not empty their bowels. The urine and faeces are absorbed by the material. Clean the kittens with a slightly damp piece of terrycloth, carefully wiping the coat, especially around the muzzle and the rectum.

Kittens without their mother are kept in a box partly covered by a lid, and in a warm environment. The best way to keep them warm is with an electric blanket wrapped in a cloth — but be careful that the kittens do not get too warm. During their first week they need a temperature of approximately 32°C (90°F) and during the next two weeks 27—29°C (81—84°F). Later they need no more than 21°C (70°F). Examine their mat after every feed and change it immediately if it feels damp. Kittens must be kept dry and in total cleanliness. Kittens reared without their mother lack colostral immunity — that is, the protection afforded by the antibodies in their mother's milk. This is something you need to take into account when vaccinating them, which must be done at an early stage and be all-inclusive. A breeder generally keeps artificially reared kittens longer since they are less resistant to infections. It is a well known fact that kittens, like other animals, reared by a human being, are very attached to that person.

Artificial raising aids for kittens.

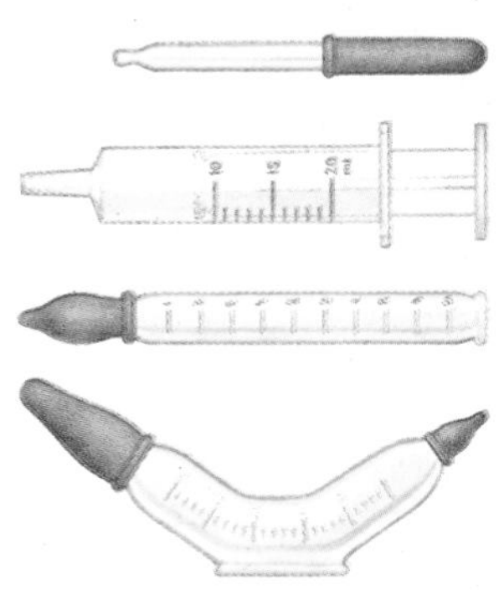

51 Weaning

If the queen has sufficient milk and there has been no need to give the kittens additional nourishment, do not offer them food until the fourth week. At first, give them one milk feed a day. Most suitable is special milk for cats or cow's milk diluted with unsweetened condensed milk. The number of feeds is gradually increased and whipped quark is added. From the sixth week begin giving them minced or scraped meat and crushed hard-boiled eggs. The weaning process takes about six to eight weeks, when the kitten eats on its own while at the same time still sucking its mother's milk. The number of feeds is increased step by step to five or six a day. A weaned kitten is fed six times a day. Weaning must be done gradually so that the kitten's digestive tract besomes accustomed to solid food. The best indication of this is the faeces. If everything is in order the kittens have a bowel movement once a day and their faeces are semi-solid and shaped.

Slowly get the kittens used to supplements to meat. By the end of weaning their food is virtually the same as that of adult cats, except that they are given more milk (two servings a day).

During the weaning process make sure the kittens learn and routinely

◁ Ten-week-old Siamese kittens are already quite independent and toilet-trained. In another two weeks they may be handed over to their new owners.

observe hygienic habits. In the fourth week, when they begin to leave their bed, place a litter tray with a low edge nearby. At first place pieces of newspaper at the bottom of the tray; these are good at absorbing dampness. Once you start to give the kittens additional food they will gradually begin to urinate and empty their bowels on their own; until this point their movements are the responsibility of the mother.

In addition to feeding and teaching the kittens hygienic habits, the breeder must take two more precautionary health measures before selling the kittens: de-worming them and having them vaccinated. The first time the animals are tested for worms is in their fourth week and the second is in the seventh week, shortly before their first vaccination. The medication and doses are determined by the veterinary surgeon. The first vaccination is administered between the eighth and eleventh week. The most important vaccinations are those against FIE and FVR (see Hint 38). Nowadays there are several combined vaccines which protect the animal against several diseases. The vaccination plan is drawn up by the veterinary surgeon, depending on the type of vaccine. At the time of vaccination the kittens must be in good health. All vaccinations are recorded in the kittens' vaccination certificates.

A queen starts to teach her kittens to use the litter box at the age of five weeks.

52 Neutering

Neutering is the most humane means of restricting the reproductive capacity of cats. It is recommended to owners of pure-bred cats who do not want further litters. Domestic cats may also be neutered, especially those allowed more or less free movement outdoors. Cats may also be neutered for various health reasons. One of the most frequent reasons for neutering males is that those kept purely as domestic pets will thereafter stop marking their territory with urine. Older breeding males are also often neutered when their breeding days are over.

•

Neutering of males (castration) is a relatively simple matter in which the testes are removed by a minor incision in the skin of the scrotum. The wound heals in a few days. Neutering females (spaying) requires somewhat more complicated surgery, together with opening the abdominal cavity, in order to remove the uterus and ovaries. Queens can also be prevented from reproducing by sterilization, which involves tying the fallopian tubes which lead

◁ The Persian Chinchilla is an example of silvery traits.

from the ovaries to the womb. Sterilization does not stop oestrus, and in later years cats so treated are more susceptible to gynaecological ailments.

All these interventions are carried out painlessly under general anaesthetic. For many animals neutering can come as a relief. Males are able to move around the house freely together with females, while spayed queens are freed of the unpleasant manifestations of oestrus which — unless it is a breeding cat — unnecessarily burden and often even exhaust them. Objections that the animal suffers by neutering or spaying are unfounded. The decline of the reproductive drive makes the cat 'forget' that it may be lacking something.

•

The important question is when to perform neutering or spaying. As a rule, only adult animals at least one year old should be castrated. In certain cases neutering is possible earlier but this must be decided by the veterinary surgeon. Too early neutering influences the animal's growth; long bones take longer to grow, extremities are generally longer and are not in proportion to the size of the head which, in case of neutered males, does not acquire its typical characteristics in terms of the size and width of the skull. Another possible complication among males neutered too early is an insufficiently developed urinary tract, which remains narrow and later causes urological complications.

The neutering surgery of a male by removing his testicles.

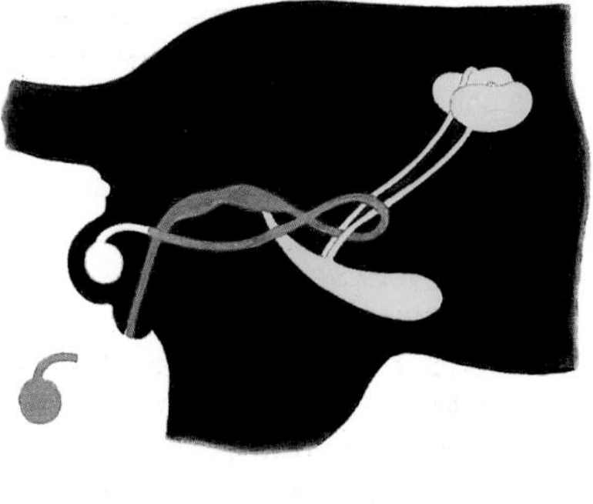

A queen's spaying consists of removing the uterus and ovaries.

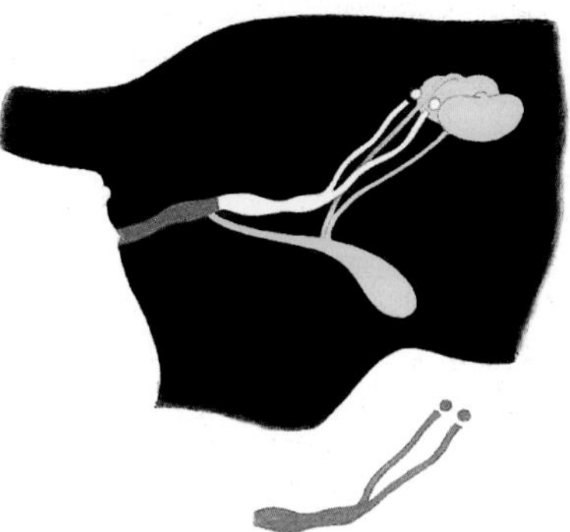

53 Post-neutering Care

After the neutering operation cats do not require any special care other than normal post-operative attention. Before the cat regains consciousness, it is placed in a restful and warm place and observed regularly. The females are given a stronger anaesthetic in view of the more complicated surgery. After regaining consciousness the animals are often restive. It is best to place them in a large carton or box with openings so that they will not hurt themselves on pieces of furniture while their walk is still unsteady. They should be given a drink only when they have fully regained consciousness. A male must not be allowed outside for two or three days, and you must make sure the wound is not bleeding. In the case of an elderly male, the wound sometimes continues to bleed; if that happens, consult your vet. In most cases, however, the male is back to normal two or three days after surgery.

The post-surgery recovery of queens takes a little longer. As a rule they refuse solid food altogether for several days, merely taking drinks. They move little and are evidently in pain. Their condition begins to improve after three days, and they should now begin to eat again. You should observe your queen to ascertain if she is urinating and emptying her bowels. The vet

◁ The Havana Oriental with its shiny, close coat resembling the colour of Havana cigars, which gave the name to this breed.

will tell you when to bring her to surgery to check on her recovery. It may be necessary to fit her with a surgical collar (see illustration, Hint 34) to prevent her from scratching the stitches in the wound. After one week the vet removes the stitches; the wound will have virtually healed and the cat will soon be back to normal.

The majority of cats do not change their behavioural patterns after neutering, although many become more placid and even more attached to the owner. However, almost all castrated males have a tendency to put on weight and this is something you must bear in mind when choosing their diet. Under no circumstances should you increase their amount of food and you should give them fewer supplements. To placate their sharper appetites, feed them smaller helpings several times a day. The coat of many neutered animals becomes thicker and richer, with the result that they shed more hair. Cats which swallow hair during their cleaning activities frequently throw up. This is quite normal, and cats often eat blades of coarse grass to help them vomit. Neutered cats have a tendency to accumulate hair balls in the stomach. You can ease the problem somewhat by daily grooming of the thick coat with a stiff brush and by feeding the cat with green food (see Hint 19).

You will find that, after neutering, a young adult male which lives with non-neutered cats will drop to a lower place in their hierarchy and may even, to some extent, be ostracized by the others. So make a point of giving him more attention and ensure that he is able to feed in a restful atmosphere — other cats are sometimes prone to chase a neutered cat away from food.

You should be aware that a male can make a queen pregnant as long as 10 days after he has been neutered because live sperm has remained in his orifice. An elderly male is generally able to inseminate a queen over a varying length of time after neutering. His behaviour with other males will for several months remains the same as it was prior to neutering: he contends with them for a place in the hierarchy just as vigorously as before.

Spaying of females is done through a small incision on the side. Barring complications, the surgical scar is totally healed in 4—5 weeks.

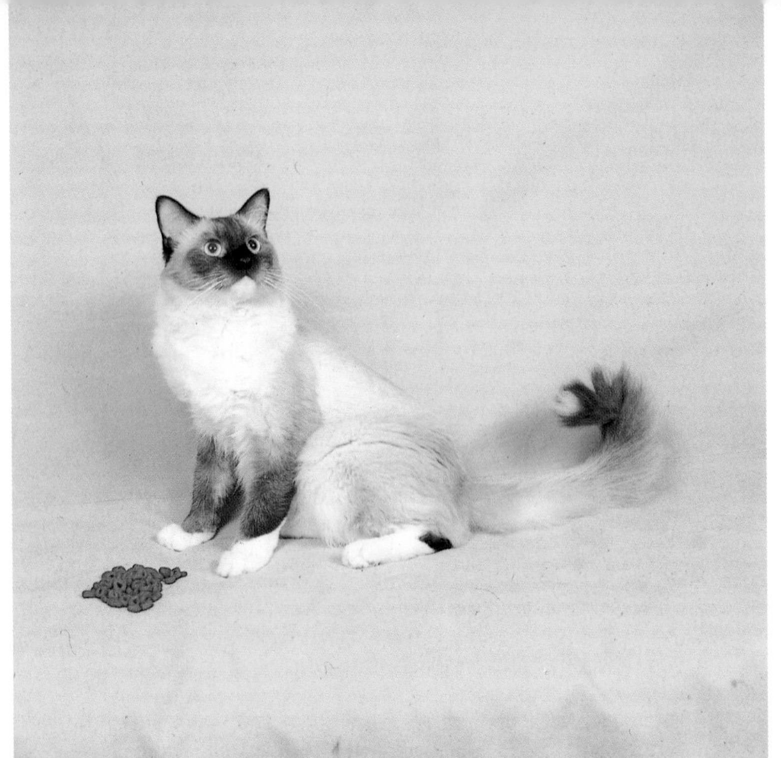

54 Body Language

Even though man has described it as a 'silent face', the cat has many ways of communicating with other animals, including man. It is well worth while spending time and effort in the attempt to understand the various means of expression of your cat; both of you can benefit from this.

•

We referred to the vocal repertoire in Hint 28. But the cat also makes itself understood by its physical attitude and gestures, each of which has specific significance. Some of the basic emotions, and their physical expression by a cat, are as follows:

Pleasure: the head and tail are raised high; the paws outstretched; eyes partly closed; slightly arched back as the cat curls around and rubs against its master's leg.

Playfulness: head held high, with ears errect; tail in the shape of a question mark; the cat jumps, runs, chases toys or other moving objects such as leaves.

◁ The Ragdoll is an extremely placid breed.

Fear: cowering posture; body low to the ground; wide-eyed, with ears flattened.
Anger: ears erect but furled back; bristling tail swishes sharply.
Defensive threat: arched bristling tail; ears flat on head; teeth bared.

The cat has countless gestures, of which the following are typical:

Rubbing its nose against you: love, trust, tenderness;
Rubbing its head: affection;
Stroking with the paw, claws retracted: closeness, affection;
Smelling: getting acquainted;
Slightly raised paw: warning.

There are situations when the cat's normal repertoire does not meet the needs of the occasion. For no apparent reason it starts to behave differently. Manifestations of such coded message include, for example, neglect of hygienic habits, an apparent desire to destroy things or excessive aggressiveness. More about this in Hint 57.

An important communication tool of the cat is mimicry. A contented cat (a) with erect ears and relaxed sensory hair; the size of the pupils is in line with available light. An angry cat (b) with ears folded back, narrow pupils and sensory hair stuck out forward. A frightened cat (c) with ears to the side and expanded pupils. A playing or hunting cat (d) with ears and sensory hair forward, expanded pupils. A petted cat (e) with half-closed eyes and relaxed sensory hair.

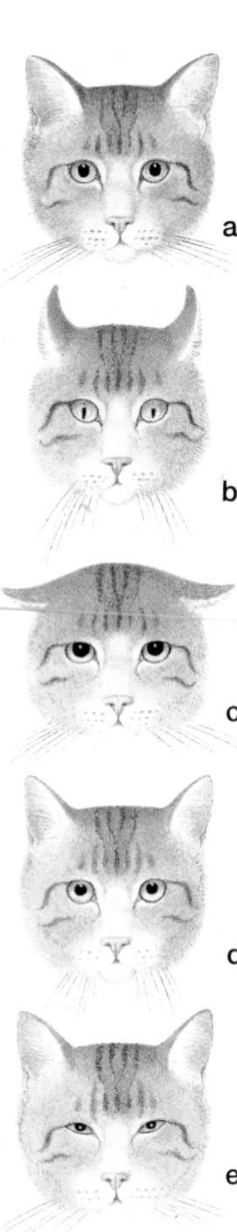

Leg rubbing is a sign of attachment and a good relationship between cat and human being.

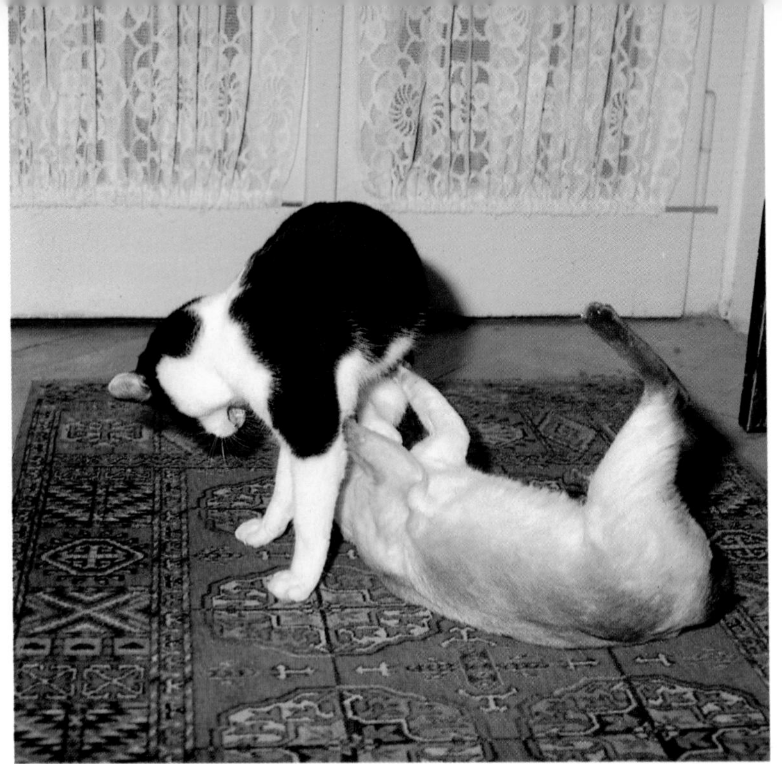

55 The Roots of Feline Behaviour

Behaviour in animals, including man, is broadly of two kinds: instinctive and acquired. Instinctive behaviour is essentially automatic and is independent of the will of the animal. It is genetically programmed behaviour and cannot be modified by experience. A so-called 'key motive' is the impulse to instinctive action, in most cases a fundamental physiological need (hunger, security, reproduction). This creates several problems for the cat owner. An animal cannot be made to alter its instinctive behaviour, or its inconvenient manifestations such as noisy oestrus seasons and claw sharpening on furniture. But we can often alleviate its effects as, for example, by providing the cat with a purpose-made claw-sharpening post (see Hint 7).

•

Acquired behaviour is most obvious in animals of a higher level of development. Only the basic disposition towards such behaviour is genetically coded: its manifestations depend on the experience accumulated by the individual; in other words, on its capacity to learn. An animal learns from its

◁ Petty fights and playing are commonplace among cats living together.

A typical posture expressing feline contentment.

own experiences as well as by observing other animals. Essentially, the ability to learn depends on the ability to see the links between cause and effect. This must be borne in mind when training the cat. If these links are to be firmly established, the cause and effect relationship must be clear and effect must follow cause in quick succession. The ability to learn varies from one cat to another. A recollection of my breeding experience might serve as an example. I had a cat which I taught to open a door by jumping onto the door handle. While that cat was alive all my other cats were able to open the door in the same way. But when the cat died, the other animals stopped opening the door and to this day none of them has learnt, or 'remembered', how to do this.

●

It is possible to divide the behaviour of a cat into a few major functional areas. These include spatial orientation; behaviour connected with food; hygiene (care of its coat); communication; self-protection; territorial behaviour (protecting its territory); reproduction; social behaviour; play; and cyclical behaviour (influenced by biorhythm). All these functional areas include elements of both instinctive and acquired behaviour in varying proportions.

Marking by male and, occasionally, by females is part of territorial behaviour. Since marking is essentially an instinctive action, it is impossible to control or eradicate by training. There are, however, steps that can be taken to alleviate the problem (see Hint 58).

56 Group Behaviour

Wild cats and domesticated ones that have become feral live in groups based on the mother-kitten relationship. Apart from the time when they are looking after their young, females keep to themselves but do not avoid contact with others. They lead a social life known as a 'cats' assembly'. Male cats generally belong to so-called male 'fraternities'. The hierarchy in these fraternities is very rigid, based on the outcome of fights within the group. Once the male cat reaches maturity he must first of all struggle to win his position. Once this has been earned, a struggle is no longer necessary unless he is driven to seek dominance over a male who is above him in the hierarchy, or if he feels threatened. Although fights between males seem to be fierce, the blows are directed mainly at well protected places on the head and on the neck and most of these blows do not cause deep wounds. A male cat defeated in a fight is always given the chance to escape. The purpose is not to kill him but to demonstrate superiority. A neutered male loses his position in the hierarchy. When a queen is in oestrus, males will often fight in her presence. However, the choice of the mate is always the prerogative of the queen and, interestingly enough, she by no means always chooses the winner of such fights.

Cat congregations, which take place mainly at night, pose interesting questions of behaviour. The queens sit for hours mostly soundless but occasionally growling

◁ Kittens enjoy many privileges in a cat family. These two Oriental males of different ages live together in harmony.

Fights between adult males always end in the submission of the weaker cat, who is given the chance of retreating.

or hissing. Although clearly forming a group, most of them keep a certain distance from each other, and only those that know each other really well sit close together. A congregation always meets in the same place, and at regular intervals. It seems to reflect an instinctive need to reinforce the cohesion, however loose and informal, of the cats in a given neighbourhood, and it appears to have nothing to do with reproductive behaviour.

Domesticated cats are compelled to live in communities, often with animals not related to each other. Cats who have known each other from their early days are able to live side by side in harmony. They share their sleeping quarters, they clean each other and are even able to look after their kittens together. Here, too, a social hierarchy develops which changes from time to time. The hierarchy among female cats is looser, based on motherhood. With each succeeding litter the mother rises in the hierarchy. During the period when she is looking after her kittens her position is strong, regardless of how many litters she has had before. If, after having one or more litters, a queen is spayed she drops in the hierarchy. Animals neutered before attaining sexual maturity win no position at all in the group.

If males are forced to co-exist in a group, fierce battles inevitably break out. Breeding males living solely in a house or with only limited outlets must be kept separated because of constant fights. A male behaves well in the company of female cats; he generally accepts the privileged position of the queen and does not have fights with her. Some males even share in the training of the kittens. Others, however, will strangle their offspring; fortunately, they are in a minority, but before allowing a male cat to remain with the mother and her kittens, be certain of how the male will behave towards them.

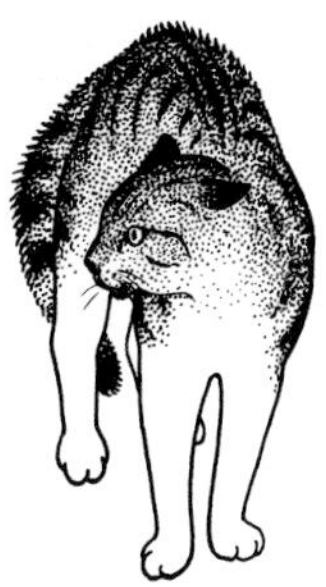

If many cats are kept in a restricted space they have a tendency to oppress those lower in the hierarchy. They will push the weaker one away from its food and from its favourite place, and will gradually make it neurotic. Neutered animals are generally the weaker individuals in groups. It is essential to ensure that the individuals of the group do not get in each other's way. It is generally accepted that each cat requires about 9m^2 (100sq.ft) of space.

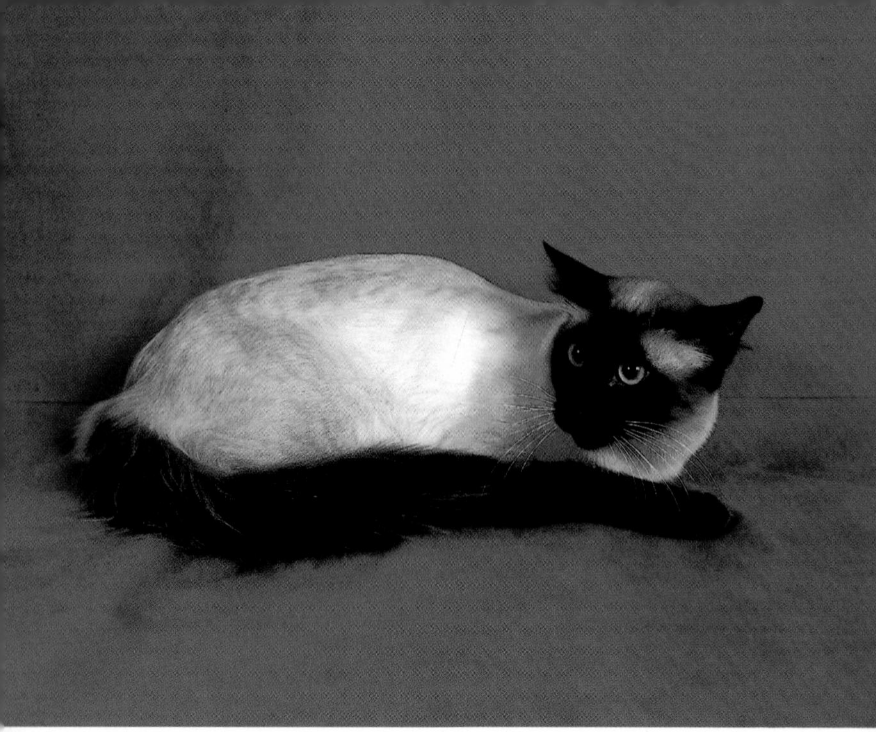

57 Signs of Stress

It is especially important for the breeder to know the causes and manifestations of stress. The conditions in which a domesticated cat lives differ greatly from the natural environment to which the species originally adapted. And even the most placid cat retains the instincts that would have enabled it to survive in the wild, so it must continuously come to terms with life in a house or flat. Serious conflicts may arise in the process since a housebound cat cannot deal with the situation by running away. It may react by changing its normal behaviour, by falling sick, by neglecting its hygiene, or by aggressive or destructive acts. Other noticeable signs of stress may be the refusal of food, devouring its own faeces, constant cleaning or even pulling out of its hair, biting its tail, uncharacteristic timidity or general depression.

•

It is necessary to look for the causes of such manifestations not in the cat but in our treatment of it, and to discover whether anything in its environment has changed. The cause might be the departure from the home of someone

◁ Balinese with dark brown markings; its posture and mimicry express fear.

for whom the cat had a particular affection, or the arrival of a new baby and the ensuing concentration of attention on it at the expense of the cat. Both cats and dogs find it difficult to accept a decline in attention paid to them, especially if they are accustomed to being constantly petted. Another cause of difficulty could be a change in the animal's regime; for example, if in the past it was used to sleeping in the owner's bedroom, but has now been banished to another room. Other reasons could be the arrival of a new cat or dog in the home, a series of visits to the vet, building work in the house, moving house, disturbed sleep or eating, inconsistent training and so on.

•

It is not easy to overcome the problem of stress once it takes hold. The owner must try to find the cause and make every effort to put things right. If the cat is suffering from lack of attention, try to devote more time to it, cuddling it and showing your affection in other ways. Cats can be very jealous of other people as well as of other animals. Everything must be done to avoid disturbing the cat when it is sleeping or eating, and you must ensure that children do not do this. If the cat neglects its hygienic habits because it does not like the location of the litter tray where it can be disturbed, look for another place until the cat is happy with it. If the cat has undergone a particular experience that has obviously caused severe stress, ask the vet to prescribe a sedative or possibly sleeping tablets.

Typical posture of a depressed cat: the animal moves very little or not at all, it is rolled into a ball with ears folded to the side and pupils expanded. In an extreme case the cat may urinate and defecate uncontrollably.

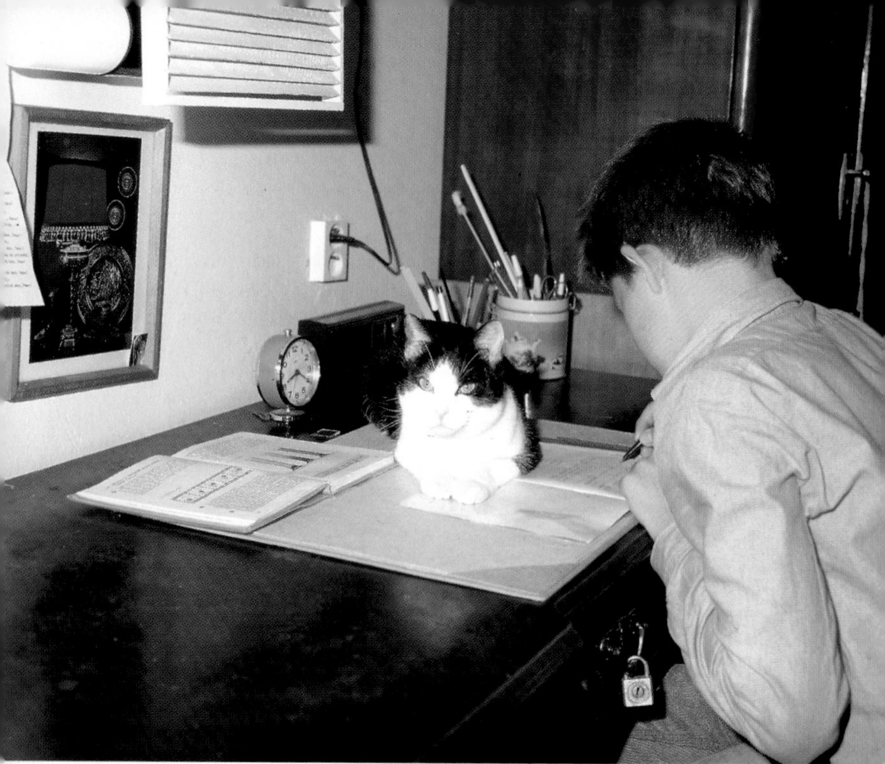

58 Cat Training

The education and training of a cat must take account of its natural inclinations and instincts. If a cat is to be rewarded, treat it to an extra helping of its favourite food, or make a point of petting it. Punishment should never be in the form of physical chastisement, which is not only wrong and in any case ineffective but will have a disastrous effect on the relationship between the cat and its owner. Some people use a water pistol to discourage bad habits — though this is hardly suitable inside the house — while others use a small ball of paper to throw at the cat; such a ball, like the jet from a water pistol, will startle but not hurt the cat. A loud 'No!' can also be a method of training. All members of the family should use the same term when they want to make the cat stop doing something.

•

A certain 'natural' type of training takes place during the very first days of a kitten's life, when it learns, by observing its mother, ways of responding to specific situations and objects, including human beings. A very nervous or neurotic queen is unlikely to give birth to well-balanced kittens. It is a well known fact that kittens (like

◁ A cat may, at least partially, be trained — but often it trains its master instead.

other young) separated from their mother at birth for whatever reason and reared on the bottle, have a very close and affectionate relationship with the human being who feeds them. We can take advantage of this by gently taking each of the kittens in our hand, making sure they do not get cold. After a few days you will find that they are no longer afraid of being picked up. On the other hand, many kittens reared in large catteries, where they have little contact with people, never succeed in becoming accustomed to the company of humans.

•

Training cats to perform various activities is essentially a process of conditioning; that is, you train the cat to except a certain, predicable sequence of events in which it has a particular part to play. The sequence is as follows: impetus (the instruction to the cat); response (the cat acts in the appropriate way); reward (praise, or a titbit). The reward must come immediately after the cat's correct response, otherwise it is useless. The same procedure must be used when disciplining an animal, the punishment must be meted out straight after the deed or, better still, the moment the cat is getting ready for it (for instance, if it squats on the carpet, preparing to urinate). Consistency of action on the owner's part is crucial in training. The animal must always be rewarded or punished, as the case may be, in the same way for the same thing.

•

Training a cat requires a great deal of patience. A cat is capable of being trained, but is unwilling to co-operate if it feels that the activity we want it to perform is meaningless. The longer it takes to teach the cat something, the longer it will remember it.

It is easy to teach the cat the rules of hygiene, since it is a clean animal by nature. A male cat can to some extent be taught to limit his 'marking' by placing a specific area at his disposal for this purpose. A cat can be taught a variety of skills, such as using a flap-door, opening the door, responding to being called, sharpening his claws only at a specified place, jumping onto one's lap, walking on a leash, and so forth.

With patience, cats can be trained to adjust to a leash. Training should begin when the animal is still a kitten.

59 Hunting

A queen teaches her kittens the rudiments of hunting at a very early stage. She brings them dead, and later live, prey. The kittens learn first to eat the prey, later to hunt it and finally to kill it. The act of killing the prey is clearly the most difficult to learn. Although cats living in a house do not go through this hunting course, they do not lack the hunting instinct. Most cats, if they become wild animals later in life, learn to hunt spontaneously even at the price of many failures. The hunting ability varies from animal to animal. Kittens of good hunters usually become equally good hunters.

Wild and domestic cats use more or less the same predatory skills. They do not pursue their prey. At first they lie in wait for quite a long time, than they stealthily approach it and pounce. Hunting uses up a lot of time and energy. It is not true that a cat, well fed by its owner, refrains from hunting. On the contrary, a well-nourished cat is in better condition and thus has a better chance of catching its prey. The fact is that cats, like all beasts of prey, hunt not only to obtain food but to satisfy their hunting instinct. Only about 25 per cent of all attempts to catch a prey are successful.

Cats kill their prey by biting it in the back of the neck; their long canine

◁ Burmese cats.

teeth penetrate the area between the vertebrae and cut the spinal cord. But often, before the actual kill, they play with their prey for a while, toss it in the air and so forth. One theory explains this behaviour by considering it as a method of practising the hunting technique. According to another theory, this is the consequence of a precisely programmed hunting instinct which requires a hunt-and-kill sequence to take a certain time.

When consuming their prey cats prefer the internal organs, especially the liver, probably because they contain vitamins, and the brain because of its amino acid content. It is evident that food consisting of offal meat alone is not sufficiently nutritious.

An interesting social phenomenon has been observed in connection with hunting. Cats frequently bring their prey to their master as a kind of gift; or they may offer it as a present to a befriended cat or, in rare cases, even to a dog. The cat deserves to be stroked for such a token of friendship.

Playing with prey is not an expression of cruelty but a central part of its hunting behaviour.

Play helps kittens to learn the technique of hunting. Even cats reared in flats are able to hunt.

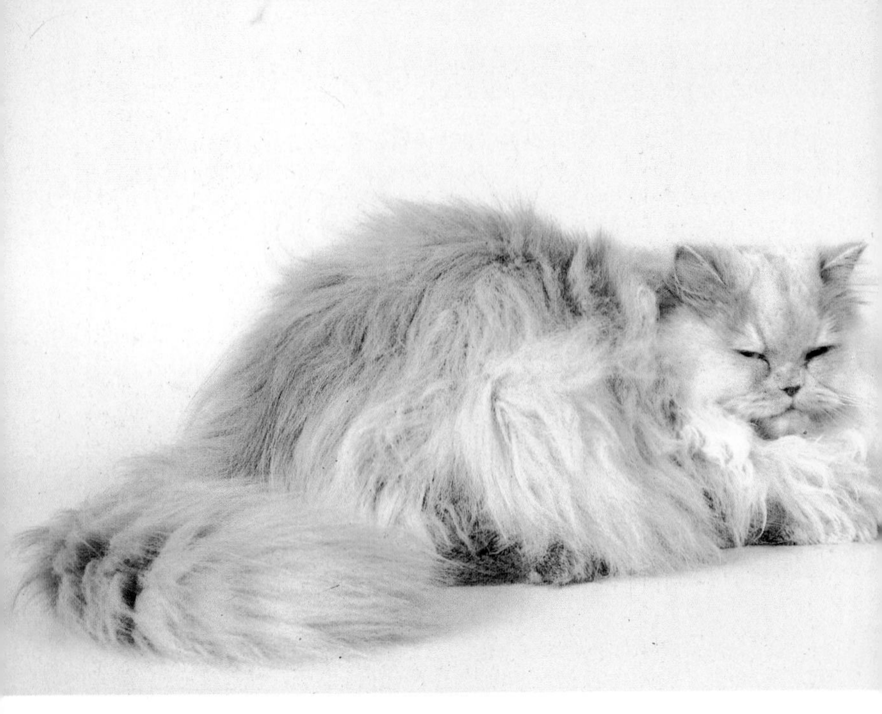

60 Sleep

A cat spends two thirds of its life asleep — about twice as long as most other mammals. It is still not clear why this is so.

•

The need for sleep changes in the course of a cat's life. Young kittens and elderly cats sleep longer than adult animals. A great deal depends on the temperature of the environment, on whether they have eaten their fill, and on their sexual activity. Recordings of brain waves show that after falling asleep the cat sleeps lightly and wakes up easily. In this sleeping phase certain groups of muscles are tense (the cat does not necessarily need to lie down to sleep) and the brain waves are high and irregular. After 10—30 minutes the sleep deepens, indicated by the so-called rapid eye movement (REM) behind closed or partly open eyelids; the muscles are totally relaxed and the eyeballs move rapidly. Curiously, the recordings show almost the same waves then as when the cat is fully awake. This deep sleep lasts 6—7 minutes. It is the most important sleeping phase, when cats have dreams. You

◁ Typical posture of a drowsing cat. It can wake very quickly from this phase of sleep.

Cats are big sleepers, spending some two-thirds of their life slumbering.

will often notice a twitching of the limbs, ears, and whiskers, and a clicking of the tongue. It is in this phase of sleeping that the nervous system is thoroughly regenerated.

Deep sleep is then followed by 20—30 minutes of light slumber. The various phases of sleep alternate regularly. Cat owners must allow a cat time for sufficient sleep in tranquility in its favourite resting place. Children should be strongly discouraged from trying to play with them at these times.

An encephalogram of a sleeping cat: (a) wakefulness, (b) drowsing, (c) deep sleep with eyeball movements, (d) drowsing, (e) wakefulness.

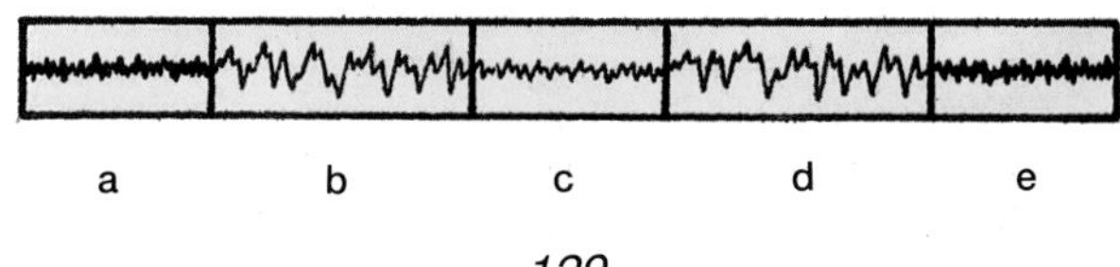

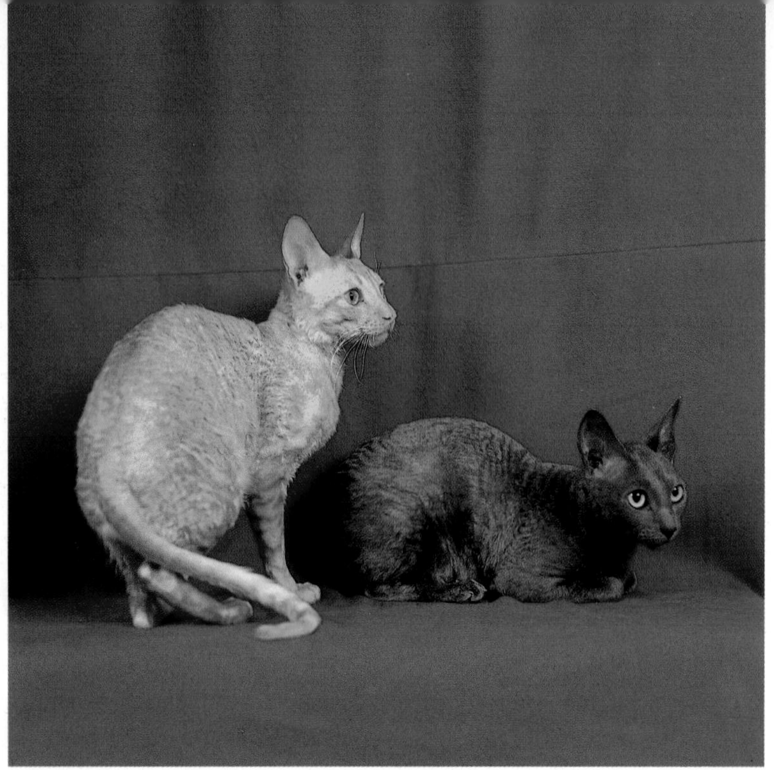

61 Feline Sexual Behaviour

Under normal conditions, as we have seen, female cats are in heat several times a year, when they are capable of conceiving. These periods are known as oestrus cycles and are accompanied by typical changes in behaviour (for more on oestrus, see Hint 29).

•

A female in heat is highly attractive to her potential partners. Each mating is preceded by a preparation, a courtship ritual. In the course of this ritual the animal must of its own free will overcome a so-called safe distance between itself and the partner without attacking, while at the same time getting hormonally and mentally ready for mating. The ritual is specifically feline and unintelligible to other species, and serves as a safeguard against intercrossing of different species. The breeder must know that the ritual must be allowed to run its course if mating is to take place.

In mating, the male approaches and mounts the female from behind and takes hold of the skin on the back of her neck between his teeth. Actual

◁ A breeding pair of Cornish Rex. If the pair lives together permanently their pre-mating ritual will be very brief.

penetration takes about five seconds before ejaculation. At this moment the female emits a loud cry, quickly retreats from the male and rolls over several times on her back. Then she chases the male away, emitting hissing sounds. This aggressive behaviour is evidently motivated by the shape of the male's penis which, with its spiny tip, painfully excites the vagina and sets in train a series of physiological reactions that culminate in ovulation. Once mating has finished, both partners meticulously clean their genitals. However, a further mating may follow and may be repeated several times in the course of the day or night.

•

Cats are not monogamous. During one and the same cycle of oestrus the female may mate with several males, so that the kittens in a single litter may have different fathers. This is something the queen's owner must remember if she is allowed to go outdoors after mating or if she is kept together with a male other than the one with whom she was mated. It is recommended that a female be prevented from contact with another male for at least 10 days after mating.

Mating position, with the male holding the female by the scruff of the neck.

62 Cat Shows

Cat shows have been held for more than a century. The first show in Europe was held at Crystal Palace in London in 1871; the first on the American continent took place in 1861. The purpose was to show the public the beauty of cats. An equally significant motive of shows nowadays is to assess the quality of cats and compare animals coming from different breeders. Only close monitoring of many animals can turn a breeder into a true expert, capable of breeding high-quality cats on the basis of theoretical and practical experience, and exhibit them with pride at a show.

•

Shows are a unique opportunity for contacts between breeders and for an exchange of information and views. Anyone looking for a kitten is able to meet many a successful breeder there. Moreover, shows are the place where one can obtain a host of information about caring for a cat, its nourishment and about how to deal with certain health and diet problems.

◁ A view of the first World Cat Show, held in Munich in 1991.

The protection of animals, cats included, has become an important public issue in recent years. Associations for the protection of animals have their stands at most shows, where visitors can get information on the subject, including ways and means of preventing the reproduction of unwanted, stray cats. Sometimes there are special shows of animals from homes for abandoned cats, which are now in excellent shape and have received all the vaccinations that are mandatory for show animals. Many a pet fancier has taken away a lovely cat to a new home from such a show.

Show cages are big enough to contain the all basic equipment. It is necessary to keep the cage clean during the duration of the exhibition.

63 Entering Your Cat at a Show

In each country where cats are bred and put on show there are one or more breeder associations that organize shows. These are generally held at weekends and last for one or two days. Nowadays most shows are arranged so that on each day a different breed category is displayed.

•

Every year there are dozens of different shows, ranging from major international events, through national and down to regional and even more localized club shows. The status of the 'prizes' to be won varies with the importance of the event. At a national show the maximum recognition conferred is to be a champion candidate (see Hint 67). The object of some special shows is to obtain a certificate on breeding qualities, but these are not held very often — in some countries not at all. Then there are shows only of kittens or of neutered animals. Exceptionally, shows are reserved for a specific breed or a group of related breeds. The shows naturally also differ in size.

◁ The Japanese Bobtail with traditional Mi-Ke tortoiseshell and white colouring is a rarity at cat shows.

Participation in a show requires membership of some breeder association or club. The organizers issue the show standards in good time, and anyone interested is told all that is needed to allow entry of the cat. The entries must be made in writing on special forms, and the last date of application is given in the show programme. Together with the application the breeder sends an admission fee. All cats participating in shows must be vaccinated against rabies and FIE; certain countries require additional immunization against FVR (see Hint 38). The cat must be healthy, and the breeder has to submit a veterinary certificate to this effect. Pregnant females are excluded from participation in shows. By his or her signature on the application the breeder undertakes to adhere to all regulations governing the show. The regulations are available from the relevant breeder club.

•

All shows are included in the calendar to enable the breeder to choose a suitable date and venue. Show calendars are issued by international breeder associations, which include clubs in various countries.

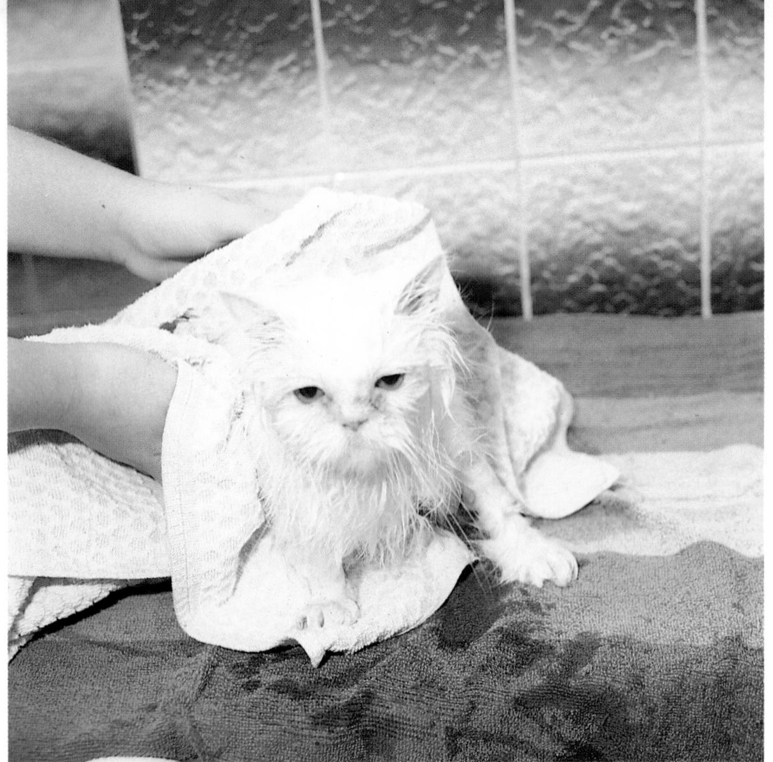

64 Preparing Your Cat for a Show

Do not leave preparation of the cat until only a few days prior to the event. Outstanding condition, which is a prerequisite of success, is the result of long-term and regular care and grooming, good quality and suitable nourishment and the animal's mental tranquillity.

The detailed preparation of cats for a show differs according to breed. Longhair breeds require more demanding preparation. About one month before the show you give special attention to the long hair. It should be thoroughly brushed every day to prevent formation of clumps of dead hair, which you would otherwise have to trim. Give the cat a bath five to seven days before the opening day. (If you bathed the animal later its coat would be drained of oil, dull and lack elasticity.) Clear-colour cats sometimes need two baths. The day after the bath, powder the coat and again brush it thoroughly. Dark coats are either not powdered at all or only lightly; instead of powder, use an anti-static conditioner after the bath. A cat that has had a bath must not be allowed to go outdoors. Great care of the coat must continue until the cat has been judged at the show; the last good brushing is given at the show. Clear-colour cats whose eyes tend to water must have the skin around the eyes thoroughly cleaned; any slight yellowing of the fur may by disguised with a touch of powder, which you

◁ A bath is an essential part of the pre-show preparation for light-coloured Persians.

Cat 'make-up': powdering the eye corners. The hair should be first thoroughly washed and rinsed with warm water and then dried.

apply carefully with a cotton wool brush. Tartar of the teeth should be removed by a veterinarian in good time. Make sure that the claws are cleaned. A slight trimming of the claws is permitted.

•

Grooming of shorthair cats is basically similar to the grooming of any other breed, except that the preparation of the coat is far simpler. One month before the show, brush the cat more thoroughly to remove all dead hair. Certain breeds — the Russian Blue, for example — can be given a bath five to seven days before the show. The bath can be replaced by a bran 'bath', which removes greasiness and dandruff (see illustration in Hint 13).

A greasy tail in a male cat creates greater problems. The tail root is degreased with the help of bran, starch or powder which must be thoroughly brushed out after 24 hours. The grooming of short hair is completed by smoothing with a chamois or silk cloth.

Siamese cats often need to go on a slimming diet before a show: they have a healthy appetite and are generally chubbier than they ought to be for a show. The loss of weight cannot be achieved by starving the animal but by better quality nourishment in smaller helpings, with fewer meat supplements.

Another form of cat grooming allowed before a show is optically 'rounding' the head of breeds which are supposed to have a rounded head and small ears. This can be achieved by gently removing hair or bristles at the tip of the ear lobe; this applies particularly to Persian and exotic cats. Dark-colour or two-colour animals sometimes have odd white hairs which may be pulled out. White patches are genetic and disqualify the animal at the show.

Cats which you intend to take to a show must be trained in good time for travelling and the presence of unfamiliar people.

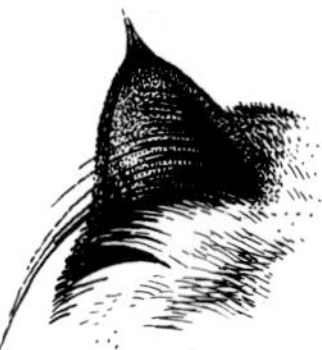

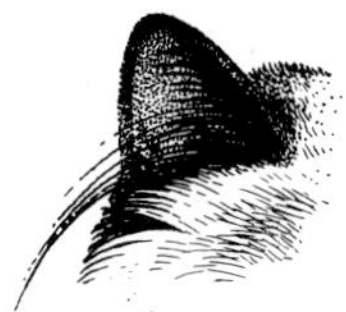

Plucking hair on top of the the ear-lobe gives the impression of a more rounded head.

65 Some Other Show Hints

When preparing for a show you must, above all, comply with the immunization requirements. Check the vaccination certificate well in advance and if necessary have the cat re-vaccinated. Combined vaccines are suitable; the administration of certain vaccines requires a certain period of time.

The cat's cage for the show should be fitted with a curtain that fits the internal dimensions of the cage: width and height 75cm (30in), depth 60cm (24in). On the bottom of the cage put either a pillow covered in the same material as the curtain, or a piece of carpeting. Most breeders try to harmonize the colour of the cage decoration with those of the coat and eyes of the cat. Place a small toilet box in the cage. Kittens and Rex breeds which need more warmth should have a blanket or a piece of cloth in the cage.

On the day prior to the show give the cat neither aromatic food nor anything that has a laxative effect. The most suitable food is poultry. It is best to avoid milk. On the morning of the show give the animal little food, and place a bowl with water in the cage and possibly a little dry food. Kittens should be given a normal portion of a light meal but not milk.

◁ A Devon Rex in a handsome and comfortable show cage.

The preparation of longhair cats of light colouring for a show is long and demanding.

The breeder must keep an eye on the cat throughout the show and keep its cage clean. Animals that are with their owner are more peaceable if he or she gives them attention throughout the event. At most shows the owner himself presents the cat to the judges.

After the show it is a good idea to keep the cat away from other animals for 10 days or so, especially if there are kittens or elderly cats in the house. Although cats which attended a show have been vaccinated, they may nevertheless fall slightly sick, and disease caught outside the home may become serious in the case of very young and old animals, since they have a lower resistance. After a show observe the cat closely to discover possible symptoms of any illness. Inspect its coat, since at shows there is always a certain risk of catching fleas.

Breeds and kittens which are fond of a warm environment should be provided with a warm blanket in their show cage.

66 Show Judging

Animals at shows are assessed anonymously. The judge does not have the animal's pedigree, and the cats are presented by a steward or by the owner with only a number to identify them. Assessment is done in public; breeders and spectators can look on. The judge generally justifies to the public the order he or she has determined, and explains the pluses and minuses of each animal.

•

When awarding points the judge is guided by specific standards for the various breeds, which give a precise description of the breed, and each feature has its own point score. Breed standards are issued in writing and new breeds and colour varieties are added regularly and then recognized by the relevant breeders' association. These standards are binding on the judges and breeders. All deviations from required standards are noted at the show and are reflected in points awarded to the animal. In addition to its actual name, each breed and colour variety has its specific code. The FIFe

◁ Judging proceeds anonymously; the cats are identified only by a number.

nowadays uses the EMS system of coding (see Hint 42 and Hint 82).

Each shortcoming in any required attribute of a breed means that a certain number of points are deducted. Assessment also takes account of the animal's age which, together with all other attributes (breed, colour, class and sex) is noted in the assessment protocol. The protocol is drawn up in the official languages of the FIFe (French, English or German) and also in the language of the country where the show is held.

•

Cats can be awarded a maximum of 100 points. Each breed has its own scale of points, which determines the assessment of individual breed attributes. The scale varies according to which appearance qualities are considered to be the most important in that particular breed. In addition, the general physical condition of the cat is also assessed and earns up to five points extra. Domestic cats which belong to no specific breed are judged according to a standard in which emphasis is placed on the harmony of the proportions of the animal's body as well as on its physical and mental condition.

Assessments within the FIFe do not record the points awarded. They merely serve as a guideline for the ultimate assessment.

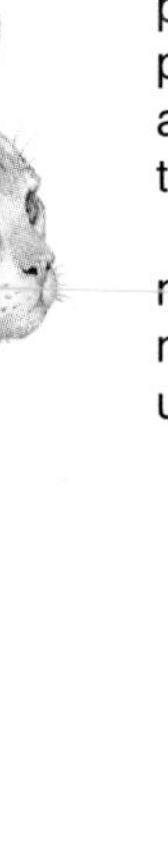

Cats must be wearing their assigned number during the entire show in order to avoid any confusion in their assessment.

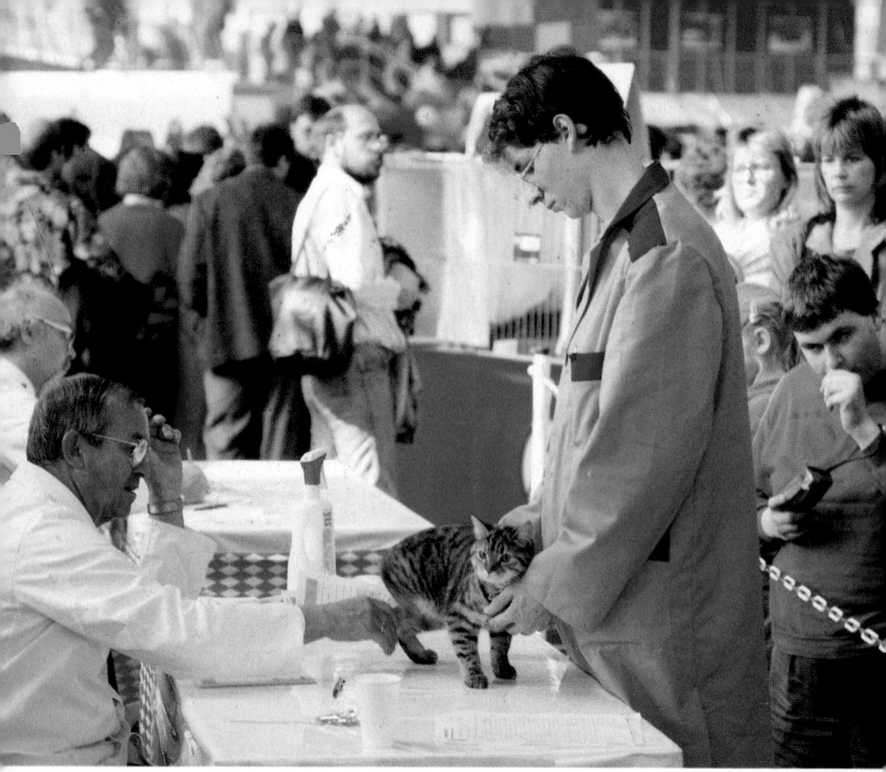

67 Show Titles and Awards

Cats are assessed separately by breed and colour variety. Animals that are comparable as regards quality and age are assessed in individual categories. Each category is divided according to sex.

•

The 'Champion' title is awarded to the cat which, in the open category, including animals aged ten months and over, has three times been awarded the title of CAC (Certificate of Championship Aptitude) by different judges at three national or international shows. For a neutered cat the analogous title is the 'Premier', which is given to the animal in the castrate category which has three times been awarded the CAP assessment (Certificate of Premier Aptitude). The CAC and CAP can be awarded only if the animal obtains 93 points or more.

•

The title 'International Champion' and 'International Premier' are awarded to animals which have three times been awarded the CACIB (Certificat

◁ Judging during the World Cat Show in Munich.

d'Aptitude au Championnat International de Beauté), or the CAPIB (Certificat d'Aptitude au Premier International de Beauté) in the champion or premier category. To reach this standard the cat must have been awarded at least 95 points by three judges in at least two different countries.

The titles 'Grand Champion' and 'Grand Premier' are awarded to animals which in the category of international champions or premiers are six times awarded the CAGCIB (Certificat d'Aptitude au Grand Championnat International de Beauté) or the CAGPIB (Certificat d'Aptitude au Grand Premier International de Beauté) by three judges in three different countries. For this award at least 96 points must have been achieved on each occasion.

•

The highest title nowadays is that of European Champion or European Premier. It is awarded to cats which in the Grand Champion or Grand Premier category have on nine occasions achieved the CACE assessment (Certificat d'Aptitude au Championnat d'Europe) or the CAPE (Certificat d'Aptitude au Premier d'Europe), from three judges in three different countries.

•

In addition to these titles, each show awards the titles 'Best Animal of the Variety', 'Best Animal of the Show', 'Best Neutered Cat', 'Best Young Cat' and sometimes 'Best of the Best' — the individual judged the best of the winners in each category. The world show, which takes place once a year, also awards the title 'World Champion'.

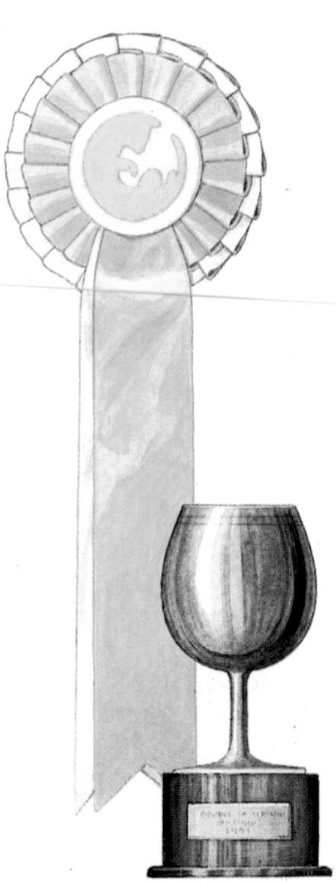

Ornamental ribbons, cups, breeders' aids and cat foods are among the prizes commonly awarded.

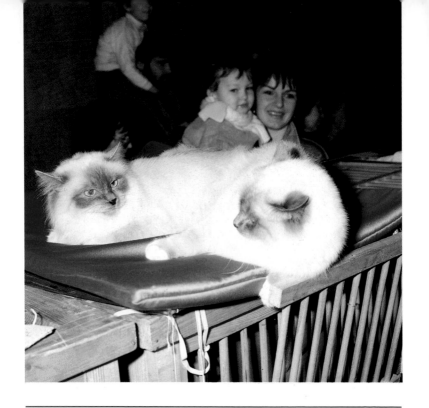

68 Show Cats: Disqualifying Defects

Cats may have certain serious shortcomings which disqualify them from entering shows. Some shortcomings are hereditary; and these lower the value of the cat for breeding purposes. Among the most serious shortcomings are an incorrect number of toes and, in the male, the absence of a testicle. Males with one or both testicles missing are not

White patches are often the reason for disqualification at a show, provided these are not imposed by the rules governing the breed. They are most common on the neck and chest, which is why they are also called 'medallions'.

◁ All breeds are worthy of admiration. This Birman attracts attention with its white 'socks' and blue eyes.

disqualified from shows before the age of 10 months. Another innate defect is a squint. This is most common among Siamese cats but is occasionally found in other breeds. White patches on the fur (not stipulated by the standards) with a diameter of more than 1cm (2/5in) are another cause of exclusion from competitions. These patches, too, are hereditary and so passed on to the young and devalue the entire breed.

Apart from innate defects, blindness, aggressiveness, miniaturization (dwarf growth), amputated toes, emaciation or obesity and doping (this applies generally to administering sedatives to tense animals) are further causes of disqualification. The absence of part of the coat, such as a bald patches measuring more than 1cm (2/5in) in diameter, is another disqualifying defect.

Pregnant and nursing females whose kittens are less than 11 weeks old, cats with evidence of poor health, dirty cats and animals with parasites are also excluded from contests. Unauthorized adaptation of the coat or some parts of the body are likewise disqualifying. Unauthorized adaptation of the coat includes any kind of dying, bleaching, trimming, shaving or excessive powdering. Cats after a tail operation (removing a kink) are similarly excluded.

A breeder intending to put his or her cat on show should know that in addition to these disqualifying defects there can be many other reasons why the animal would not win a title. These include all deformations of the tail (with the exception of neutered cats, where this is tolerated), an injured eye, abnormal depressions, protrusions and crevices on the skull, any deformation of the thorax bone, deformity of the thorax or spine, and a permanently protruding tongue and teeth.

All these and other negative provisions are meant to ensure that only healthy animals are used for breeding, not those burdened by defects. In recent years certain cats have been bred purely for their appearance without the breeder paying sufficient regard to the production of healthy animals. Breeding for the sake of appearance alone runs counter to ethical principles since it is liable to produce animals who, throughout their life, suffer from a variety of ailments which they pass on to their offspring.

Some breeds are freely allowed any amount of white colour. For example, in the Rex breeds white medallions are among the permissible colours of the hair.

69 Heredity in Cats

A solid grounding in genetics is important if you hope to engage in successful breeding of cats. Knowledge of genetic laws is essential not only for the production of sound new varieties and breeds but for everyday breeding procedure.

Gregor Johann Mendel (1822—84), an Austrian monk and botanist, was the founder of genetics; his scientific experiments established the principles that govern the inheritance of characteristics in plants and animals.

A gene, the fundamental genetic unit, is a segment of a chromosome in which individual traits are çontained in code. A group of genes of the individual is known as genotype. The numbers of chromosomes in each organism is stable: a cat has 38 chromosomes in each cell. Two of these are sexual (labelled X or Y) and determine the sex of the individual: female cells carry identical chromosomes (XX), males different ones (XY).

Genes exist mostly in pairs of functional forms known as alleles. An allele is either dominant (it is expressed as an italic capital letter) and is always evident: for example *L* signifies short hair; or it is recessive (expressed as an italic lower case letter) and is manifested in the absence of a dominant allele

◁ The striped Siamese was the outcome of an experiment by a Swedish geneticist to test the propensity of the pattern effect together with that of the Siamese colouring. This cat achieved considerable popularity.

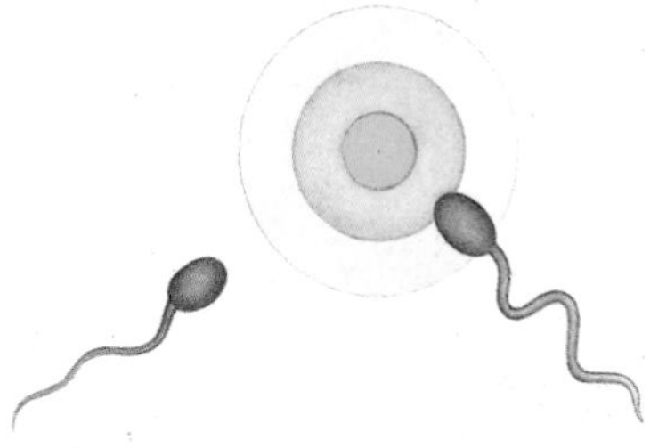

A sperm (male sex cell), consisting of a head, collum and flagellum, fertilizes a mature egg.

of the same gene (e.g. *l*= long hair). In body cells alleles exist in pairs (in two chromosomes). If both are identical (whether dominant — *LL*, or recessive — *ll*), they are called homozygous. A combination of a dominant allele with a recessive one (*Ll*) is called heterozygous. An organism's characteristics — its size, shape, hair and eye colour — which represent the outward manifestation of its genotype, are known as the phenotype. Certain traits are determined by combinations of genes.Those combinations consisting of major genes are known as modifiers, and those involving genes whose individual effect is small are called polygenes.

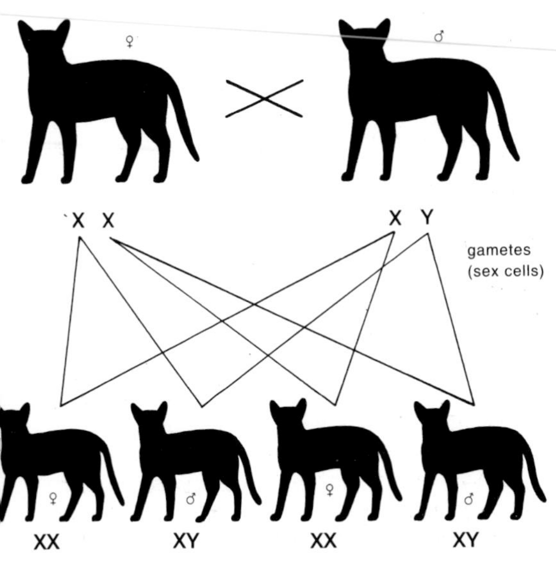

Foetal cells contain only half the normal number of chromosomes (19). The sexual chromosome of male cells is always X, while half of the sperms contain X and half Y. When the egg (X) merges with sperm X, the result is a female (XX); after merger with sperm Y the result is a male (XY). The ratio of male and female foetuses is 1:1.

70 The Known Genes of Cats

The genes listed below are those that are known to determine some of the physical characteristics of cats. There are others whose effect is not known in detail and which in most cases do not even have a special name.

- *A:* agouti (the colour of the coat between the stripes of tabby). This gene causes an uneven pigmentation of the hair (ticking); the colouring is also called zonal or 'wild'
- *a:* non-agouti; determines a uniform colouring of the hair without a design and without ticking — i.e. self colouring, solid colouring
- *B:* black (undiluted) colour
- *b:* chocolate dilution
- b^1 (b^l): light chocolate dilution (cinnamon)
- *C:* full colouring (without mask)
- c^b: Burmese colouring
- c^s: Siamese colouring (blue iridescent)
- *c:* total albinism
- *D:* undilued colour
- *d:* blue dilution — black is diluted to blue, red to cream; with gene *b* it produces lilac colour, with gene b^i fawn colour
- *Fd:* folded ears

◁ Persian Blue — one of the best known Persian varieties.

fd: normal upright ears
Hr: normal hairy body
hr: hairless body
I: inhibitor — pigmentation in the lower section of the hair is suppressed, only the tips of the hair are coloured (tipping)
i: pigmentation of the hair throughout
L: short hair
l: long hair
M: tailless or short-tail Manx cats
m: normal length tail
O: red colouring (orange), tied to chromosome X
o: black colouring
Pd: polydactyly or extra toes (usually on front paws)
pd: normal number of toes
R, Re, Rg, Ro: normal structure of the coat
r: curled coat, awn hairs are missing (Cornish Rex)
re: wavy and short hair (Devon Rex)
rg: wavy and short hair (German Rex)
ro: wavy and short hair (Oregon Rex)
S: white patches
s: colouring without patches
$T\ T^{+}$: tiger pattern
T^{a}: Abyssinian tabby
t^{b}: marble tabby colouring
W: white hair
w: any colour of hair other than white
Wh: excessively curly and wiry coat
wh: normal hair structure

A blue colouring is one of the longest known colour mutations in cats. The records go back to 1558, when the breeders were probably Carthusian monks. The blue dilution is very common in present-day breeds.

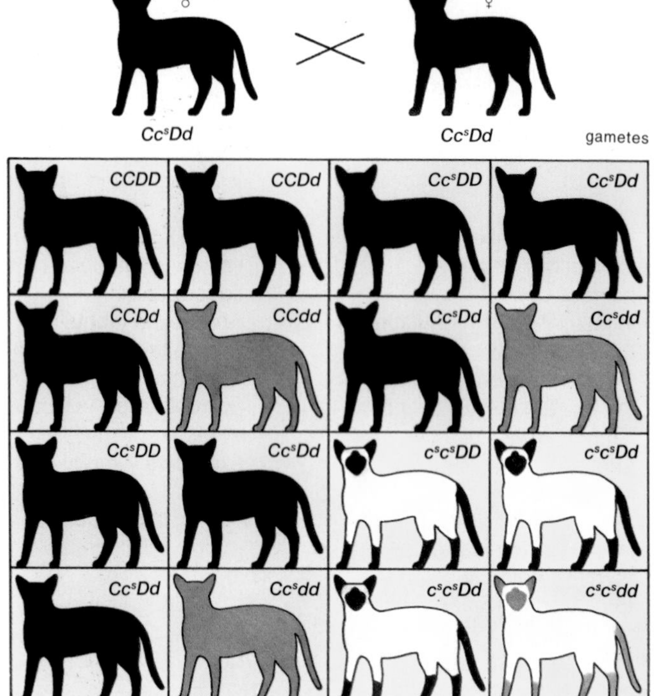

4

71 Using Genetic Laws in Cat Breeding

The Mendel-Morgan laws give the breeder a good basis for breeding work and explain individual rules in specific situations which occur regularly in the process of breeding.

The law on the uniformity of the generation F_1 and the identity of reciprocal crossing says that when mating other homozygous individuals of the parent generation (P), the first filial generation (F_1) is uniform. An example is the mating of the Siamese male (c^sc^s) with the Oriental female with homozygous traits for the full colouring (*CC*). All their offspring (generation F_1) will have identical, heterozygous traits Cc^s (see Fig. 1). The same result occurs if we mate an Oriental male (*CC*) with a Siamese female (c^sc^s), i.e. by a reciprocal combination.

The law on the purity of traits and the segregation of signs says that in the mating of individuals of the F_1 generation among themselves, a division occurs in the F_2 generation. Dominant and recessive alleles do not mix: they remain pure. Recessive alleles become 'visible' the moment they unite, and a homozygous individual results — in our case a Siamese female (c^sc^s) (see Fig. 2).

To prove that traits carry over into sex cells in a 'pure' form and retain independence, Mendel used the breeding method known as back-crossing, from

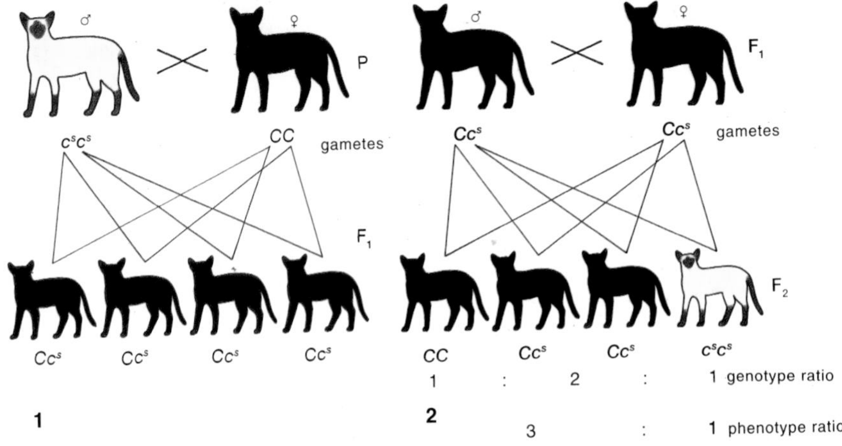

which a B_1 generation results. He mated a homozygous offspring of the F_1 generation with its homozygous parents. In our case, this would mean crossing a heterozygous Oriental individual (Cc^s) with its Siamese parent (c^sc^s). The result of this mating are the two parent forms in the generation B_1 — Oriental and Siamese kittens (see Fig. 3).

The law on the free combination of traits says that if the parents differ in two or more pairs of characteristics, these characteristics are inherited independently of each other. The alleles of the father and mother genes combine freely, but only on condition that each pair of characteristics is on a different chromosome and they are not in interaction. This law can be well demonstrated by the mating of two black Oriental cats which are heterozygous, first for colour dilution (they carry a trait of blue dilution, *d*) as well as for Siamese coloration (they carry one c^s trait each). The parents differ in two pairs of characteristics (Cc^sDd); this is an example of bifactorial heredity (see Fig. 4). The result is a permanent, unchangeable segregation ratio in the offspring (which, however, becomes fully evident only if there is a sufficient number of offspring): 9 black Oriental cats, 3 blue Oriental cats, 3 black Siamese cats and one blue Siamese cat.

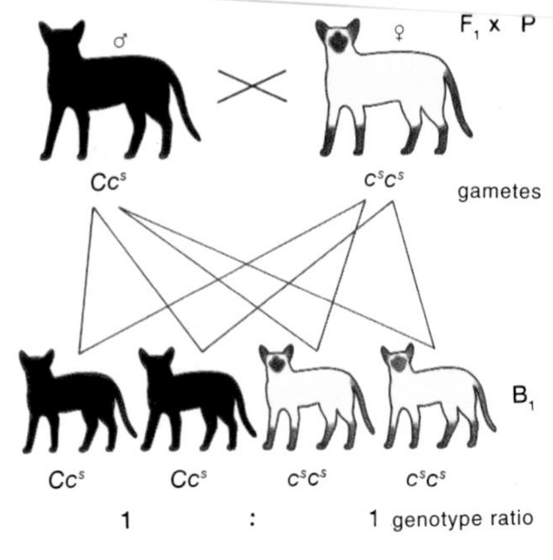

3

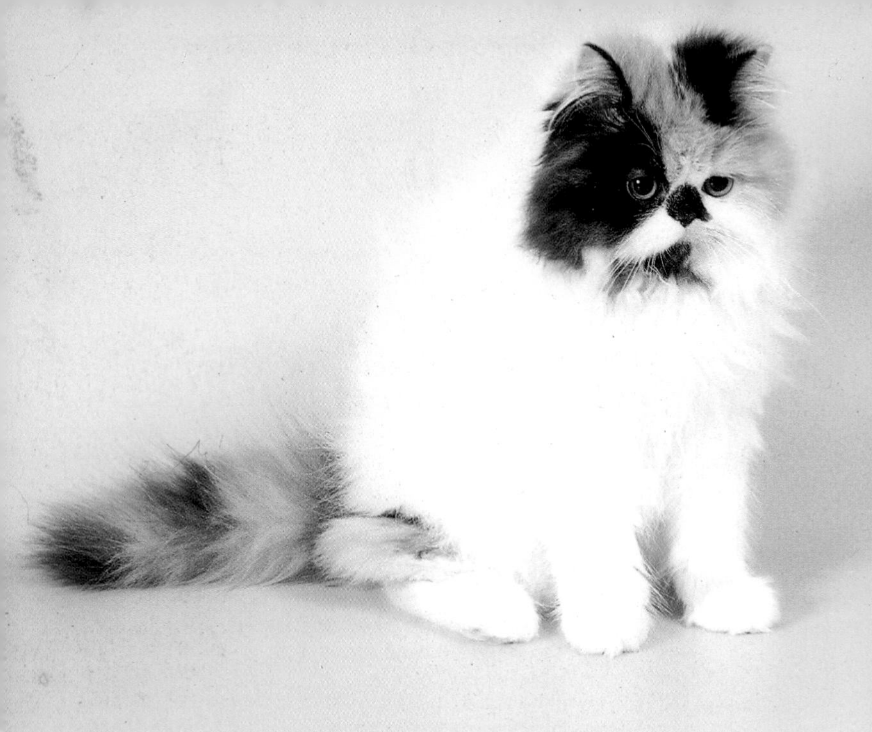

72 Breeding Methods

One of the most frequent breeding methods is where more or less closely related animals are deliberately mated; the object is to stabilize certain desirable features. The degree of relatedness is defined as close, near and remote. An extreme example of close relationship breeding is incest — mating of siblings or parents and their immediate offspring. Less related animals are used more often — half-siblings, cousins, grandparents, etc.

Relationship breeding increases homozygosity in breeding: genes are stabilized and a genotypical uniformity of the animals is created. The method can be used to reinforce certain desirable features, but at the same time it creates a greater chance that recessive genes will appear, bringing about negative features or even defects. These genes would not appear in breeding non-related individuals. From this point of view we can consider the breeding of relatives as a means of discovering these desirable and undesirable tendencies.

A number of systems have been developed showing how to make planned use of relationship breeding in suitable proportions. An example is so-called line breeding, in which a certain part of the genes from an exceptionally high-quality ancestor is passed on to the offspring; the amount of these genes is estimated theoretically in advance.

Van Tortoiseshell Persian in white: the colour is present only on the head and tail.

It is best to establish relationship breeding with a large number of animals simultaneously so that there can be regular crossing only within the system and 'foreign' animals are totally excluded. By establishing a broader breeding base, you can also eliminate too-close relationships, which could have undesirable repercussions.

Selection is another breeding method. The selection of breeding individuals is the basis of successful breeding and it must be done carefully and in well considered manner. The aim, which is easier to state than to achieve, is to select only individuals with desirable features that are unburdened by defects.

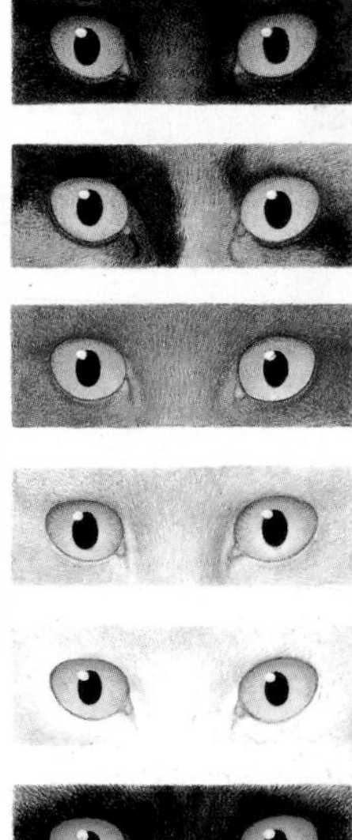

The colour of the iris is a significant mark in the breeds of cats. Here the breeder must resort primarily to selection, since the majority of shades are based on polygenes. In certain instances alone the colour of the eye is tied to the coat (blue eyes of cats with acromelanic colouring and in white cats).

H ♀	F	C	
			C
		D	A
	E	C	
		B	

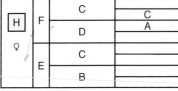

Specimen of a pedigree with line breeding.

In mating the male cat C passes on half the genes to his offspring. If his daughters are mated with him, the ratio of genes of male C is increased in the offspring. The proportion of foreign, less desirable propensities is reduced by the same ratio. If exclusively foreign, unrelated males are used for mating the offspring which resulted from this union, the share of the ratio of genes of male C is gradually reduced in subsequent offspring. Seven generations later its genes have been virtually excluded by the process know as suppresive crossing.

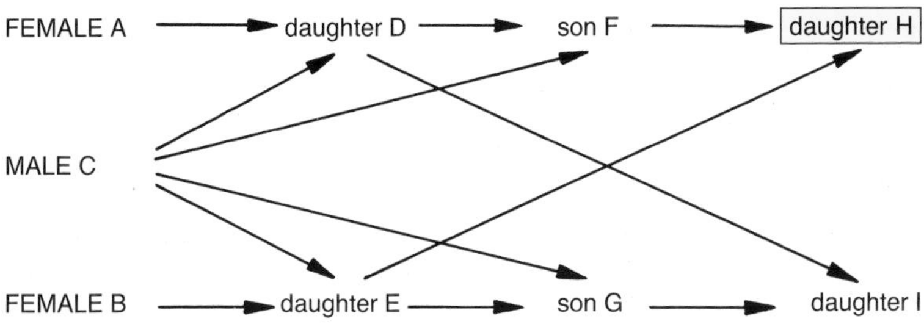

73 Diluted Coat Colours

One of the many gene mutations in cats are the so-called 'diluted' colours of the coat. Recessive genes produce a different concentration of pigment (colouring matter) in the fibres of the coat which to the eye looks like a different colour. The fundamental undiluted colours include black and red. The impact of diluting propensities on these colours gives rise to a vast selection of colours. Diluting genes occur among solid-colour (self-colour) cats as well as on cats with a pattern of coat colours. The occurrence and combination of diluting propensities for the colour of the coat is most important for breeders. Knowledge about the impact of these genes allows them to achieve a vast range of officially approved colour mutations. The FIFe today recognizes over 4,000 colour varieties and more are added every year.

The blue-green colour, known as blue, is created by the diluting gene *d* which dilutes the black colour. All blue cats are recessively homozygous (*dd*). Blue dilution has been known in cats for a very long time; today the great majority of breeds include this colour, and some of them consist only of blue (Russian Blue, Chartreux, Korat). The blue colour has different shades in individual breeds, from dark blue to a light blue with a touch of silver, caused (in the Russian blue) by light tips to the bristles. Breeders achieve the ideal shade by selecting animals for later breeding.

◁ Burmese Lilac. The colouring is determined by two diluting genes (gene *d* for blue and gene *b* for chocolate dilution).

If the *d* gene acts on the red colour, a delicate pastel beige colour is created. Brown or chocolate colouring is determined by a recessive propensity *b*, which dilutes the black colour. Brown colouring, too, exists in many shades. The most desirable is a warm pastel colour, which is also achieved by selection. Chocolate dilution is used less frequently. The chocolate colour was originally recognized among Siamese cats since it existed already in their original habitat. Chocolate dilution is not permitted among many breeds because it did not exist among them originally and would be an artificial crossing. These include the Maine Coon, the Norwegian Forest and European cats. If a diluting gene *b* emerges in a red cat it does not influence its colour.

The simultaneous impact of genes *d* and *b* creates a delicate pastel mauve. Mauve cats are, thus, dual recessive homozygotes (*dd bb*). The b^l or b^1 (light brown) gene produce a light brown colour called cinnamon or sorrel. This colouring is termed 'non-sex-linked red' since it is not produced by the same propensity which creates the classic red. It occurs most frequently in Abyssinian and Somali cats and, more recently, in Orientals. The interaction with a propensity for blue (*dd* b^lb^l) creates the delicate pastel colouring known as fawn.

A table of so-called classic colours (according to J. Kilborn) was originally drawn up for Siamese and Oriental cats, but it applies equally to other breeds where these colours exist. It reveals what types of offspring and in what ratio we may expect from various matings.

1 Seal Point/black with no diluting propensities – 2 Seal Point/black with propensity for blue colour – 3 Seal Point/black with propensity for brown colour – 4 Seal Point/with propensity for blue and brown colour – 5 Blue Point/with no further diluting propensities – 6 Blue Point/blue with propensity for brown colour – 7 Chocolate Point/brown with no further diluting propensities – 8 Chocolate Point/brown with propensity for blue colour – 9 Lilac Point/lilac

Example: A black female with propensity for brown colour (3) mated with a blue male with propensity for brown colour (6) will have half her kittens black with both diluting factors (4), a quarter of the kittens will be black with the blue factor (2) and a quarter will be brown with the blue factor (8). If both parents also carry a propensity for Siamese colouring, a quarter of the kittens will be of adequate Siamese colour (see Hint 71).

	1	2		3		4				5	6		7	8		9
1	1	1	2	1	3	1	2	3	4	2	2	4	3	3	4	4
2		1	2	1	3	1	2	3	4	2	2	4	3	3	4	4
		2	5	2	4	2	5	4	6	5	5	6	4	4	6	6
3				1	3	1	2	3	4	2	2	4	3	3	4	4
				3	7	3	4	7	8	4	4	8	7	7	8	8
4						1	2	3	4	2	2	4	3	3	4	4
						2	5	4	6	5	5	6	4	4	6	6
						3	4	7	8	4	4	8	7	7	8	8
						4	6	8	9	6	6	9	8	8	9	9
5										5	5	6	4	4	6	6
6											5	6	4	4	6	6
											6	9	8	8	9	9
7													7	7	8	8
8														7	8	8
														8	9	9
9																9

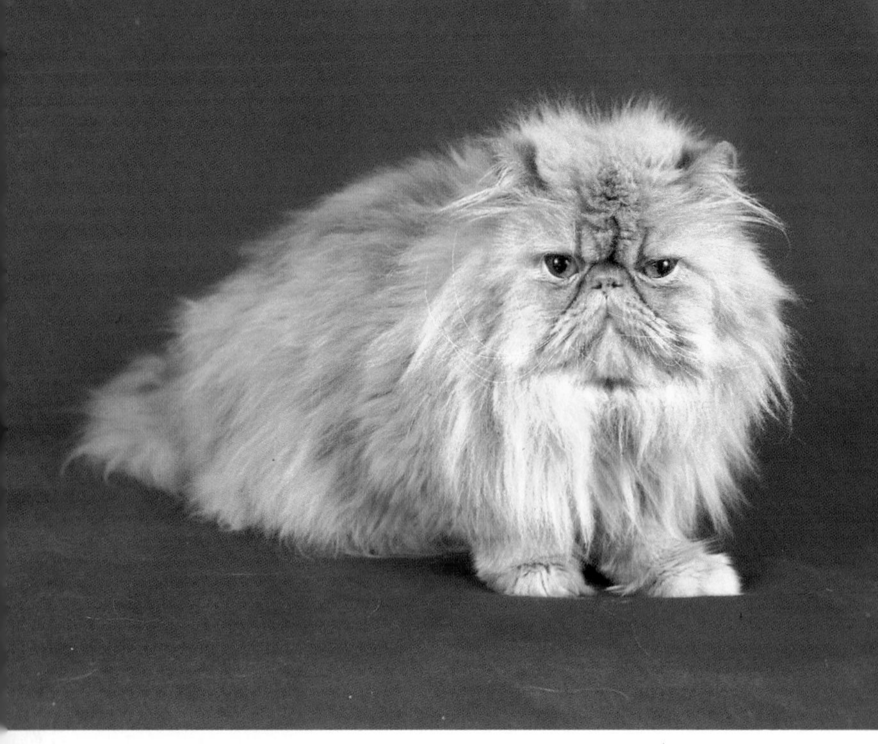

74 Red and Tortoiseshell Colouring

The red colouring is produced by the gene *O* (orange), situated in the sex chromosome X. It is thus inherited on the basis of the sex of the individual and is termed 'sex-linked red'.

The red colouring of the female cat is determined by one presence of the gene *O* on both X chromosomes. If the gene *O* is present only in one chromosome X, tortoiseshell colouring arises, characterized by irregular red and black spots. If, in addition, diluting inclinations are present, a blue tortoiseshell, chocolate tortoiseshell or mauve tortoiseshell colouring may result.

Under normal circumstances males have only one chromosome X in the cells, so the red colouring arises by the presence of one gene *O* on this chromosome. Tortoiseshell males are extremely rare and their colouring shows an anomaly in the number of sex-linked chromosomes — they have one additional chromosome X (XXY). These individuals are called 'intersex' and are generally infertile. In appearance they often resemble a female cat: they are smaller and have an atypically small head. Over the past few years there have been extremely rare fertile tortoiseshell colour male cats. A number of theories have been put forward to account for them, including one that explains it as a rare case of extra-chromosome heredity.

◁ Red Persian: this colour is determined by gender.

The colour red has many shades. The most desirable is a deep red achieved by selective breeding. The variability of the red colour is attributed to the group of modifier genes and is called 'rufism'. Another quality of the red colour, which causes difficulties to breeders, is that it is virtually impossible to bread a totally one-colour red animal. Each of them has a more or less clear pattern in the form of stripes on the legs, tail and so forth. This is due to the genetic essence of the red colour and it is very difficult to influence it except by careful selection.

Tables of mating of animals with propensity for red colouring. In the presence of diluting propensities a corresponding dilution of these basic colours takes place.

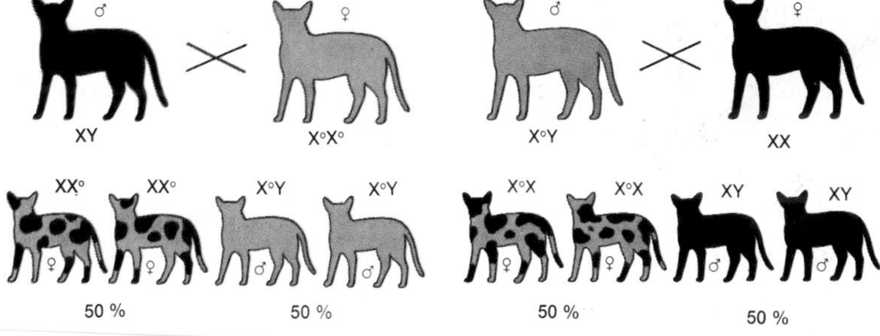

a — Mating a black male and a red queen.

b — Mating a red male and a black queen.

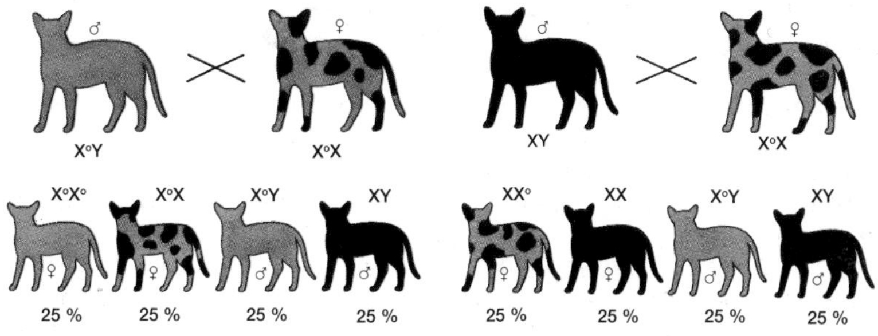

c — Mating a red male and a tortoiseshell queen.

d — Mating a black male and a tortoiseshell queen.

75 Coat Patterns

There are four types of coat colour pattern on cats. The most common is mackerel tabby, determined by the dominating gene *T* in interaction with gene *A* for agouti (see Hint 70). The term mackerel tabby refers to colour stripes going from the line of the spine vertically down the sides of the body, as in a tiger. In the original, so-called wild (undiluted) form the stripes are black and the basic colour of the coat is sandy yellow. The hair has clear ticking (see Hint 76).

•

In the Abyssinian tabby, gene *T* is suppressed by gene T^a. This type of colouring is characterized by the presence of ticking and a minimum of stripes on the legs and the tail; what is visible is just the small 'eel' stripe on the side and a black tip to the tail. This is found in Abyssinian and Somali cats where selection has excluded the presence of all stripes on the legs and tail.

The blotched tabby and the classic tabby are due to the recessive gene t^b. The marking consists of three side stripes and an oval pattern on the sides of the torso. The tabby pattern varies somewhat in different cats, but a sym-

◁ British Silvery Black Tiger: apart from its propensity for pattern, it is also affected by a propensity for silvery colouring.

British Red Marbled cat – a very attractive breed.

metrical pattern on both sides of the body is required. The face, legs and tail have clear stripes. Since the allele t^b is recessive it appears only in the homozygous state *(t^bt^b).* This pattern is less common than the tabby but occurs in many breeds.

The last type of pattern consists of blots, as in the spotted tabby. Expert opinions differ about its genetic origin. Some experts maintain that it is a heterozygous state of the allele *A* and *T* (either *Aa TT,* or *Aa* Tt^b); others argue that it is a tabby or tiger-type pattern influenced by modifier genes. Spotted breeds are required to have regular and contrasting spots. Only a slight stripe on the side is tolerated; the face, legs and tail have stripes. Spots exist in many breeds; in some, such as the Ocicat and the Egyptian Mau, it is the only colouring.

All types of patterns can occur in different breeds in various dilutions as well as in combination with other propensities (silver shade, white spots, acromelanotic colouring, etc.). Irrespective of breed, cats with patterns are among the most popular animals.

Basic pattern types: (1) marbling – blotched tabby, (2) tiger – mackerel tabby, (3) spotting – spotted tabby, (4) Abyssinian – Abyssinian tabby.

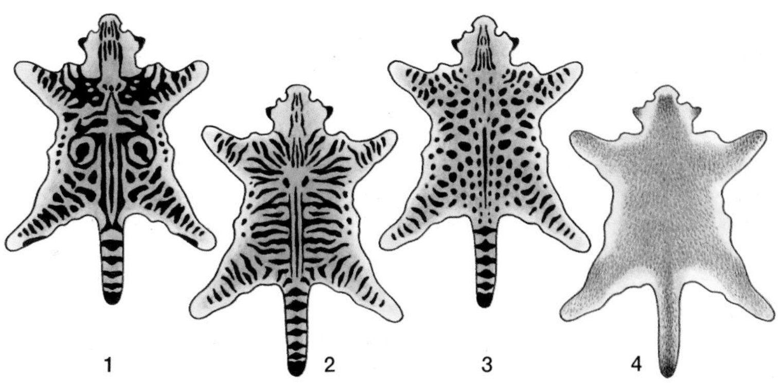

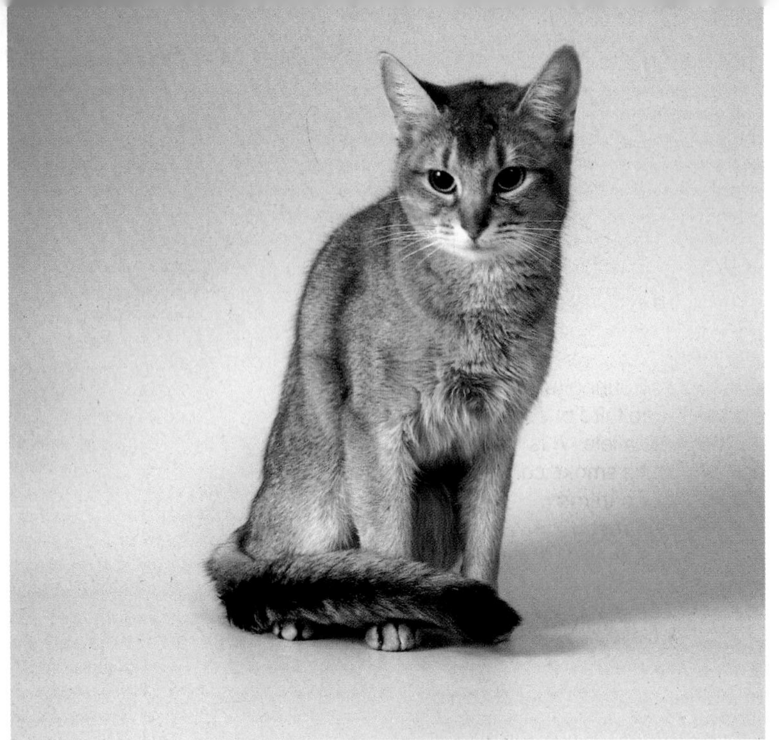

76 Ticking and Tipping

The original colouring of domestic cats as well as of their wild ancestors was based on the presence of the gene *A* for agouti or wild colouring. The gene *A* causes the so-called zonal colouring of the hair known as 'ticking', in which light and dark zones alternate on each hair shaft. With the simultaneous presence of some of the propensities for the pattern (see Hint 75), the pattern is determined by gene *A*. On the hair of cats with ticking we distinguish between the ticking colour, which in undiluted form turns black, and the basic colour of the hair, which is sand yellow. Depending on the presence of diluting propensities, the both colours can change. For example, a blue diluting gene produces a steel blue colouring of the ticking as well as a light cream shade of the basic colour. One of the oldest mutations in cats is that of the dominant gene *A* on the recessive gene *a,* which in the homozygote state (*aa*) determines the solid or self colour of the coat.

Tipping affects only the tips of the hairs; the rest of the hair is silvery white. The silvery white colouring is determined by gene *I* (inhibitor), which prevents the creation of pigment in part of the hair. The intensity of the effect of gene *I* is influenced by polygenes. In the case of cats with a patterned coat, gene *I* produces impressive silver tabby varieties. Another colour produced

◁ The Ruddy Abyssinian cat represents a breed in which ticking — zonal colouring of the hair — is evident.

An Exotic cat displaying rare shaded cameo colouring.

gene *I* is chinchilla (shell), in which only one-eighth of the hair is coloured; the rest is silvery white. When the colouring is shaded, one quarter to one third of the hair is coloured. The allele *I* is least pronounced in the smoke colour, where one half to two thirds of each hair is coloured; the rest is silver. The colour of the tips may be influenced also by diluting, so there is a broad range of silvery shaded cats.

If gene *I* acts together with gene *O* to create red, the colouring known as 'cameo' occurs. The colour intensity may vary: the silver is most evident in cameo shell, less so in cameo shaded, and least of all in the red smoke variety. In connection with gene *O* there are, naturally, tortoiseshell cats also in all the silvery forms mentioned above. A similar black tip colouring of the hair exists also among golden cats; the remaining segment of the hair is of a warm cream colour, which indicates that the golden variety has a different genetic foundation from that of the silver variety. The cream colour is evidently determined by polygenes, influencing the intensity of the impact of gene *I* on silvery cats. This proves that golden animals occur in litters of silvery cats which are not homozygous for the gene *I*.

Tipping; (a) shell (chinchilla) colouring, (b) shaded colouring, (c) silver tabby colouring on the bristle and down hair, (d) smoke colouring, (e) golden colouring.

Ticking: (a) on the bristles; (b) on the down hair.

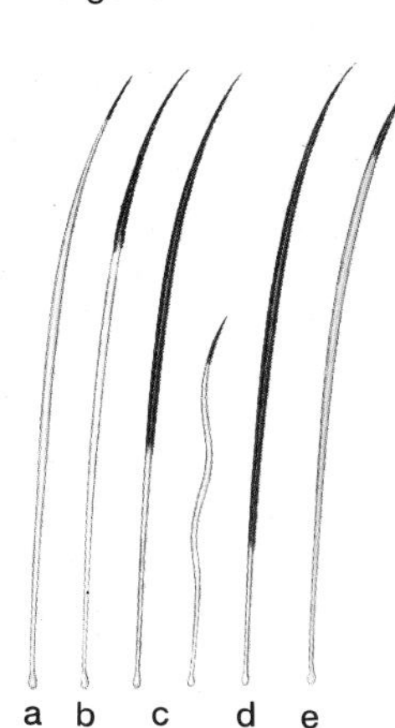

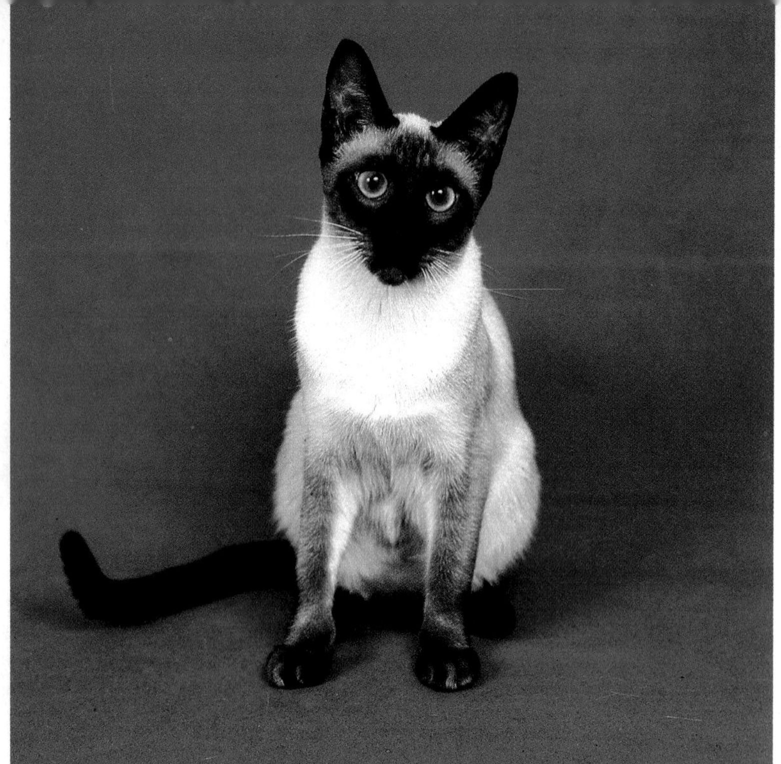

77 Albinism and Partial Albinism

Albinism and partial albinism are caused by the genes of the so-called albinotic series. Each of these genes limits to a varying degree the creation of pigment in the coat, skin and the iris of the eye. All these genes are recessive towards the full colouring of the coat.

The best known and most frequent gene in this group is c^s for Siamese colouring, acromelanism. As a result of its influence, the body of the cat is very light to white, only the points (extremities) of the body being coloured. The eyes of Siamese cats are always blue. However, gene c^s makes the colour of the points lighter; thus the black (seal point) Siamese has genetically dark brown points. The colour of cat pointing with acromelanism depends, however, on the presence of diluting genes; these cats occur in all dilutions as well as in the red colour, even with a pattern.

Another gene of the albino series is c^b for Burmese colouring. In Burmese cats the colour contrast between the body and the points is far less than in Siamese cats. Gene c^b also influences the point colour: the brown Burmese is in fact genetically black. It also influences the colour of the iris: the eyes of Burmese cats are jade or yellow.

The interaction of these two similar genes is interesting. If we cross a Siamese with

◁ This Siamese cat is a semi-albino of oriental origin.

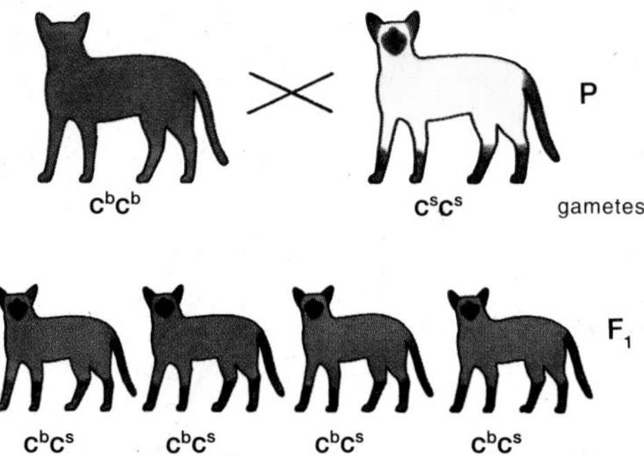

Crossing a Burmese and a Siamese produces a Tonkinese, which has a smaller contrast between the colour of its body and the colour of the pattern than the Siamese. Tonkinese have turquoise eyes and their body structure is midway between the two breeds.

a Burmese, we obtain cats with a body frame and coat colour as well as eye colour exactly between these two breeds. They are called Tonkinese, and when a pair are mated they produce kittens whose colouring varies between Tonkinese, Siamese and Burmese. The interrelation of alleles c^s and c^b is an example of an intermediate type of heredity in which both genes have an equal impact.

The last genes of the albinotic series are genes c^a and c. Gene c^a causes the absence of pigment in the coat, but a certain amount of pigment is preserved in the iris, which is blue. In the case of total albinism caused by gene c, pigment is lacking also in the iris, which is pink. Albinotic cats must be distinguished from white cats of a different genetic foundation (see Hint 78). They are bred only to a limited extent in the Siamese type and they are recognized only by certain American clubs.

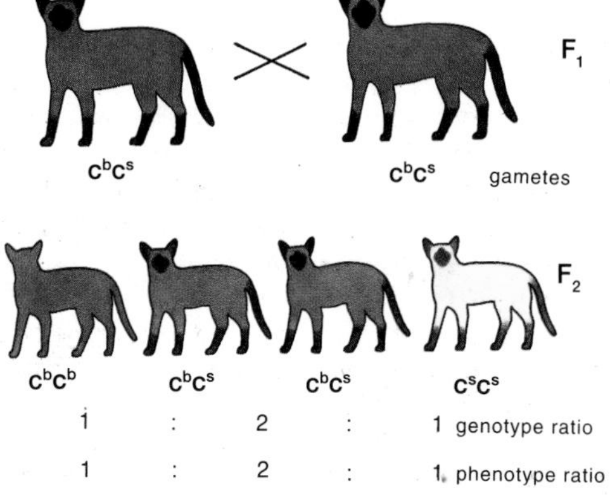

When crossing two Tonkinese the result is 50 per cent Tonkinese kittens, 25 per cent Burmese kittens and 25 per cent Siamese kittens.

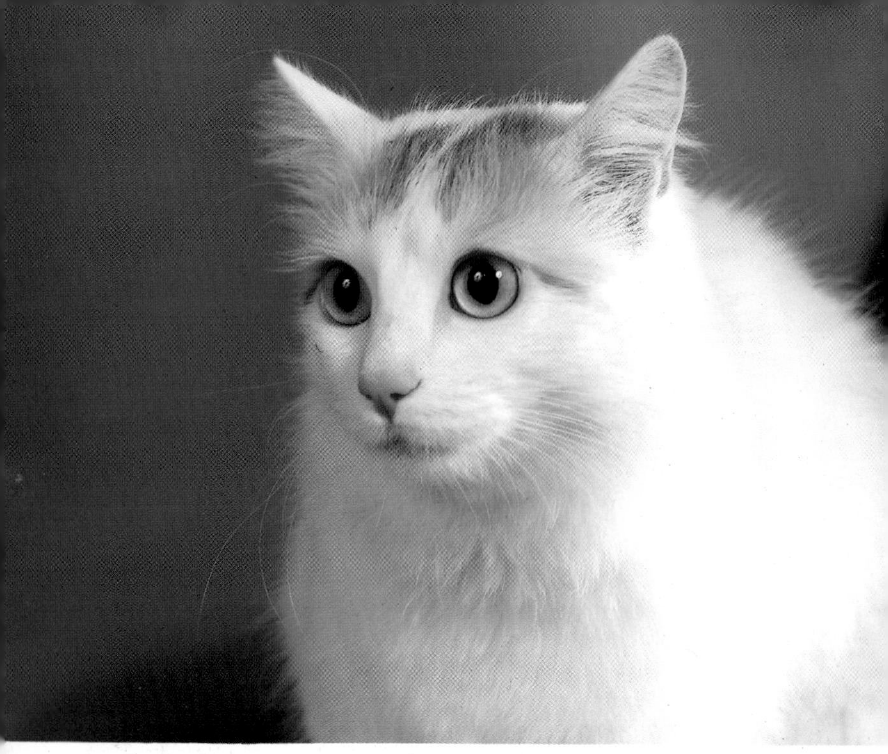

78 White Colouring and White Spots

White coloured cats occur in the majority of breeds as well as in domestic cats. Their eyes are orange, yellow or blue, or each eye has a different colour (one blue, the other orange); this latter colouring is called 'odd-eyed'.

The white colour in the coat is determined by trait *W* (white), which suppresses the effect of all other propensities on colour. In theory, a white cat can carry propensities for any other colouring, which may well appear only in its offspring. It can be either heterozygote (*Ww*) and, when mated with a male of a colour other than white, 50 per cent of the kittens will be white; the colour of the other 50 per cent will depend on what propensities the white female and her partner have, or on the homozygosity: all offspring of a homozygously inclined female are white irrespective of her partner's colour.

White kittens are often born with a coloured patch on the head which reveals the kitten's colour propensities. Spots are tolerated on the young, but they disappear in adulthood. White cats (especially blue-eyed) are known for the fact that they are more frequently deaf than cats of a different colour. This is an innate deafness caused by degeneration of the cochlea of the inner ear.

White spots on cats are determined by the dominant gene *S* for patching, which is highly variable in its manifestations. Its action causes anything from small spots in the

◁ The Turkish Van gave its name to a type of colouring found in two-coloured cats.

coat to totally white with only remnants of other colours. We distinguish between three degrees of white patches: bi-colour, where one third to half the coat is white; harlequin, where white covers two thirds to three quarters of the coat; and van-type, in which colour is confined to parts of the head, tail and legs.

•

Generally it can be said that the heterozygous state of the allele (*Ss*) is responsible for a smaller proportion of the white colour, and the homozygous state (*SS*) for a larger proportion. In practice, allele *S* does not always behave entirely according to this rule and thus causes breeders considerable difficulties. For example, a heterozygously inclined animal may have a larger proportion of white than a homozygote. The size of patches is clearly also determined by other genetic influences (polygenes) and probably by non-genetic influences during embryonic development. However, this does not make cats with white patches any less attractive, and they are bred in large numbers.

Turkish Angoras are one of the breeds in which the two eyes are of different colour (one is amber, the other blue).

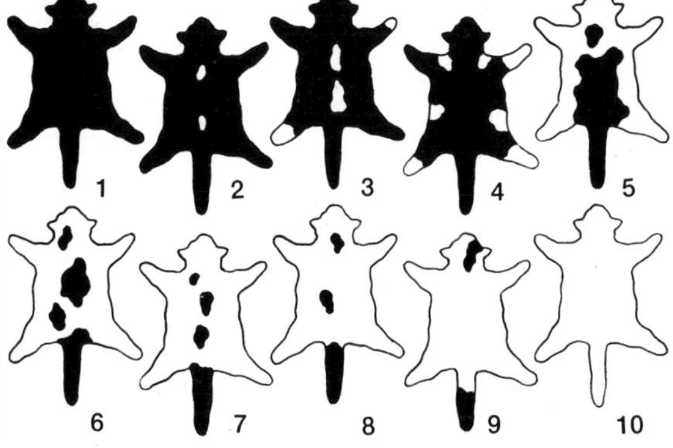

The heterozygous state of allele *S* causes, on average, a colouring of degree 4–6, the homozygous state a colouring of degree 5–8, although there are many exceptions.

79 Hair Length and Structure

The wild ancestors of the domestic cat had short hair, though it is not certain whether in some areas long-haired cats did not exist even before domestication. The mutation of gene *L* for short hair to gene *l* which determines long hair is among the oldest known mutations among cats. The impact of this recessive gene in the homozygous state (*ll*) makes the hair long; its length varies between 12 and 13cm (4 $^{3}/_{4}$ and 5in), depending on the breed and individual breeding lines. Although gene *l* is present in many breeds (Persian, Maine Coon, Norwegian Forest, Turkish Angora, Turkish Van, Ragdoll, Somali, Javanese), these breeds differ in the length and structure of the hair, which is influenced by many more polygenes. Some breeds are required to have certain other qualities — fine hair, hard bristles, etc. Consistent selection stabilizes these marks caused by polygenes.

Mutation in the structure of the hair is represented by a group of cats with curly hair. The Rex breed was 'discovered' in several places (Britain, Germany, the United States) in the mid-20th century. Individual types of Rex differ in their genetic essence as well as in the appearance of their coat and body. We know three recessive alleles causing the Rex-type: *r* (Cornish Rex), *rg* (German Rex), *re* (Devon Rex) and *ro* (Oregon Rex). Crossing reveals that the Cornish Rex and German Rex types were

◁ The coat of the Cornish Rex is curly and lacks bristles.

identical, whereas the other Rex types were created by mutations in various loci (the places on a chromosome where specific genes are located). In certain types of the Rex breed we see changed bristles — from very short, curly and with a plush appearance (Devon Rex) to strongly curled hair (Cornish Rex), resembling an astrakhan fur.

A typical head shape of the Devon Rex. A Rex with an acromelanic colouring is called a Si-Rex.

The Cornish and German Rex, moreover, lack bristles. The inclination to a curly coat is inherited independently of any colour, so there are Rex breeds of every possible colour including Siamese-pattern types, unofficially known as Si-Rex.

The coat of the American wirehair cat differs from that of all Rex breeds. It is determined by the dominant allele *Wh*. The coat feels rough and wirelike. All types of hair (flue, bristles, as well as covering hair) are strongly and irregularly curled.

Cats of Canadian origin, known as Sphinx, are hairless. Their body is covered by negligible fine hair; traces of the coat are found at the tip of the tail, on the muzzle, on the lower parts of the legs, and on the scrotum. Hairlessness is caused by the recessive allele *hr*.

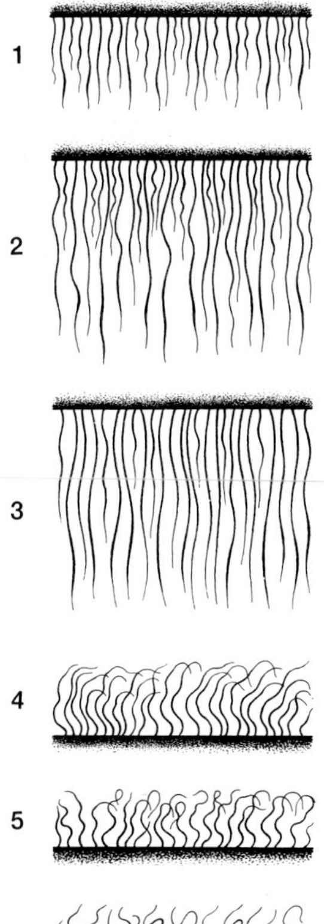

Types of hair: 1 European cat, 2 Persian longhair with well developed undercoat, 3 Turkish Angora with minimal undercoat, 4 Cornish Rex, 5 Devon Rex, 6 American wirehair, 7 Sphinx.

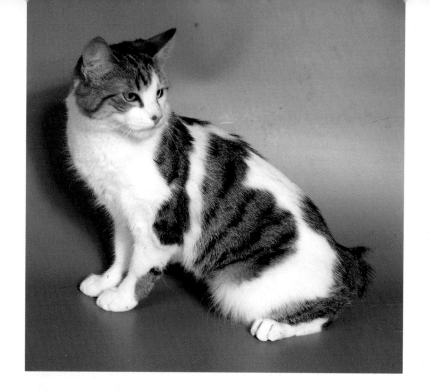

80 Genes and Body Shapes

The structure of the body of individual breeds of cats differs mostly in regard to size and, above all, to the shape of the head. Breeds strongly differing in shape or those lacking a part of the body are in a minority. One of the few breeds marked by such a deviation is the Manx, a tailless cat from the Isle of Man. Taillessness is caused by the dominant gene *M*. Manx cats can be bred only as heterozygotes; the homozygous state of allele *M* (*MM*) is lethal and kittens die while still in the embryonic stage.

Ideally, rumpy Manxes have a little hollow in place of their tail. In addition, there are genetically identical (i.e. heterozygous) Manxes known as stumpies, with a tail stump of varying length. Both types are used for breeding. Manx cats with a normal tail (longies) do not carry

The Manx can be bred in all existing colours.

◁ In the stumpy Manx the tail stump has been preserved.

Table of mating of two Manxes: 25 per cent of the embryo die, 50 per cent of the kittens are Manxes and 25 per cent of the kittens have a normal tail.

♂ × ♀ P

Mm Mm gametes

MM Mm Mm mm

† F_1

25 % 50 % 25 %

allele *M*, but they are used for breeding because they have other characteristics of breed (shape of the head, texture of the coat) which would be lost if allele *M* types were crossed with other breeds. At times, evidently because of a shortage of animals, British or European cats are also used to breed the Manx variety.

The Japanese Bobtail is another breed with a different shape of the tail. Its tail is shorter and kinked; when stretched out it measures 12cm (4 $^{3}/_{4}$in) at the most. The gene determining this deviation of shape has not yet been thoroughly examined but it appears to be recessive and has been stabilized by long-term selective breeding (Bobtails have been bred in Japan for some 1000 years). Research so far does not show that the gene has deformating effects on the other parts of the skeleton or is harmful in any other way.

Ears that are normally folded forward and lie almost flat on the head are the most striking characteristic of the Scottish Fold, a breed whose progenitor was discovered in Scotland in 1961. The folding of the ears is determined by the dominant allele *Fd* and is due to the deformation of the ear cartilage. The symptoms first appear in kittens in their fourth week. The fold may be single or double. Fold-ear cats may be heterozygous or homozygous; in the *FdFd* configuration the gene does not have a lethal effect. In certain, mainly homozygous Folds, various bone and joint deformations in limbs and tail have been recorded. That is why the Scottish Fold is not recognized by all breeders' federations. In Britain and other European countries it is one of the non-recognized breeds, whereas in America it is popular and widespread.

The folding of the ear flap gives the Scottish Fold a melancholy expression.

81 Hereditary Defects

One of the best-known hereditary defects of cats is an above-normal number of toes (polydactyly), caused by the dominant gene *Pd.* This defect exists mainly on the front paws, where there may be six or seven toes instead of the normal five. In view of the dominant nature of the gene it is fairly easy to eliminate this defect in breeding. Similarly, the defect of a less than normal number of toes (oligodactyly) is also hereditary. It is called split-foot and is caused by the dominant gene *Sp.*

It is far more difficult to remove from a breed defects of a recessive character, such as squint eyes, anomalies in the jaws and teeth (overbite or abnormal positioning of the teeth), or a deformed tail. Whenever these defects occur, a strict program of selection is essential and the descendants of the siblings of animals with any such defects must be carefully observed because they can transfer the defects in a concealed manner. Naturally mating with an animal from which such a defect originated must not be repeated.

•

A squint is most common in Siamese cats, but it also occurs in other breeds. In the case of squint-eyed Siamese it has been found that cats suffering from this defect have an abnormal sight nerve which passes erroneous perceptions from the eye to

◁ Burmese Red. The colour of the body is slightly lightened by a gene for the Burmese colouring belonging to the so-called albinotic series of genes.

the vision centre, which would normally give a cat double vision. The squint, however, compensates for this defect, so that the animal may see normally. We still lack final information about the heredity of this defect, but it cannot be ruled out that two or more genes are responsible for its origin.

A squint means disqualification for a cat at a show and reduces its breeding value.

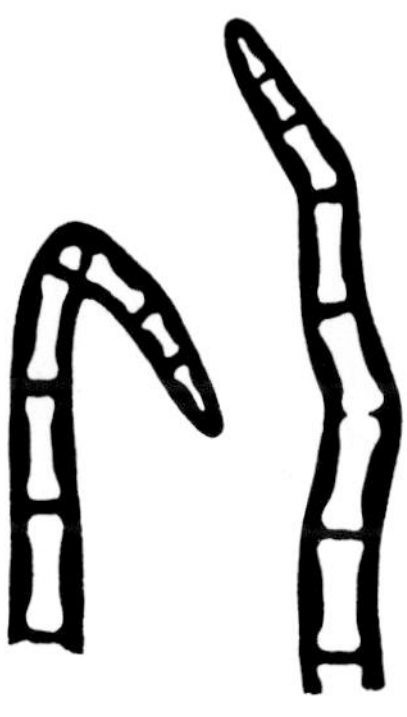

The notches are due to a deformation of the tail vertebrae. When this deformation appears also in the lumbar or chest bones, the nerves emanating from the spinal cord are compressed; the animal is in pain and becomes paralyzed.

Deformations of the tail in the form of a curve, bend or kink were in the past observed mostly in Siamese cats. Nowadays they occur occasionally in all breeds. Experimental crossing of Siamese cats in the past suggests the breed has a recessive inclination towards this defect. There has so far been no experimental crossing of other breeds.

Hydrocephalus (gene *hy*), abnormally high fluid pressure in the brain; ataxia, or defective coordination of movements (gene *At*); and porphyria, a hereditary defect of the metabolism, are other hereditary conditions in cats.

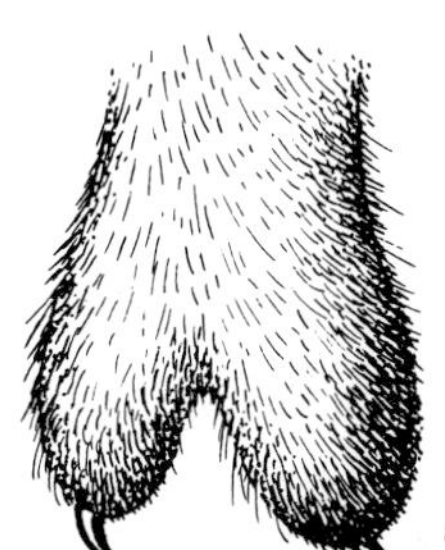

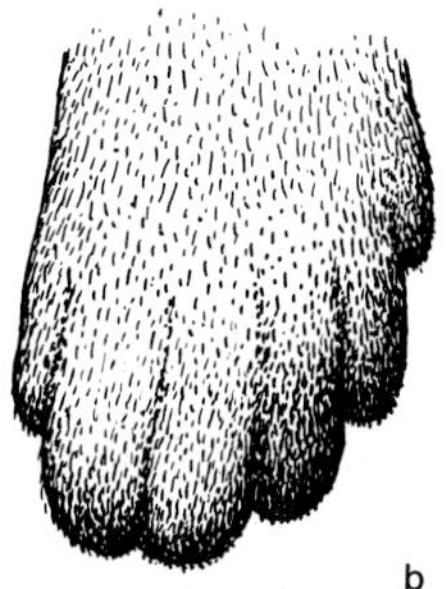

(a) oligodactyly,
(b) polydactyly

82 Cat Breeds

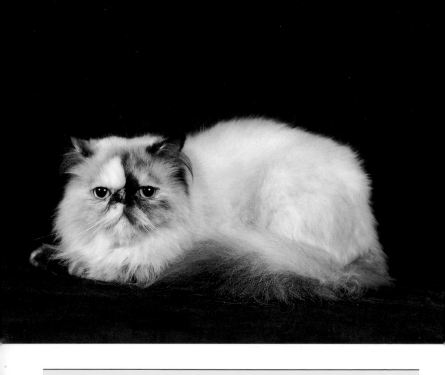

The number of breeds recognized by different international breeders' federations varies. Today the FIFe (Fédération Internationale Féline) recognizes 29 breeds; others, for example the various American federations and associations, recognize even more breeds. FIFe divides the breeds into four categories according to the structure of the body and the length of the hair:

1. Persian and Exotic cats,
2. Semi-longhair cats,
3. Shorthair and Somali cats,
4. Siamese and Oriental cats.

Suggestions have been made with a view to amending this divi-

Semi-longhair Maine Coon: blue marbling with white.

◁ Persian with tortoiseshell marking (tortie point).

Siamese with blue points.

sion, but for the moment no other classification has been approved. In each breed there are several colour varieties. Given the immense variations in cat colours, the number of these varieties is huge: at present more than 4,000.

•

Domestic cats, that is to say those which belong to no breed, are classified at shows in the category of Domestic cats. Cats of a breed not recognized by the FIFe are judged separately, provided such a breed has at least a provisional standard.

Each breed and colour variety has an abbreviated mark, a code made up of letters and numbers. (See page 186.)

Blue Exotic cat.

Russian Blue.

83 Longhair and Exotic Breeds

Although this group consists of only two breeds — Persian and Exotic cats — it is a very big group. Persian cats remain the most frequently bred. It is an artificially created breed: to produce it longhair cats of quite different origins (from Turkey, Iran, Armenia) were used. Selection has created a cat with a robust frame on strong legs and with fine silky hair. The most characteristic feature of Persians is their typical head with a round face and a round understructure where the nose and front bones meet, i.e. a 'stop'. The eyes are expressive and round.

•

Persians have been bred for more than 100 years and have 278 colour varieties. They are bred in all diluted and non-diluted colours, in all types of patterns, with acromelanic points and tipping. Certain colour varieties are most common, others are rare; some exist only in theory. Recognition of these theoretically derived colours gives breeders the possibility of register-

◁ Exotic Cream Marble.

ing such animals and expanding the breed. The creation of such new colours is helped by theoretical findings about their heredity and its application in cat breeding.

●

Originally Persians were bred in blue, black, red, white, black marble and silvery marble colours. The other colours arose gradually from a variety of combinations and crossing with cats of other breeds.

●

Persians are known for their quiet poise and are usually easy to get on with. However, their disposition varies from animal to animal. Persians reach adulthood fairly late, the female's first heat occurring at the age of about one year, and taking place twice a year thereafter.

●

The second breed in this group are the Exotic cats which emerged in America. They are shorthair varieties of the Persians. They have identical body proportions, and differ only in the length of hair. Exotic cats of the same colour behave just like Persians, yet the history of their breeding is much shorter. The FIFe did not recognize them until 1984.

Persian Red.

84 Semi-longhair Breeds

This group consists of six very different breeds whose popularity has increased greatly over the past few years. The hair of these cats is lengthened by the same gene as in the longhair cats, but it differs both in length and texture. From the strictly genetic point of view these are longhair cats, but traditionally they are described as a semi-longhair breeds. The Birman is an attractive cat of uncertain origin which attracts attention by its colouring — it has acromelanic points in combination with white patches in the form of 'socks' on all four legs. Its eyes are blue. The Birman is bred in 20 colour varieties. Breeding is difficult since not all kittens are born with ideal (show-worthy) patches on the legs.

A breed which has been becoming increasingly popular of late is the Maine Coon. This big, athletic cat, probably a native of the state of Maine in the north-eastern United States, is bred in many colours. According to colour, the Maine cats are divided into nine groups. It is a natural breed of great resilience.

The European equivalent of the Maine Coon is the Norwegian Forest cat which comes from northern Scandinavia. It differs from its transatlantic

◁ The pure black Maine Coon is relatively rare.

counterpart in the shape of the head and, above all, in the texture of its coat, which is water-repellent. It too is a resilient, natural breed and very popular. It is bred in the same colours as the Maine Coon. Both breeds are also notable for their fine bushy tails.

The Angora, originally from Turkey, is a slim, graceful cat. The body coat is medium-long. Until recently it was bred only as a white cat but since 1993 the same colours as in the Maine Coon and the Norwegian Forest have been recognized.

The Turkish Van is an endemic breed which comes from the country of its origin in the region around Lake Van. It differs from the Turkish Angora by its more robust structure and in its colour. Its typical features are red or cream patches on the head and tail, the rest of the body being white. This type of colouring, Van, was named after this breed. Many Turkish Vans are good and enthusiastic swimmers.

The last breed in this group is the American Ragdoll. It is a large, heavy cat which was artificially created by deliberate crossing. It is bred in three types (colourpoint, mitted and bi-colour); at present the FIFe recognizes only the bi-colour type. It exists in seal point, blue point, chocolate point and lilac point colours.

Turkish Van.

85 Shorthair Breeds

Because of its great variety, the group of shorthairs includes 17 breeds. All breeds differ from each other in their body proportions and coat textures. British cats are robust animals bred in England from domestic cats. The breed has many colours, and a typical feature of the animal is its gentle disposition and affectionate nature. The European cat has a similar origin. It was created by breed crossing of domestic cats. It is less robust than the British cat and does not have such a round head.

The Abyssinian cat is a graceful animal originating in Ethiopia. It is bred only in Abyssinian tabby colouring, although in different dilutions as well as in silvery forms. Its longhair equivalent is the Somali, which originated in the United States.

The Russian Blue most probably comes from the Arkhangelsk region of northern Russia and its breeding has a long tradition. It is bred only in blue colouring, similar to that of the French Chartreux breed.

The Manx tailless cats originated by isolating the cat population on the Isle of Man, and their breeding is not easy (see Hint 80). They are bred in all colours.

◁ The Japanese Bobtail is winning admirers because of its exceptionally sweet nature.

In origin, the Burmese cats are distantly related to the Siamese. The first species were brought from Bangkok (Thailand) to the United States in 1930, where they were bred to their current appearance.

The Cornish Rex is an animal with a curly undercoat. It was first discovered in Cornwall in England. Crossing this mutation created a new breed. The Devon Rex from the neighbouring county has a similar origin, yet its genetic disposition is different. These Rex species differ from each other by the structure of the body. The German Rex, found in Germany, has the same genetic disposition as the Cornish Rex but has a more robust body structure. It has become extremely rare, and there are fears that this breed will become extinct.

The Korat is a placid animal. This blue cat is a native of Korat province in Thailand. Its breeding is based entirely on imported individuals. The Korat is not very resistant to feline diseases; that is why their immunization is vital.

The Japanese Bobtail is a shorthair that has been kept in Japan for some 1,000 years. It adapts easily to human company and wins affection by its extremely congenial temperament as well as by its unusual appearance.

A new shorthair breed is the Sokoke, a silvery African marble cat originally from Kenya. The latest recognized breed is the Burmilla; it is the result of crossing the Persian Chinchilla with the Burmese cat in a breeding programme that lasted 15 years. The last two breeds in this group, the Ocicat and Egyptian Mau, are bred in only one type of pattern — spangled. Their dots are quite regular and most attractive. The Ocicat is a hybrid breed, bred in the United States with the help of Siamese and Abyssinian cats. The Egyptian Mau has been in existence since the time of the pharaohs, as attested by ancient temple wall paintings.

Abyssinian Red.

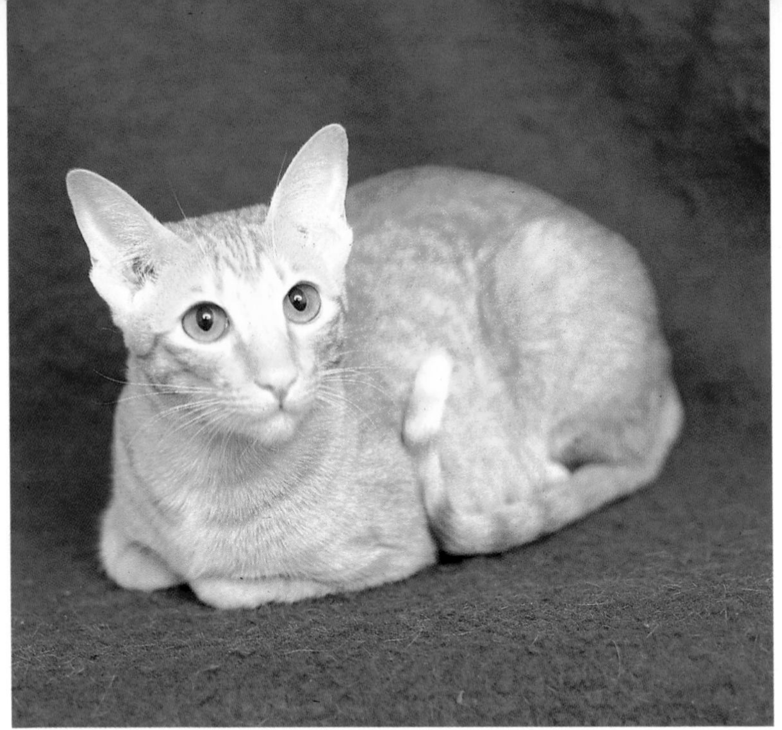

86 Siamese and Oriental Breeds

This group consists of four breeds, and its members can be inter-crossed. All these breeds have identical body proportions and differ from each other only in their colouring and length of coat. They are slim but muscular, with a long and delicate-looking head. They have large ears and a long thin tail. The temperament of the Siamese and of the breeds derived from them is well known: they are active and sprightly cats, communicating very well with humans and reaching adulthood at an early age.

•

Siamese cats, from which all other breeds in this group have been derived, were imported into England from Siam (modern Thailand) in 1884. However, over years of breeding they have undergone many changes. They have long ceased to resemble the original obese and squint-eyed cats with 'knotted' tails. Siamese cats are nowadays bred in 20 colour varieties, including classic colours (seal, blue, chocolate and lilac point), as well as colours determined by sex (red, tortoiseshell), colours based on the presence of a pattern (tabby point), and also pure white.

◁ Oriental cats have the same body structure as Siamese; they are also called Siamese without marks. This is a red spotted Oriental.

Oriental cats differ from Siamese merely by the colour of their eyes and body. They do not have acromelanic points and their eyes are always green. They are bred in a huge variety of colours; all dilutions are recognized, including the cinnamon silvery varieties, as well as all types of pattern. In Europe, white patch cats are as yet not recognized. Although Oriental cats were recognized much later than the Siamese, they long existed in Thailand, as did their acromelanic relatives. They were forgotten for some time and later imported and bred into their present appearance. We can therefore refer to them as a natural breed.

The longhair mutations of these two breeds were created artificially in the United States. They are the Balinese (longhair Siamese, recognized in the same colours) and Javanese (longhair Orientals, also bred in the same colours). These graceful longhairs cannot conceal their Siamese ancestry as regards their personality, but are somewhat more placid.

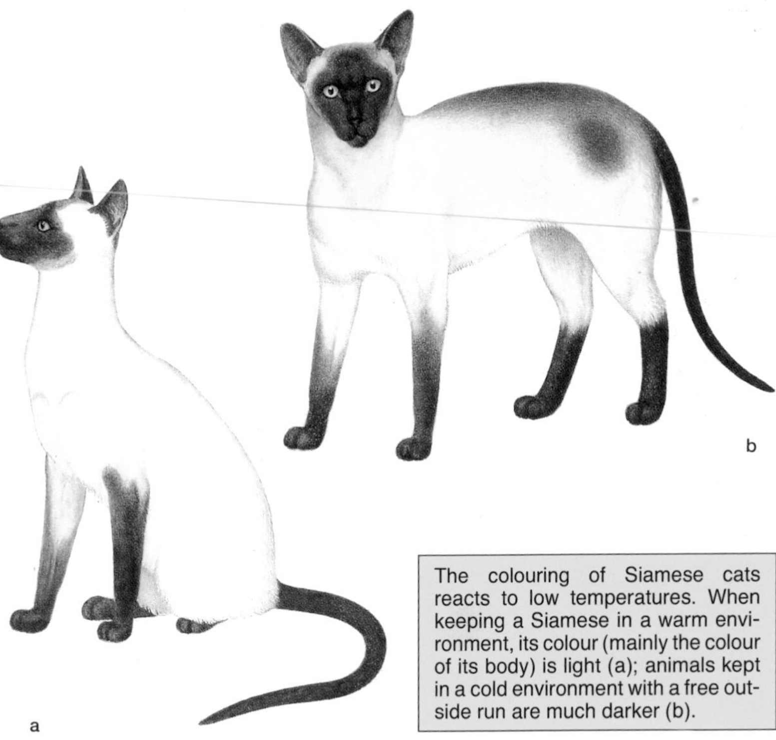

The colouring of Siamese cats reacts to low temperatures. When keeping a Siamese in a warm environment, its colour (mainly the colour of its body) is light (a); animals kept in a cold environment with a free outside run are much darker (b).

87 Non-recognized Breeds

These are breeds not recognized by some national or international cat associations or clubs, but they have their specific standards: other organizations may recognize them. Some of these breeds exist in large numbers of individuals and have their traditions, while others are only in the first stages of breeding and for the moment do not exist in sufficiently large numbers to allow us to speak of a definite breed.

•

Non-recognized breeds include those which are the result of crossing established breeds. They include the Burmilla – recognized in 1994 as a breed – which is the result of crossing the Burmese cat with the Persian Chinchilla. Such breeds are called hybrids, and they include also the Tonkinese, Poodle and Snowshoe cats.

Other non-recognized cats are characterized by the addition of the blood of wild cats by the crossing from which they originated. The Bengal breed is the result of crossing the Bengal cat (*Felis bengalensis*) with the domestic cat, and the Safari cat by crossing Geoffroy's cat (*Felis geoffroyi*) with the

◁ A representative of non-recognized breeds: the Bohemian Rex, a Czech curly cat. It is a Persian with curly hair.

A semi-longhair Siberian cat is a beautiful animal.

domestic cat. Although these are very beautiful animals, their breeding is difficult. In the first generation there is reduced fertility and even sterility; and the cats inherit a natural timidity from their wild ancestors.

There are also many breeds which are not very numerous or occur only in certain countries or regions. They include the Siberian cat, the Czech curly cat, the American wirehair, the Singapura, the Ceylon cat, the Cymric (a longhair Manx), the Scottish Fold, the Sphinx (hairless cat) and certain others.

The Cymric cat is a longhair Manx cat and is among the rarest breeds.

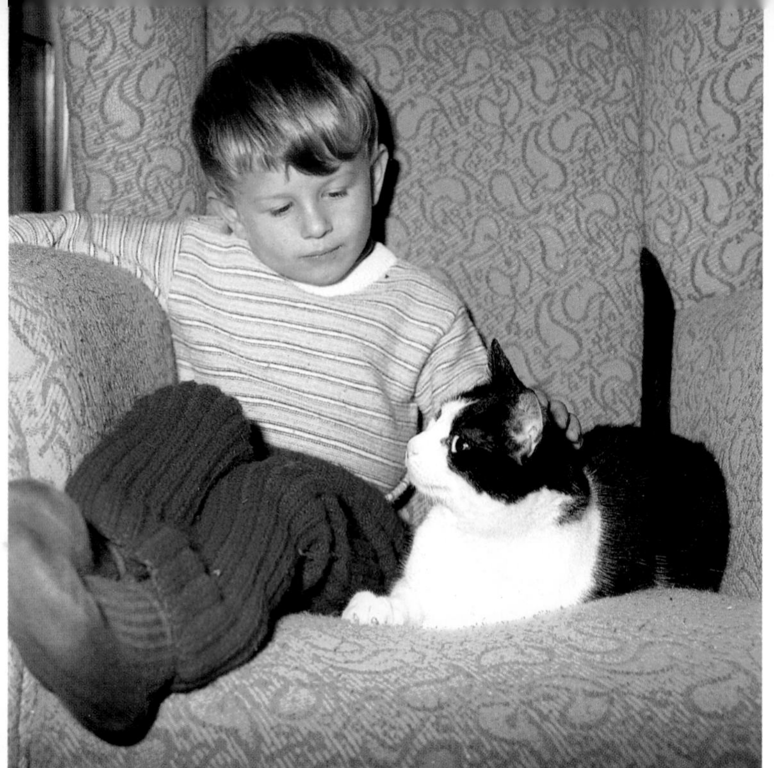

88 Breeding Ethics

Nowadays hundreds of thousands of people throughout the world go in for cat breeding. It is a fascinating hobby which fills our free time. The cat is gradually becoming more and more a social animal, kept for its beauty and pedigree and not only to kill mice, as in the past. In most cases, breeding is done on scientifically established foundations. Unfortunately, there are instances when certain breeders concentrate more on the commercial aspect of cat breeding than on genuine breeding, which requires considerable resources as well as endless hours and a sincere passion.

•

The cats of such commercial breeders are being used excessively for breeding; they are mated too frequently and once they have served their purpose and grow old, the 'breeder' gets rid of them in order to reinforce his or her breed with fresh stock. A genuine breeder loves his or her animals and allows them to live out their days in the tranquility of their home.

◁ The cat can be a friend as well as a lifelong hobby of man. This relationship frequently begins in childhood.

Cage (Volière) breeding is not suitable for cats. By losing direct contact with the human being the cat also loses some of that which makes it a human's friend. In my opinion an animal with perfect appearance which has no contact with humans is something like a beautiful painting or a voiceless sculpture, lacking life. It is also extremely doubtful if a cat can feel happy in a cage, albeit equipped to perfection and enjoying every care.

If you are thinking of starting to breed cats, stop and consider whether you have sufficient money and time, whether you are prepared to give up this or that because you will have to consider your animals, even when going on holiday or when you have a lot of work or other interests; whether you are willing to look after the animals even when they are sick (and pay the veterinarian bill); whether you are aware that a cat lives for 10, 15 and more years, and that throughout this time it will depend on you and that you will have to be there until the very end. If you have answered 'yes' to all these questions, you know what you are doing, and all that remains for me is to wish you the best of luck in your breeding venture.

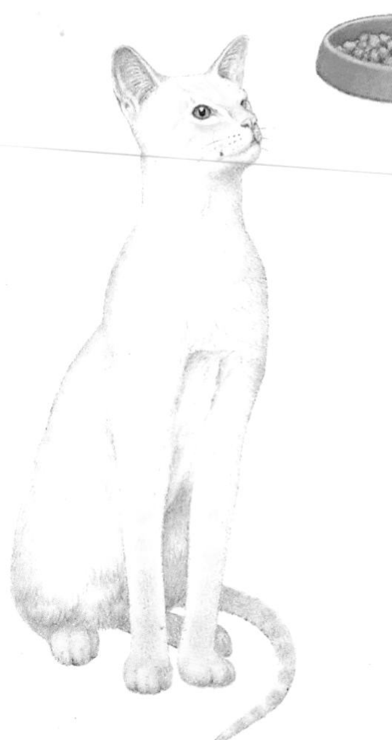

THE EMS SYMBOL SYSTEM

BREEDS

ABY	Abyssinian	MAN	Manx
BAL	Balinese	MCO	Maine Coon
BML	Burmilla	NFO	Norwegian Forest
BRI	British	OCI	Ocicat
BUR	Burmese	ORI	Oriental
CRX	Cornish Rex	PRE	Persian
DRX	Devon Rex	RAG	Ragdoll
EUR	European	RUS	Russian Blue
EXO	Exotic	SBI	Birman
GRX	German Rex	SIA	Siamese
CHA	Chartreux	SOK	Sokoke
JAV	Javanese	SOM	Somali
JBT	Japanese Bobtail	TUA	Turkish Angora
KOR	Korat	TUV	Turkish Van
MAU	Egyptian Mau	X	non-recognized breeds

COLOURING

n	black (basic)	j	lily tortoiseshell
a	blue	o	red-brown (sorrel)
b	chocolate	p	fawn
c	lilac	q	sorrel tortoiseshell
d	red	r	fawn tortoiseshell
e	cream	w	(dominant) white
f	(black) tortoiseshell	s	silvery tipping
g	blue tortoiseshell	y	gold tipping
h	chocolate tortoiseshell	x	non-recognized colouring
var	variant		

EXTERNAL CHARACTERISTICS

01	white patches 'Van'	32	Tonkinese depigmentation
02	white patches 'Harlequin'	33	Siamese depigmentation – points
03	white patches 'Bicolor'	51	Manx rumpy
04	white patches 'Mitted'	52	Manx rumpy riser
09	unspecified white patches	53	Manx stumpy
11	shaded	54	Manx longie
12	tipping-shell	61	blue eyes (on white cats)
21	agouti (general striped)	62	orange eyes
22	marbling	63	different colour of each eye
23	tiger	64	green eyes
24	spotted	65	Burmese yellow eyes
25	ticked tabby	66	Tonkinese turquoise eyes
31	Burmese depigmentation	67	Siamese blue eyes

STAMBOOM

STAMBOEK
NEDERLANDSE VERENIGING VAN
FOKKERS EN LIEFHEBBERS VAN KATTEN
Opgericht 28 januari 1934
Lid van de Fédération Internationale Féline (F.I.F.E.)

Van: NIKE VAN JUARRO
Nederlands Kattenstamboek No: K 42-224 Geboren: 5 juni 1976
Ras: siamees Geslacht: poes
Kleur: red-point(32a)
Gefokt door: Mevr.J.E.Coree-Smit,Landbuurt 12-14,Leeuwarden.

	Ouders	Grootouders	Overgrootouders	Betovergrootouders
Vader:	Bodante Bronc Buster NKS K 41-261 Import 32a	Felitan Gulliver of Bodante CFA 272-27143 V 107 24	Dahin's Pasha of Petmark CFA 272-25338 V 105 24	Dahin's Deino of Rendara 24
				Gr.Ch.Miss Karma of Dahin 24
			Ch.Felitan Golda CFA 273-30540 V 103 24	Gr.Ch.Sia-Mews Blue Cavalier of Che-Ree 24
				Gr.Ch.Gaidon Lolita of Felitan 24
		Bodante Sandpiper CFA 299-0104 V 107 32a	Ch.Angkor Rose Red Rid'R of Chalonai CFA 278-0403 V 103 32a	Bo-Be's Red Fanci of Angkor Rose 32a
				Ch.Tsu-Kee-Ah-Kee Roja of Angkor ?
			Solitaire Fireopal of Bodante CFA 279-0286 V 102 32a	Solitaire Tagetes 32a
				Embee Prajan 32b
Moeder:	Int.Ch.Aphélandra van Juarro NKS K 30-393 32b sealtortie	Ch.Zapatski v.Marantish NKS K 17-207 32a	Gulden Tibeert v.Maupertuus NKS K 16-321 32a	Int.Ch.Chiccona Fandango 24
				Int.Ch.Kernow Thani Imp.sealtortie 32b
			Int.Ch.Asuni Ang Pow NKS K 16-498 Import 32a	Ch.Pitapat Toosin 32a
				Ch.Asuni Ki-Sin sealtortie 32b
		Manon del Promesa NKS K 16-542 24c	Int.Ch.San-T-Ree Caress Tangle NKS K 14-500 Import 24b	Bemans Montasser 24b
				Purr-Du Caress 24b
			Delila del Promesa NKS K 12-951 24c	Int Ch.Arkas van Asgard 24c
				Nicolle van Umuiden 24a

Gewaarmerkt d.d. september 1976

Stamboek sekr. (stempel: Vereeniging van Fokkers en Liefhebbers van ...)

voor de afd. Siamezen adj. sekr.
Mevr. A. v. d. Bos - Bloemhofstraat 5 rd
Haarlem - (023 - 31 18 10).

FIFe (Fédération Internationale Féline) Members

Argentina
Asociación Felina Argentina
Rodriguez Peňa 36 1 piso B
1020 Buenos Aires

Austria
Österreichischer Verband für die Zucht und Haltung von Edelkatzen (OVEK)
Liechtensteinstrasse 126
A – 1090 Wien

Klub der Katzenfreunde Österreichs (KKÖ)
Castellezgasse 8/1
A – 1020 Wien

Belgium
Fédération Belge des Chats Clubs a.s.b.l.
Albert I. Promenade 3/13
B – 8400 Ostende

Brazil
Clube Brasiliero do Gatto (CBG)
Rua Almirante Tamandaré 280
CEP – 09310350 BR – Mauá SP

Byelorussia
Felinolog
Logojski trakt 39-1 327
220090 Minsk

Croatia
Savez Felinoloskhi Drustava Hrvatske
Vinogradska 2a
41000 Zagreb

Czech Republic
Český svaz chovatelů
Maškova 3
CZ – 182 53 Praha 8

Denmark
Landesforeningen Felis Danica
Esbjergparken 5
DK – 9220 Aalborg

Estonia
Felix
Pardi 23
EE – 0013 Tallin

Finland
Suomen Kissaliitto r.y.
Tohlopinkatu 2
SF – 33310 Tampere

France
Fédération Féline Française (FFF)
75 Rue Claude Decaen
F – 75012 Paris

Germany
1. DEKZV – Erster Deutscher Edelkatzenzüchter Verband
Berlinerstrasse 13
D – 35614 Asslar

Great Britain
The Cat Association of Britain, CA
Mill House, Letcombe Regis
Oxon OX 12 9 JD

Hungary
Magyar Macskabarátok es Tenyesztok Országos Egyesulete (MMOE)
Rószua u. 64
H – 1064 Budapest

Israel
Amil
PO – box 11070
91110 Jerusalem

Iceland
KYNJAKETTIR
Havalagata 40
101 Reykjavik

Italy
Federazione Felina Italiana (FFI)
Via principi d'Ajaca 20
I – 10138 Torino TO

Latvia
Mooncat
Dzirciema 4 – apt. 7/2
Riga

Liechtenstein
Aristocat
Gapont 34
FL – 9495 Triesen

Lithuania
Bubaste
Kapsu 83-2
3005 Kaunas

Luxembourg
Lux Cat Club (LCC)
B.P. 526
L – 2015 Luxembourg

Malaysia
Kelab Kucing Malaysia
P.O. Box 11591
50750 Kuala Lumpur

Mexico
Asociación Felinofila Mexicana A.C.
(AFEMEX)
Cerro del Otate
Col R. de Terreros
04310 Mexico D. F.

Netherlands
Felikat
Vuurtorenstraat 7
NL – 1976 CJ Ijmuiden

Mundikat
Kerkstraat 12
NL – 9649 Muntendam

Norway
Norske Rassekattklubbers Riksforbund
(NRR)
Hammerfestgt. 2C
N – 0565 Oslo

Poland
Stowarzyszenie Hodowcow Kotow
Rasowych v Polsce
ul. Bonifacego 79 skr. 68
PL – 02 945 Warszawa

Portugal
Clube Portuguez de Felincultura
Rua Republica da Bolivia nr. 53-5 Dt
P – 1500 Lisboa

Russia
The All Russian Cat Club Associacion
Ul. 800 letia Moskvy 3-2-139
127 591 Moskva

Slovakia
Slovenský zväz chovatelov
Krížná 44
824 76 Bratislava

Slovenia
Zveza Felinoloskih Drustev Slovenije
Kraigherjeva 7
SLO – 63000 Celje

Spain
Asociación Felina Española (ASFE)
Paseo de Extremadura 8, 10 C
E – 28 011 Madrid

Sweden
Sveriges Kattklubbars Riksforbund
(SVERAK)
Johannelundsgatan 3
S – 50235 Boras

Switzerland
Fédération Féline Helvetique (FFH)
Solothurnerstrasse 83
CH – 4053 Basel

Ukraine
Ukrainian Felinology Associacion
Ulica Gogola 11/91
270100 Odessa

Index

The figures refer to the hints (not page numbers)